Writing for TV and Radio

Sue Teddern's TV credits include:
Birds of a Feather
Bosom Pals
Happy Together
Homefront
My Family
My Parents are Aliens

Radio credits include:
From Galway to Graceland
In Mates
Sad Girl
soloparentpals.com (five series)
The Charm Factory (two series)
Westway

Nick Warburton's TV credits include:
Born and Bred
Doctors
EastEnders
Holby City
Jupiter Moon

Radio credits include:
Beast
On Mardle Fen (six series)
The People's Passion
A Soldier's Debt
Tommies
Witness

Writing for TV and Radio

A Writers' and Artists' Companion

Sue Teddern and Nick Warburton

Series Editors: **Carole Angier and Sally Cline**

Bloomsbury Academic India
An imprint of Bloomsbury Publishing Plc

BLOOMSBURY
NEW DELHI • LONDON • OXFORD • NEW YORK • SYDNEY

First published in India 2018
First published 2016

Bloomsbury Academic India
An imprint of Bloomsbury Publishing Plc
BLOOMSBURY, Bloomsbury Academic India and the Diana logo are trademarks of Bloomsbury Publishing Plc

This edition published with permission from Bloomsbury Publishing Plc, 50 Bedford Square, London, WC1B3DP, UK

British Library Cataloguing-in-Publication Data
A catalogue record for this book is available from the British Library.

Library of Congress Cataloging-in-Publication Data
A catalog record for this book is available from the Library of Congress.

ISBN 978 93 88038 22 5

For sale in the Indian subcontinent only

Bloomsbury Publishing India Pvt. Ltd
Second Floor, Building No. 4
DDA Complex LSC, Pocket C – 6 & 7
Vasant Kunj, New Delhi 110070
www.bloomsbury.com

Series: Writers' and Artists' Companions
Typeset by Integra Software Services Pvt. Ltd.

Digitally Printed and bound in India by Replika Press Pvt. Ltd. In 2019.

Sue Teddern

To Edward and Ruth for their love and patience

Nick Warburton

To Jennifer

Contents

Part 3 Write on – getting it right, getting it written

Preface

Writing for TV and Radio, the eighth in our series of writers' Companions, may be the liveliest. These writers for TV and radio can do voices, and seem to speak directly to us, as though we were all in a room together – or in The Room, which is (we learn) what the industry calls the creative space where writers and producers meet for story conferences.

Everything they tell us is memorable. Discussing the differences between TV and radio writing, Nick includes a paradoxical piece of advice: 'If you're writing for TV, think about words. If you're writing for radio, think about pictures.' Unexpected, but profound – you must stir the imagination to provide what isn't there. Talking about writing TV sitcoms, Sue tells us that 'Three laughs per page used to be the industry standard', but it's now four. We won't forget that in a hurry! She goes on to test an idea for a sitcom set in a café, called *Crunch Time*; we promise you won't forget that either.

In Part 2 we hear from a fascinating cast of guests, including fifteen British writers, three Americans, a Canadian and a Dane. You mustn't miss any of them, but as an example: read what Jeppe Gjervig Gram says about the Double Story, and you'll understand what made *The Killing* and *Borgen* such remarkable television.

In Part 3 we're back with Sue and Nick, and the nuts and bolts of TV and radio writing, complete with exercises for classes, or for writers working alone. They explore where ideas come from, and how to find them; how to create characters – interestingly, sitcom characters mustn't change (Sue), but most dramatic characters do, spurred on by their Driving Condition (Nick); how to manage plot and structure – for sitcoms, Sue has what she calls SHIGWIGB (see page 167), while Nick solves the age-old problem, to plan or not to plan, by planning, writing, and planning again. They also explore, in detail, thorny subjects such as voice and narration, dialogue (leave the most important thing *un*said), script layout (with intriguing and entertaining examples from their own work) and many more. This book is as close to The Room as you'll get before you enter it yourself. Which, with the help of *Writing for TV and Radio*, we hope you will.

Carole Angier and Sally Cline
Series Editors

Foreword

Richard Schiff

Some great writer, it might have been E. L. Doctorow, said something like: 'The minute I know what the next sentence is, I stop writing.' If he didn't say it, he should have. Or could have. What that means to me is that his writing, his creative flow, is coming from somewhere behind the brain, or below it, from that unknown source. Once, my niece had painted a beautiful, soulful portrait of a woman – an impression so fluid and stunning it stopped me when I first saw it. I told her it was brilliant, this painting is stunning and brilliant. She ducked her head and said: 'No, I didn't do anything. It's just nothing.'

We tend to want our brilliance to come from sweat and arduous effort, like a marathon runner finally breaking the tape just before collapsing or a mountain climber as he or she reaches the Everest summit. Some colossal struggle to overwhelm the greater elements, the mythic forces of opposition. We want to be heroes.

When I'm acting I like to not know what is next. I like to be active and present so much to the point that I am unaware or don't remember the next line or moment. Hopefully, I will have crafted the character so that the truthful, whole reaction will be educed from what is happening now. I like to 'E.L. Doctorow' my acting. When that happens it feels effortless and I get the thrill of surprise in moments I didn't expect. When it happens on stage it feels like flight. When it happens on a TV or movie set it feels like I am intimate with some otherworldly thing, something greater than me. It feels, and don't laugh, like love.

I have been lucky to embody the characters and speak the words of some wonderful writers: Eugene O'Neill, David Mamet, Lanford Wilson, Arthur Miller, Aaron Sorkin, David Kelley, David Milch, Jason Katims, Nick Hornby,

Jonathan Franzen, to name a lot. All of these writers have a thing in common: they give me the tools to build my platform for flight or craft my house of intimacy. An actor is a detective who combs scripts like a Cold War spy until he finds those elements that unlock the secrets of the soul of his character. The reason he exists, in this story, and in the world. What are the clues? Well, to name a few: How does he speak? Is he shy or verbose? Does he speak openly, unapologetically? Or is he obtuse and sneaky or close to the vest to protect himself or someone close? What does he communicate and how? Is he physically imposing, threatening? Is he timid? Is he accepting and open? How does he present himself? His clothing: Is he a dresser, a slob, someone who does the minimal presentation to get by but not be noticed too much? Has he been on a bender? Does he stink from drink and smoke? We look for every clue to answer the first essential question: Who am I? And then I look at what he does and why. How he goes about it, his actions. What he is willing to risk? Where and who are the obstacles or enemies? Where the hell am I anyway? My home? What does that mean to me? What are the clues? Is it a well-appointed home? Are there servants? Is it lived in? Comfortable? Is there a woman's touch? Then, of course, comes the forensics on the words themselves. Does he speak in quick phrases? With eloquence? A high vocabulary that might actually mask his meaning more than illuminate it? Is he a liar? Is he pathologically truthful? Does he have an accent? How long has he been away from his homeland? Why did he leave? Is this why he is so quiet? Protective? Scared? Each beat is explicated, each moment examined, each word chewed and swallowed. David Mamet writes like jazz, sometimes scat jazz; Eugene O'Neill with the lyric street folklore of the 1920s; Aaron Sorkin in metered eloquence and quick quips. Jason Katims in a sort of middle-American, muted, rock ballad and David Milch in a harsh, gutter symphony. Each writer has wonderfully different music to the language and each challenges us to find their rhythm and play in a cohesive band. But these writers – and there are plenty more – have one thing in common: their characters are steeped deep in the world of the story. The clues they leave for us actors are rich and complex and sometimes require extraordinary techniques of excavation, examination and exploration. They know the deeper they bury, the more obsessive we will be to dig it out.

Does this intimidate you, the writer? It should, but don't let it. We need you. Imagine doing all that work we do as actors with a lousy script. I've done it and it's not fun, let me tell you. We get awards for some of our finer work but the reality is that the most challenging work in my career has come from trying to create a life in a character written by a lazy writer. There should be awards given to actors making mediocrity out of crap! Don't get me wrong, writers have every right to want to murder some actors who've butchered their words. And I'm sure I've been in some writers' crosshairs more than once. It can become a nasty battle were it not for the saving grace of those few very special chances in our careers when the right actor and the right writer meet. That's what keeps us climbing Everest and running that marathon. The sweat, the heartache, the psychic ache and pain come from the bad shit; when our writing or acting gets stuck in some purgatory of mediocrity.

What E. L. Doctorow knew, what my niece knew unwittingly, what I have been graced enough to know here and there in my creative life is that when we hit that sweet spot, when all the dreams come into the light at that right time, when the pavement gets hit at full speed – that's where we bleed and sweat to get to. That's when we don't know what the next sentence will be or the next moment. And that's when we feel, as my niece did, like we 'didn't do anything'. That 'it's just nothing'. Please, please, I want to not do anything always! Whether I can get there or not, that's up to you. We need you writers. Not just us actors for our collaborative sport, but all of us, need you: to tell us your story, in a way only you can do.

Introduction

Sue Teddern and Nick Warburton

We hope that what we say here will encourage you to get on and write something. However, we won't be suggesting that there are any shortcuts or that writing for TV and radio is easy. If you're looking for a quick pathway to your first broadcast, you won't find it here. Writing for TV and radio takes hard work and application. But that's part of the fun.

In this book we concentrate on writing drama, and most of the drama we talk about is narrative drama. We don't have anything to say about journalism or features, about 'reality' or game shows. And our comedy expertise is of the sitcom and comedy-drama variety; we can't offer any useful pearls of wisdom if you're interested in sketch shows or stand-up comedy.

It may at times look as if we're setting out rules for writing but we aren't really doing that. We're talking about what we've learned from years of experience in the business. There *are* rules for writers but they tend to be rules writers make for themselves. They also tend to differ from writer to writer. Of course, all writers feel – or should feel – at liberty to break the rules they've set themselves, at least once in a while.

Because we each have different ways of working – and not working – we mightn't always offer identical advice. When we do, it will be useful for you to see that this particular tip or technique has at least two proponents. When we offer contradictory advice, we leave it to you to experiment with the bits that resonate and discard the bits that don't. We won't be offended. As writers, we all find our own strategies for filling those scary blank pages.

Many of the examples we quote are from our own work. There are two reasons for this. The first is that we know what we were trying to do when we were writing. The second is that we'll feel free to refer to things that didn't work as well as those that did.

There are three basic requirements a writer needs to make a go of it: talent, luck and stamina.

You can get by on two of those but you'll need all three to make a living.

Part 1

Reflections and experiences

Back story 1: My journey as a writer

Sue Teddern

So many journeys are uncharted and unplanned. Or they're changed by circumstance, a fork in the road, the wrong kind of leaves on the line. Or you're on a train from London to Brighton but you're diverted at East Croydon. Or transit workers are on strike so you have to walk. (Yes, yes, we get the idea!)

Some writers painstakingly plan their writing careers, know the route and won't deviate from it: A to B, script to screen, wannabe to BAFTA winner. Writers half my age may have studied creative writing at uni, followed by an MA in The Screenplay, with the sole aim of having something on the telly before their thirtieth birthday. Good luck to them.

When I was in my teens, there were no courses in screenwriting. Or if there were, I wasn't interested because my ambition was to become a window dresser. So this would have been the first destination I logged into my career satnav.

At school, like so many other writers, I was hopeless at Maths and good at English. I didn't see my writing skills as anything special so I chose not to go to University. Instead, I got a Diploma in Design and Display from a college in Watford. Two years into my window-dressing career, including a crème de la crème job at John Lewis in Oxford Street, I realized it was time to 'come out' and admit that I'd meandered down a pointless cul-de-sac.

My aim, at this point, was magazine journalism. So I took a quick course in typing and speedwriting and worked my way up the greasy pole of publishing: secretary to sub-editor to feature writer to deputy editor. I worked on teen mags, women's mags, even *New Scientist*. Jobs weren't hard to come by and if you didn't like one, you left on the Friday and found another.

A major junction on my journey came while working as assistant editor for a group of in-flight magazines in Amsterdam. It was from my quaint canal house near Dam Square that I wrote a week of episodes for *The Archers*. As you do. Let me explain.

One of the magazines we produced was aimed at European business travellers and one of the destinations was Birmingham. I'd settled in Amsterdam without a TV and had become accidentally hooked on the world's long-running soap, *The Archers*.[1] I still listen, even though it sometimes drives me potty.

When my editor said we should run a feature about this Birmingham-based phenomenon, I asked to write it. I flew over and watched some episodes being recorded – my first experience of a radio studio – and thought: I could do that. And I did, while still living in Amsterdam, and again when I moved back to London. But they didn't keep me on. I am a nano-blip in *The Archers*' archive.

From this stage of the journey, I was driven – no pun intended! I went on an Arvon residential course, Writing for TV with Paula Milne and Geoff McQueen. I found an early version of my writing voice during this week and I've kept a tight hold of it ever since. I know what makes a Sue Teddern script. I came away with a better sense of the journey ahead.

An evening class in radio drama followed. I started a radio play and got heartily sick of it. Why was it taking so long? But I finished it, so that I could allow myself to start something new. I sent it in. And it was produced.

My first radio play, called *Sauce*, was inspired by my time writing restaurant reviews for the magazine in Amsterdam. I listened to it recently. It's a bit creaky – I was a real novice – but I'm not ashamed of it.

In my chapter, 'Having a Laugh',[2] I describe my route to writing for the BBC sitcom, *Birds of a Feather*. The tools and technique for crafting thirty minutes of comedy were acquired on the job and I'd be lying if I said it wasn't tough, scary and occasionally just plain impossible. Why did the producers think I could do it? What if I couldn't? Could I slope off quietly, change my name and never write another word again?

I survived *Birds*, with thirteen episodes to my name. In fact, it was mostly a hugely enjoyable experience. And it gave me the validation to carry on.

[1] See 'Ten landmark radio dramas and comedies', Part 1, page 17. The Archers is recorded in Birmingham.

[2] Part 1, page 69.

That said, there have been times during this journey when I wanted to jump out of the moving car. The way ahead was too demanding, the holes in the road too deep, the obstacles too insurmountable.

Writing for radio is mostly wonderful. Writing for TV can occasionally wring the very essence out of you. Notes are contrary, deadlines shift, requirements change with the arrival of a new commissioning editor or the re-casting of a lead character. It can be tough and confidence sapping, but stage fright is part of the process.

That's what I tell myself, anyway.

But when an actor soars with that problematic speech you sweated blood over, or an audience guffaws at your favourite gag, those moments make the ill-planned, uncharted journey worthwhile.

I didn't know I'd end up here, when I set off. Or that my detours and diversions would be part of the journey. But here I am. And I can't complain.

Back story 2: My journey as a writer

Nick Warburton

A few writers have complete confidence in their own ability. Even fewer are right to feel so confident. Most of the writers I know remain insecure.

Some years ago I met David Ashton, the award-winning writer of *McLevy*. I hadn't seen him for a while and I asked him how he was doing.

'Oh, you know,' he said, 'still waiting to be found out.'

I knew exactly what he meant.

If you wanted to be a writer where I grew up – in East London in the fifties and sixties – you kept that ambition to yourself. You would've been laughed at for being both pretentious and hopelessly unrealistic. What you had to do – what everyone tried to do – was get a Proper Job. Writing wasn't a Proper Job. And in many ways it still isn't a Proper Job, even now. But that's another story.

It wasn't just the fear of being laughed at that stood in my way, though. I knew that I had neither the *qualifications* nor the *experience* you needed to be a writer.

Even though writing isn't a Proper Job, you still have to be qualified to do it. And you qualify by being clever and by belonging to the middle or upper classes. So I didn't qualify, not even halfway. And as for experience, I didn't have any. I had nothing to write *about*. Real writers sailed the world under canvas, like Joseph Conrad, or did time in a blacking factory, like Charles Dickens. I had a paper round.

So I had very little choice: I had to stop thinking about writing and get a Proper Job.

My school offered its leavers two pieces of careers advice: go into banking or become a teacher. You could take your pick. The paper round showed me I was poorly equipped for counting money, so I became a teacher, but I still wanted to write.

As it turned out, I was wrong about the qualifications. It can help to be conventionally clever but it's not essential. And sometimes cleverness gets in the way: there are plenty of clever people who can't write. What you need instead is an ability to recognize a story. An ear for the language and a visual imagination are also useful.

Class shouldn't matter at all. If I'd realized that years ago I wouldn't have spent so long feeling I was trespassing in someone else's garden.

I was also wrong about experience. The paper round *would* count, as would the fear of being laughed at. The American short-story writer Flannery O'Connor said, 'Anybody who has survived his childhood has enough information about life to last him the rest of his days.' In other words, get to the age of five and you'll have material enough to be a writer.

When I was thirty-something I realized that, if I reached sixty-something without having made the attempt to be a writer, I'd regret it. So, unqualified and inexperienced as I was, I gave up my regular, steady Proper Job and tried to write. Give it two years, I thought. See what happens.

For a year and ten months, nothing much happened at all. I wrote and sent things off and waited for them to be sent back, which they always were. In those days you posted manuscripts with a large stamped and self-addressed envelope so they could be returned with the minimum of effort. So you learned to recognize the sound of these envelopes thumping on the doormat. Once a rejected manuscript came through the letter box and hit me on the back of the neck as I was tying my shoelace. This time, it seemed to be saying, it's personal.

Then, out of the blue, a contract turned up. It fluttered to the mat.

It came from the BBC without any kind of preliminary letter so I had to read it several times before I realized what it was. I'd never seen a contract before. It looked vaguely legal and I wondered, briefly, if it might be a court order telling me not to send them any more scripts. But, no: it was a contract for my first play.

The play itself was full of blunders and clumsiness, but the experience of hearing it broadcast was enough to make me think that maybe I could carry on trying to write.

And I still am. Still trying to write.

So I'm one of the many writers who feel insecure about writing. I felt insecure about it long before I started doing it seriously and I still feel insecure about it. Now, however, I know that a little insecurity can be my friend. It can prevent me being too satisfied too soon with what I've done.

Too much insecurity will get in the way. It'll stop me getting anything done at all. The best way to prevent that, I find, is to cut out introspection.

Don't think about yourself as you write your script – pretentious, inexperienced, not worth listening to. Don't think about the people who'll read it – superior, highly educated and scoffing. Think only about the story you have to tell and the way it has to be told. A writer loses a sense of self when the writing is going well.

When you've finished the script – at least as far as the First Draft[3] – you can go back to feeling insecure again.

[3] For what I mean by the First Draft see Part 3, page 268.

Ten landmark TV dramas and comedies

Sue Teddern

Choosing ten memorable, important, groundbreaking TV comedies and dramas is an impossible task. My long list covered two single-spaced A4 pages. Somehow I whittled it down to ten.

I'd love to have written about *Widows, Queer as Folk, I Claudius, Cops, Edge of Darkness, The Quatermass Experiment, The Prisoner, Friends, This Life, Rock Follies, Scenes from a Marriage, The Royle Family, ER, Six Feet Under, Cracker, Happy Valley, The Likely Lads, Twin Peaks, Coronation Street, The Wire, Clocking Off, MASH* and many, many more.

- What would be your ten most memorable TV shows?
- Why?

Z-Cars *(UK, 1968–1972)*

Police dramas were already part of the TV schedules in the 1960s, but *Z-Cars* was the first to portray a realistic, warts-and-all precinct, with absolutely no gentleman-detective revelations in the country house drawing room.

Set in the fictional northern city of Newtown, *Z-Cars* reflected influential 'kitchen sink' British films of the period, like *Billy Liar* and *A Kind of Loving.* The characters were, for the most part, lowly uniformed coppers like Jock and Fancy, who drove the police cars, and were kept in check by their superiors: Sergeant Lynch, DCI Barlow and DS Watt.

Cases failed to be closed, cops were fallible and dialogue was more authentic than anything that had come before, thanks to great scripts by writers like Alan Plater, Allan Prior, Troy Kennedy Martin and John Hopkins.[1] It could be argued that without *Z-Cars* there would have been no *Hill Street Blues, NYPD Blue* or *The Wire.*[2]

The Forsyte Saga *(UK, 1967–1968)*

In the days before boxed sets and catch-up TV, you had to watch your favourite programme when it was on. Or you missed it. At the height of *The Forsyte Saga*'s popularity, pubs closed and church services were brought forward so that families could cluster round the telly, in shared pre-*Downton* harmony.

Dramatized in twenty-six episodes from John Galsworthy's series of novels (by writers including Donald Wilson and Constance Cox), this classic serial took off slowly on BBC Two. The repeat on BBC One a year later reached unheard of audiences of 18 million for the final episode. It was also a massive hit around the world and the first series to be sold to the Soviet Union.

Emotionally stifled Soames' brutal rape of his reluctant wife Irene and flighty flapper Fleur's affair with her cousin Jon were just two highlights of the most successful classic drama of all time, proving that we could all be drawn into the lives of these rich, pampered, compelling characters. A 2002 remake, starring Damian Lewis as Soames, was unable to capture the same massive audiences.[3]

Breaking Bad *(USA, 2008–2013)*

'A good person doing bad things for good reasons.' Some of TV's best dramas have kicked off with this simple premise.[4] But none have taken it to the very farthest, darkest extreme, as *Breaking Bad*'s creator Vince Gilligan

[1] See *Talking to a Stranger*, page 13.

[2] Just as *Cagney and Lacey* paved the way for *Prime Suspect, Scott and Bailey, The Killing, The Bridge* and *Happy Valley.*

[3] Including episodes by Jan McVerry, see Part 2, page 105.

[4] e.g. Frank Sobotka in season two and McNulty in season five of *The Wire*, Dexter Morgan in *Dexter.*

did with the saga of science teacher Walter White. He's a decent man who starts cooking crystal meth in order to support his family after a terminal cancer diagnosis.

As season one unfolds, we're rooting for Walter. We tolerate his business partnership with dissolute ex-pupil Jesse Pinkman and we fear Jesse will drag him down. But as the five seasons unfold, Walter loses his moral compass and Jesse finds it.

Breaking Bad crept up on its audience via word of mouth, boxed sets and Netflix. People were judged on how late in the day they came to it. (What do you mean, you *still* haven't seen it?) Certain moments – often end-of-season cliffhangers – are as good as TV will ever get. Ever! We laughed, cried, gasped, cheered and gasped again. A tough act to follow for all concerned.

The Avengers *(UK, 1961–1969)*

Watch the very first episode through 2015 eyes and it's slow, wooden and laden with clunky dialogue. You have to remember how things were back then. Life was still fairly monochrome; TV certainly was. Created by Sydney Newman, *The Avengers* didn't land on our screens fully formed as cult viewing. Early episodes had John Steed in a minor role, minus bowler hat and umbrella. It was only the eventual inclusion of a feisty female partner – most memorably Cathy Gale and Emma Peel – that gave it legs. Literally.

These women were not ditzy dolly birds: Dr Gale was a thirty-something anthropologist who wore leather jumpsuits. Mrs Peel was a sassy, trouser-suited widow, memorably pushing hair out of her eyes with a revolver in the groovy opening credits. At the height of its success, *The Avengers* overlapped with 007 for wit, style, kinky boots and comic-book capers. It became one of the first British series to be aired on prime time TV in the USA, and in 2007 it came in at number twenty in *TV Guide*'s top cult shows ever. Fab!

Cathy Come Home *(UK, 1966)*

Written by Jeremy Sandford, this drama highlighting homelessness via the story of one struggling young family is as powerful today as it was when it was first broadcast as a BBC Wednesday Play. You try watching the final five minutes, when Cathy's children are wrenched from her by social workers in a busy London station, without filling up. The improvised agitprop documentary style, exemplified by director Ken Loach, was a real game changer at the time, and so realistic was the drama that for years afterwards Carol White, who played Cathy, would have cash thrust at her by sympathetic strangers who thought she must still be homeless.

Few dramas change public policy and perceptions but *Cathy Come Home* did just that. Shelter, the charity for the homeless, had coincidentally just launched, and gained huge support as a result. In 2005, *Cathy Come Home* was voted the UK's most influential TV programme of all time by *Broadcast* magazine. Ken Loach went on to make countless TV dramas and films that packed a punch,[5] but none more than this one.

The Office *(UK, 2001–2005)*

Inspired by documentary-lite series like *Airport* and *Driving School*, where certain participants became 'reality TV stars', Ricky Gervais and Stephen Merchant's comedy, *The Office*, depended on its audience finding the central character of David Brent utterly compelling, despite his politically incorrect asides and unreconstructed observations.

Gervais' performance as a man hiding his insecurities under a camouflage of bluster and matey-ness was a tour de force. Cynical underling Tim saw through him while man-child Gareth regarded his boss as a role model.

It took just fourteen episodes of the British series to generate a US version, featuring Steve Carell as an American Brent.[6] 'We love the Scranton crew,' proclaimed *Entertainment Weekly*. 'But Ricky Gervais' mockumentary series about sadsack employees in Slough, England, is the undisputed champion of awesomely awkward cubicle hell.'

---

[5] *Up the Junction*, *Days of Hope*, *The Price of Coal*, *Ladybird Ladybird*, *Sweet Sixteen*, to name but a few. He also directed episodes of *Z-Cars*.

[6] Aka Michael Scott. Paper merchants Wernham Hogg became Dunder Mifflin.

Grange Hill *(UK, 1978–2008)*

Children are a discerning audience. Patronize them at your peril. This was Phil Redmond's ethos when he created a gritty drama serial for kids about a realistic school, just like the ones his young TV audience attended. If *Doctor Who* fans have their favourite Time Lord, you can age a grown-up by who the presiding *Grange Hill* head teacher was over thirty years of episodes: Mr Starling? Mrs McLusky? Miss Gayle?

Critics often accused the serial of being too issue led, most famously Zammo's heroin addiction. Bullying, rape, Asperger's, dyslexia, knife crime and a gay teacher were also covered in *Grange Hill* storylines and the cast of kids included actors with disabilities; groundbreaking stuff in a show for children.

When the BBC announced plans to change the nature of *Grange Hill*, Redmond, in typical fiery fashion, called for it to be scrapped. The BBC obliged. Grange Hill occasionally tub-thumped but it always treated its audience with intelligence and it changed perceptions of kids' TV and kids in general.

Seinfeld *(USA, 1989–1998)*

'No hugging, no learning.' This was Larry David's golden rule for the sitcom he created with Jerry Seinfeld. It was an antidote to the *Brady Bunch* gloop of the Seventies and maybe even to the witty cuteness of its comedy contemporary, *Friends*.[7]

There were no moments of revelation; lynchpin Jerry kept his cynical stand-up schtick, George Costanza remained stingy, petty and whiney, Elaine stayed super honest and over-reactionary, with a hatred of *The English Patient*... and Kramer was, well, just Kramer, the 'hipster doofus' who liked to burst through Jerry's front door.

If you were a fan, you'll know the joy of episodes like *The Contest*, when all four competed to remain 'masters of their domain',[8] or Kramer's invention

[7] *Friends* ran from 1994 to 2004.

[8] Cryptic code words for refraining from masturbation.

of a brassiere for men,[9] or George's fiancée's demise, after licking toxic glue from the cheap envelopes he'd bought for their wedding invitations. And ever since Seinfeld, haven't we all blanched when someone 'double-dips' a tortilla chip? If not a comedy catchphrase, then a rule for life.

Blue Remembered Hills *(UK, 1979)*

One cannot compile this list without mentioning Dennis Potter. He exemplified the truly original voice of British drama. *Pennies from Heaven* and *The Singing Detective* showcased his use of actors miming to classic songs from the Twenties and Thirties. But for me *Blue Remembered Hills*[10] is the one that still resonates, thirty-six years on.

A gang of seven-year-olds play in sunlit woods and fields; the setting is Potter's childhood stamping ground of the Forest of Dean. Allegiances are observed, hierarchies are tested. One of the group, nicknamed Donald Duck, is bullied and picked on and ultimately dies when the rest of the gang won't let him out of a barn, unaware that he's set light to it.

The USP (an acronym that would have appalled Potter) is that the children were played by adults: Helen Mirren, Colin Welland,[11] John Bird, Janine Duvitski, Robin Ellis, Michael Elphick and Colin Jeavons as poor old 'Quack-Quack'. *Blue Remembered Hills* is as chilling as *Lord of the Flies* but with a heightened sense of discomfort because of the utterly believable child-adult cast.

Talking to a Stranger *(UK, 1966)*

Three of these four linked plays, shown in weekly instalments, ran to 96 minutes, with the final part coming in at 102 minutes. The culture back then was: if it's good, why cut it to fit a slot? This tradition of public service

[9] The 'Bro' or 'Manssiere'.

[10] The title comes from A. E. Housman's poem 'A Shropshire Lad'.

[11] Famous for saying 'The British are coming' when he won an Oscar in 1982 for his screenplay of *Chariots of Fire*. He also played PC Graham in *Z-Cars*.

is impossible to imagine now. Or that the writer, John Hopkins, delivered the scripts seven months late.

Talking to a Stranger told the story of a momentous weekend, related by four members of one family, each from their own point of view: a mother, father, brother and sister, after the mother's suicide. The daughter was played by a sparky young Judi Dench and the performance won her a second BAFTA. The dialogue is surprisingly naturalistic for its time and the long multi-camera scenes give a real sense of intimacy and urgency.

Observer TV critic George Melly wrote that 'on the evidence of this work alone, the medium can be considered to have come of age'. It's also said that Alan Bleasdale refused to allow *Boys from the Blackstuff*[12] to be repeated as part of a major BBC Two retrospective unless *Talking to a Stranger* was also included.

[12] See Yosser Hughes, 'Ten memorable TV and radio characters', Part 1, page 47.

Ten landmark radio dramas and comedies

Nick Warburton

One of the things that radio drama has in common with the novel is that, at regular intervals in recent years, its demise has been predicted. New technologies, people say, will be the death of both. Books? Who needs them when you have a personal computer in your pocket? And who's going to tune in to a *wireless* when it gives you words without pictures? But we still have novels and we still have radio drama, and in some ways radio drama is stronger than it's ever been.

One of the reasons radio drama is still doing well is that the new technologies that were supposed to kill it off have made it much more flexible and accessible. People can listen to radio while they're doing other things. You can experience a play while you're having a bath or cooking an omelette. While you're on the move – in cars, trains or planes, on runs or walks – you can be transported to Ancient Rome or Dublin, to outer space or Ambridge.

All this began less than a hundred years ago. Here's a brief history of radio drama centred on ten plays or series. Some represent key moments in the development of radio, in the technology or in the way stories are told. Some are simply examples of excellence.

Twelfth Night *(1923)*

Shakespeare's *Twelfth Night* was the first complete play performed on radio specifically *for* radio. Before that plays had been broadcast but rather apologetically. 'You can't see what's going on,' seemed to be the suggestion, 'but we can help you.' So the announcers of the British Broadcasting Company (as it then was)[1] would read the stage directions between bouts of dialogue, almost like a sports commentary. ('Muriel crosses to the coffee table and picks up the cigarette lighter.') The experience for the 1923 audience must have emphasized its sense of being absent. 'You're not actually here, but other, luckier people are.'

J. C. W. Reith, the first General Manager[2] of the BBC, wanted to give people something better than that. He wanted the production itself to do the work of the announcer, and the play he chose for this experiment was a comedy that depends on visual clues – girls dressed as boys and twins mistaken for each other. But Reith insisted that it could be done, and so it was. Getting rid of the announcer was a simple but important development.

David Pownall's 1998 radio play, *An Epiphanous Use of the Microphone*, was written to mark the seventy-fifth anniversary of this first production, and it tells the story of Reith's endeavour brilliantly.

A year after *Twelfth Night*, the BBC broadcast the first play written specially for radio, *Danger* by Richard Hughes (1924), which showed a shrewd understanding of the exciting new medium by setting the drama in a coal mine, in the dark.

The War of the Worlds *(1938)*

Howard Koch, who also co-wrote the script for *Casablanca*, adapted H. G. Wells' science fiction novel for *The Mercury Theatre of the Air* in the United States. The original novel tells the story of a Martian invasion of Earth and much of it takes place in the English countryside at the end of the nineteenth century. Koch's adaptation makes a number of significant changes. To begin with, it locates the story in New Jersey, so making it seem very close to home for its listeners. It sets it not forty-odd years ago but in the present. It also makes use of a narrator who speaks directly to the audience, not simply to tell the story but to convince them that everything is happening here and now, that it's not, in fact, a story but real events in real time.

---

1 The BBC became the British Broadcasting Corporation in 1926.

2 Reith became Director General in 1927, and Lord Reith in 1940.

Listeners heard a kind of prologue, spoken by the director (Orson Welles), which referred to the millions of Americans who happened to be listening to the radio on that particular October evening in 1938. This was followed by a weather report and then music, live from New York. Then came the first of a series of announcements – 'we interrupt this programme . . .' – which informed people of the invasion from Mars.

If you missed the titles and the prologue and tuned in for the music and the interruptions, you might conclude that the safest thing to do was to get out of the city and head for the safety of the open countryside. Which, according to legend, is what thousands did.[3]

Orson Welles and his team showed how powerful and convincing radio drama could be, especially if you were prepared to experiment with the medium itself.

The Archers *(1950)*

Shortly after the end of the Second World War the BBC was planning a series of programmes aimed at encouraging and informing the farming community. In the early stages of discussions someone suggested the best way to do this might be to follow the lead of the melodramatic and hugely popular *Dick Barton – Special Agent*, which the BBC broadcast daily at the end of the 1940s. If they dressed their farming facts in daily dramas they might be more effective. So *The Archers* was launched, with some of the *Dick Barton* writers on the team. It's been running ever since and shows no sign of fading away. These days it's less concerned with informing farmers than it is with telling stories.

Its fans may be found all over the world and in all walks of life[4] and it has even attracted members of the Royal Family to make guest appearances.

[3] It's unclear how many people actually fled the cities. The controversy was real enough, though, and showed how radio can shock and disturb. When Dorothy L. Sayers' dramas based on the life of Jesus (*The Man Born to Be King*) were first broadcast by the BBC in 1941/1942, some people were so incensed at the thought of an ordinary man acting the part of Christ that they blamed the fall of Singapore, in February 1942, on the production.

[4] I once spoke to a captain of the England cricket team who confessed to being 'a bit of an Archers man'.

Over the last sixty-odd years, it has chronicled both large and significant changes in society, and the small, apparently inconsequential events in the lives its Ambridge inhabitants. Its real strength, I believe, is in the telling of these small stories. The characters in *The Archers* are, for a lot of listeners, like neighbours. People care about who Lynda Snell is going to cast in her next pantomime.

What's different about writing for *The Archers* – and some other long-running serials – is twofold. Writers can take advantage of the organic nature of the process by following where their characters lead; see what takes off and go with that. They also have time at their disposal. Because *The Archers* runs almost daily – from Sunday to Friday every week – and for years, enterprises of great pith and moment can be addressed without having to set up and resolve everything within an hour or forty-five minutes (or even four times forty-five minutes).

The Goon Show *(1951/1952)*

When I was about eleven my friend Stewart and I hauled a simple reel-to-reel tape recorder into the garden shed so we could create our own surreal stories and thread them through with cartoonish sound effects. *The Goon Show* was our inspiration. It was one of the biggest and most influential radio comedies of the 1950s. The other was *Hancock's Half Hour*.[5] Both were played before a studio audience and both had a clear understanding of how the medium operates. *Hancock's Half Hour* worked largely through character. It centred on the life of an ordinary man with dreams of greatness which were at odds with his mundane surroundings (Railway Cuttings, East Cheam). He was brilliantly realized by Tony Hancock, who created the bumptious, pretentious and permanently underachieving 'Tony Hancock'.

The Goon Show also gave us character – an array of vivid and bizarre creatures like Eccles, Bluebottle and Major Dennis Bloodnok – but its success was more to do with the imaginative way it used words and sound to

[5] Written by Ray Galton and Alan Simpson.

create unexpected and surreal worlds. In one episode, for example, the hero, Neddie Seagoon, attempts to auction the equator.

The show began in 1951 as *Crazy People* and starred Spike Milligan (who did most of the writing), Harry Secombe, Peter Sellers and Michael Bentine. It also featured a real and highly respected BBC announcer (Andrew Timothy) to make the whole thing sound authoritative and reasonable.[6] Bentine left the show in 1952 but the others continued to tell their wild and subversive stories for the rest of the decade. At times it made BBC executives nervous because they were never quite sure how rude and offensive it was being.

It was tried on television, in 1963, but was at its best on radio.

Under Milk Wood *(1954)*

The period from the late Forties, through the 50s and into the 60s was in many ways a golden age for radio drama with a variety of imaginative and groundbreaking works. Many of these were written by poets like Louis MacNeice or Henry Reed, or occasional poets like Samuel Beckett or Harold Pinter. The best known and arguably the greatest of the plays from this period is Dylan Thomas's *Under Milk Wood.*

His 'play for voices' was produced not by the Drama Department but by Features. It breaks many of the 'rules' of drama. It has over sixty named characters, which is far too many for any listener to keep track of; great chunks of it are directly narrated; there is little or no dramatic tension or conflict. The day begins before dawn when the little seaside town of Llareggub[7] is sleeping. Its people dream, then they wake, go about their business in a desultory sort of way, and then they sleep again. Nothing much happens. No one is on 'a journey', or has a crisis or is significantly changed.

And yet it's a work of lasting genius and profound humanity. It's poetic and funny. If you listen to a recording of the first public reading of *Under Milk Wood,* at The Poetry Center, New York, in 1953, you can hear the audience

---

[6] This role was later taken by Wallace Greenslade.

[7] You probably know this already, but read the name backwards to get an idea of Thomas's take on what tended to happen in the little Welsh town.

adjust their responses to it. It begins in respectful silence ('this is poetry, we must listen intently') and gradually moves to a much warmer appreciation, and to laughter ('this is about real people and it's funny').

I've mentioned *Under Milk Wood* elsewhere because it's such an important part of what radio has done and can do. It teaches us that rules are there to ignore, as long as the final result 'works'. It demonstrates the powerful link between word and image. It relishes character. So listen to it, if you can. Read it. But don't try to emulate it. You have to do what you can do, not repeat what Dylan Thomas did more than sixty years ago. That's one of the rules.

Albert's Bridge *(1967)*

Albert's Bridge is one of Tom Stoppard's early radio plays. It won the *Prix Italia* in 1968. It's in the tradition of Giles Cooper's *The Disagreeable Oyster*[8] and *Under the Loofah Tree*[9] in which apparently ordinary people are shunted into doing extraordinary things by following a seemingly logical course of action. This one tells the story of Albert, a dreamy student of philosophy. He wants to continue his studies but the university won't keep him on, so he gets a job as a painter on the Clufton Bay Bridge. The work seems dull and repetitive, ill-suited to someone with Albert's intellectual training, but he finds he likes it. It allows him to be on his own and to think. He becomes obsessed with bridge painting.

In *Albert's Bridge* Stoppard, as he does in a lot of his plays, dramatizes ideas. It's touching, in the way that the philosophy of the human condition can sometimes be touching, but it's predominantly thought provoking and dazzlingly playful.

It's interesting to compare *Albert's Bridge* with one of Stoppard's later plays for radio, the masterful *In the Native State* (1991). This play is much richer in character and has greater emotional depth, but the playfulness and the dazzle are still there, and both are perfectly suited to radio.

---

8 See also 'A most delicate monster – voice', Part 3, page 193.

9 See also 'Hearing their dreams – the nuts and bolts of radio', Part 3, page 230.

The Hitchhiker's Guide to the Galaxy *(1978)*

The Hitchhiker's Guide to the Galaxy, created by Douglas Adams, began as a series of six science fiction radio comedies broadcast, as much of radio comedy and drama still is, with little in the way of announcement or fanfare. Because it was both comedy and science fiction – two reasons for some people not to like it – it wasn't popular with everyone but those who understood what Adams was doing liked it a lot and it became a word-of-mouth success. A television series followed, then a 'trilogy' of five novels, and a film, but it was born on radio and its purest and, many would argue, most successful manifestation was on radio.

It seems to me that the main reasons for this are to do with the nature of radio, which is perfect for positing strange new worlds and then asking the audience to picture them. (In the Fifties the BBC had great success with *Journey into Space*, a long-running science fiction drama serial written and produced by Charles Chilton.) Other factors in its success were its use of sound, which was, as *The Goon Show* had been, inventive and funny, and Adams' writing which was consistently witty and surprising.

The voices on *Hitchhiker* were perfectly matched to the roles. This was particularly the case with the voice of Peter Jones as the Book (the eponymous Guide).[10] Jones sounded both authoritative and comfortingly unperturbed by all that was happening in this bizarre universe. There were, of course, other memorable voices. One only has to think of Marvin the Paranoid Android to hear Stephen Moore intoning, 'Life, don't talk to me about life.'

Dreams, Secrets, Beautiful Lies *(1986)*

I was particularly influenced by a number of exceptional radio plays written in the 80s – to mention only a few, *Daybreak* (1984) by Don Haworth, *Outpatient* (1985) by Rhys Adrian, *Languages Spoken Here* (1987) by Richard Nelson and the almost perfect *Cigarettes and Chocolate* (1988) by Anthony

---

[10] Peter Jones was a practised radio narrator as can be seen in his own series, *J. Kingston Platt*.

Minghella.[11] It's a diverse collection and each attempts and achieves different things, but they all make the most of the intimacy of radio and draw the listener into a private world, and they all demonstrate the importance of language, not just as the carrier of the story but as part of the experience of listening.

One of these Eighties plays was *Dreams, Secrets, Beautiful Lies* by Robert Ferguson (directed by another significant name in radio drama, Richard Imison). It's a contemporary play about, among other things, what people say to each other and what they avoid saying, about lies and truths and the territory between. It makes use of the fact that, in 1752, the country changed over to the Gregorian calendar and so, apparently, 'lost' eleven days. In that year the 2nd of September was followed by the 14th of September and people thought time had been stolen from them. *Dreams, Secrets, Beautiful Lies* is set in a similar period of supposed lost time, the missing eleven days in September. We follow its characters as they try to understand what they are losing. I remember listening to it on my own while I was doing something else, and being stopped in my tracks.

Spoonface Steinberg *(1997)*

Spoonface Steinberg by Lee Hall is part of a quartet of plays for radio called collectively *God's Country*. They were all produced and directed by Kate Rowland. This particular play, the last in the series, is a monologue for a seven-year-old autistic girl. That in itself is quite a challenge – expecting a complete play, as subtle and complex as this one, to be carried by such a young actor. In the event, Spoonface was played, with heartbreaking simplicity, by Becky Simpson. The fact that this little girl is also dying of cancer presents another challenge. The writer has to steer a narrow course between despair and mawkishness. Lee Hall avoids mawkishness by keeping faith with the girl's voice: this is not an adult speaking in the voice of a child; she

[11] All Giles Cooper Award winners. See also Peter Tinniswood, David Cregan, Michael Wall, Andrew Rissik, William Trevor and others.

has wisdom but it's not beyond her years. He avoids despair by making the short time we spend in Spoonface's company so uplifting. She's afraid at times but she has no self-pity.

What we can learn about radio from *Spoonface Steinberg* is first the great virtue of simplicity. Only one voice speaks to us – directly to us, as if she knows who we are and trusts us – though we also hear the recorded voice of Maria Callas in full-throated song.[12] (Compare this to the vast cast of *Under Milk Wood.*) It's as simple as it can get: one voice talking to a single listener – me.

The other thing we can learn from it is how important it is to put heart into what we write.

Ulysses *(2012)*

The BBC has an honourable tradition of presenting great novels as serialized dramas. Most have appeared in the Classic Serial slot, usually broadcast on a Sunday afternoon or a Saturday evening. In recent years, though, some dramatizations have been given more inventive scheduling. In 1999 *Bomber*, adapted by Joe Dunlop from Len Deighton's novel,[13] was aired in several episodes on a single day. In 2011 Kenneth Branagh and David Tennant starred in an eight-hour dramatization of Vasily Grossman's masterpiece *Life and Fate*. Its thirteen compelling episodes, written by Mike Walker and Jonathan Myerson, were broadcast in a variety of different slots throughout an entire week. At the other end of the scale, the BBC has also commissioned trailer-length plays, little more two minutes long.[14]

A recent example of this kind of scheduling was a fine adaptation of James Joyce's novel *Ulysses* by Robin Brooks. It was produced by Jeremy Mortimer and Claire Grove and was one of the last productions the exceptional Claire Grove worked on before she died. The seven episodes, broadcast across five and a half hours, were directed by Jeremy Mortimer and Jonquil Panting.

[12] See also 'Hearing their dreams – the nuts and bolts of radio', Part 3, page 232.

[13] Directed by Adrian Bean and produced by Jonathan Ruffle.

[14] See, for example, *Two-minute Tales* broadcast on BBC Radio 4 Extra.

The novel is set on 16th June 1904 and follows the fortunes and misfortunes of Leopold Bloom (Henry Goodman) and Stephen Dedalus (Andrew Scott), as well as almost everyone they meet, during their wanderings through the streets of Dublin on this one unexceptional day. All seven episodes of Robin Brooks' adaptation were broadcast through the entire day of 16th June 2012, in slot lengths that varied from fifteen to seventy-five minutes. This huge project also managed to find the drama in the book, as well as keeping faith with its spirit and with the voice of James Joyce.

Horses for courses: TV, radio or both?

'I've written a play...'

Nick Warburton

Before you start

Before you start writing for radio or TV there are a few questions it's useful to ask yourself. (It's useful to ask some of them during and after the writing as well.) They're questions about the nature of TV and radio drama and about their audiences.

I've written a play...

A would-be writer once said to me, 'I've written a play; what should I do next?'

I said, 'Well, what sort of a play is it? Is it for the stage, or radio, or TV . . . ?'

'Oh,' she said, 'at the moment it's just a play. I thought I'd decide about all that later; see who might be interested.'

'In that case,' I said, 'why not give up now and get a Proper Job? You don't know what you're doing.'

No, I didn't say that. Of course not.

For one thing, I want to be kind. People were kind to me when I started writing. For another, I've made plenty of foolish mistakes myself – not just when I started writing but at regular intervals since.

There are lots of mistakes out there waiting to be made and lots of pitfalls you're not even aware of when you set out. The more you write the more you begin to see the pitfalls and the harder it all becomes as a consequence. What looked like a long straight road gradually turns into a twisting and tricky one. At least it does in my experience.

And anyway it's a common enough question to ask – I've written a play; what should I do next?

But it's not the first question you should ask yourself.

The first question to ask is: 'What sort of play should I be writing?'

You can't really start to write a play without knowing what sort of play it is. That's like saying, 'I thought we'd play a ball game, and decide exactly what sort of ball game, after the first half. See how we all feel about it then.'[1]

What sort of idea . . . ?

In fact, this notion – knowing what kind of thing you're writing – applies to all forms of writing. The writer Roy Apps once said to me, 'One of the first things you need to know about your idea is what sort of idea it is. Is it a Poem Idea? Or a Short Story Idea? Or a Stage Play Idea . . . ?'

A lot of good ideas are spoiled by being forced into the wrong box. ('I've come up with a fantastic idea about a man's obsessive hunt for a great white whale . . . and I think it's going to be a limerick.')

So ask yourself what sort of an idea you've just had, and if the answer is a Play Idea, you should then go on to ask what sort of a play.

It's possible to have a good idea that *might* become both a radio play and a TV script – or something else. I've rewritten radio plays as stage plays and vice versa. There's nothing (well, not much) to stop you doing that – or, at least, trying to. But each attempt must be a fresh start – a wiping clean of slates and a reduction of the idea to its bones. And you'll end up with two plays, not one that might more or less work in either medium. And each fresh start should lead you to another question.

In our case, that question is, how can I best tell this story *on radio,* or *on TV?*

So, to return to my would-be writer and her innocent question, what I suspect she meant was, 'I've written some dialogue; what should I do next?'

---

1 Of course, you *can* start writing without knowing exactly what you're doing, and that might yield something interesting, but it's unlikely to yield a radio play or a TV script. It might yield something that could *become* a radio play – but only after you've worked on it.

(Incidentally, Christopher Moltisanti, in *The Sopranos*, was faced with a similar question. When he asked his girlfriend Adriana what she thought of the film script he was writing, she told him she'd have to know the whole story before passing judgement. 'Well, I thought I'd start with the dialogue,' he said.)

A play is more than people talking to each other. It has many more working parts. How you set about writing it will depend on whether it's for stage, radio or screen. So decide before you start: not just a play, but a stage play or, in our case, a radio play or a TV script. And think about what that means.

Strengths and weaknesses...

Both radio and TV drama have strengths and weaknesses so it's sensible to be aware of that from the start and to focus on the strengths rather than the weaknesses. If, for example, you decide to write a radio play, you'll know that your audience can't see the people to whom you're giving voices. The question to ask next might seem to be: 'How can I tell this story when no one can see the characters?' But it's better to ask how you can exploit the fact that your audience can't see these characters. There are advantages to not seeing. What are they? How can you make invisibility a strength rather than a weakness? Similarly, if you're writing a TV script, ask yourself what it is about TV that will help you to tell the story in a uniquely TV way.

The strengths of radio and TV are partly what this book is about.

Audiences

As well as questions about the nature of the medium you're working in, there are also questions to ask about its audience.

Who will see your TV drama or hear your radio play?

Is the experience of a radio audience significantly different from that of a TV audience? (Or any other kind of audience for that matter?)

How do you want your audience to react and how can you make that happen?

The audience game...

What you're doing with your audience when you write is playing with them. You're planning surprises for them. You're leading them to expect one thing to happen and then confounding that expectation by making something else happen. Sometimes you do this for the sake of a powerful dramatic and ironic twist, sometimes for the sake of a joke.

So you plant questions and then delay answering them. Or you don't answer them at all. You leave some things unsaid, or half said. You show things without completely explaining their relevance or significance. And these are all ways of playing with your audience, invitations for them to become involved.

When you write – at least, when you write narrative drama – you are in a sense doing two things at the same time:

- You're creating a story and responding yourself to the way it develops.
- You're checking the effect of the story might have on an imaginary audience.

Or, to put it another way, you're dealing both with the story you have to tell and the way you tell it.

Everyone will manage this in his or her own way. Most people will probably consider the story to be of prime importance. If the story's good and sound your audience will follow. No need to think too much about them. Let them keep up if they can. Others will be much more conscious of the game they're playing with the audience and the reaction they want.

I tend to concentrate on the story first – who the characters are; what they do and why they do it; the internal logic of the piece – and then think more about the audience in a vague, back-of-the-mind way when I'm working on a second or third draft.[2]

I might, for example, say to myself, 'This is how the narrative unfolds: the girl goes up to the castle to find out what's happened to her brother. Yes, she does, but perhaps it would be more interesting to make the audience think she's going there to betray him.'

It's almost as if I have to play the game with myself before I can play it with anyone else.

---

[2] *My* second or third draft, not the Second or Third Draft sent out into the world. Again, see Part 3, page 268 for the difference between First Draft and first draft.

Some writers would no doubt say that the two things – the story and how it's told – are so closely related that they can't be separated. And, for them, they're probably right.

Some examples …

Here are three examples of playing games with an audience, of leading them to think one thing and then surprising them with another …

1. The first time we meet Don Draper in the first episode of *Mad Men* persuades us that he's a free-spirited office Lothario, independent and single and cynical about marriage. When he goes home at the end of the episode, we're shocked to find he lives in a conventional suburban house, complete with neat lawn and hat-stand. There's a wife waiting to greet him and there are two children innocently asleep upstairs. The writer (Matthew Weiner) has pointed us in one direction and then, at the last moment, taken us somewhere else – 'Don Draper's not the man you thought he was. Keep watching and I'll tell you more.'
2. In *Porridge*, Fletcher is being escorted to prison to start serving his sentence. When the van breaks down on the moors, he manages to escape his escort and break out of the farmhouse where they've put up for the night. He roams for miles across the open countryside until, hungry and tired, he sees a small farmhouse and breaks in. We're led to believe he's taken his chance and managed to put miles between him and his escort. But we discover with Fletcher that he's broken into the very place he escaped from only hours before and he's back where he started.

   (Incidentally, both these homecomings – Draper's and Fletcher's – are more or less wordless. They're televisual moments. Nothing else needs to be said when we see Don with his children. And Fletcher's realization that his long and arduous escape has brought him back to his starting point can be seen, wonderfully, in his face.)
3. An example from radio. I wrote a play called Catching Heathcliff about Lindsey who was trying to live a wildly romantic life in down-to-earth, mundane circumstances. The play is about, among other things, the

contrast between ideals and reality, between the way Lindsey wanted things to be and the way they actually were. So it begins like this ...

MUSIC. A WILD WIND IS BLOWING ACROSS WUTHERING HEIGHTS. IN THE DISTANCE, HEATHCLIF IS CALLING WILDLY – 'Cathy! Cathy! Hear me, my heart's darling! Cathy!' DIP UNDER AS LINDSEY READS.

LINDSEY: Oh, I wish I were a girl again, half savage and hardy, and free! Why does my blood rush into a hell of tumult? I'm sure I should be myself were I once among the heather on those hills –

GRAHAM: Do you want that biscuit?

THE STORM STOPS ABRUPTLY. IT'S GONE AND SO HAS HEATHCLIFF. WE'RE IN A SMALL BACK ROOM IN A CHURCH HALL.

I was trying to send the audience down that wildly romantic track – Lindsey as Cathy – and then throw a switch to direct them into a humdrum little siding – the church hall with unimaginative Graham.

Where to draw the line ...

It requires a sense of balance, this game you play with the audience. They don't know what you're going to say or do next but you want them to guess. If you say too much, if you give too many hints, they'll see where you're leading them before you arrive and they may lose interest. If on the other hand you don't say enough, if you're too obscure, they might become confused and lose interest.

So do you risk saying too much or too little?

In fact, it's almost always better to say too little, to challenge your audience to keep up with you, than it is to underestimate them by telling them too much. Audiences are fairly sophisticated at seeing what's coming and filling in gaps. They can read pictures and manage unanswered questions and things unsaid. But they won't like deliberate obscurity.

Drama is a collaborative activity and you'll probably find yourself working with producers, script editors or actors who'll disagree about where the line should be drawn. They'll urge you to tell your audience more, or to reveal less,[3] so you might need to argue your case, and you might, on occasions, need to yield.

This notion of collaboration is important, not just for programme makers but for audiences too. Michael Tolkin, talking about his co-written script for the film *Changing Lanes*, mentions the 'handover'. At each stage in the process, he points out, a story, a script is handed over – from writer to director, from director to actors, from actors to audience – and all these people, including the audience, must be left with something to do, something to contribute. If they're not handed something to do, they won't feel part of the game.

The TV audience...

What's the nature of a television audience? It's huge and diverse and usually watches at home, surrounded by the distractions of home. Some will watch with rapt attention but for others the story you've laboured for months to tell will be little more than background – with the remote within arm's reach. It's easy for a television audience to opt out. This can lead to a writer becoming intimidated by the audience.

You'll want to counter the distractions of home and the ease of opting out. You'll want to catch your audience's attention and hold it. And you'll be tempted to do this by employing shock tactics – increasing the dramatic tension, upping the ante, raising the stakes, throwing in more and more twists and surprises. The danger here is that you do these things not because the *story* demands that they should be done, but because the *audience* does. Or because you think it does. Then what you end up with is contrivance. Instead of true drama you get melodrama and cliché, and instead of properly earned tension you get a kind of surface tension.

It's not the fear of the audience that should dictate the way a story goes, it's the story itself, and its characters.

There's also a law of diminishing returns with shock tactics. This is illustrated, I always think, by the use of the crash trolley in medical dramas. When a patient is in some sort of medical crisis, someone thumps a red

---

[3] Usually it's more.

button and a trolley laden with life-saving equipment comes skidding to the rescue. If it's properly prepared for, this can indeed be dramatic. But it must be used sparingly. My crash trolley rule is this ...

- One crash trolley in an episode may be dramatic
- Two is probably heading towards the melodramatic
- Three is almost certainly courting indifference in your audience

So what can you do about holding on to a television audience? The ante can be upped, the stakes raised and so on, but those things must be done organically, as a natural and proper part of the writing process and not as a kind of literary crash trolley.

In spite of all these anxieties, a writer can tell stories that will engage this huge and varied audience, and make them care, and keep them watching.

The radio audience ...

In the UK it's likely that hundreds of thousands of people will be listening to a radio play at any given time, but it's not the number of listeners that defines this audience. It's more useful to think of the writer for radio as addressing an audience of one. There are three main reasons for saying this.

- The first is that people are more likely to listen to a radio play on their own
- The second is that, because of the way listening to radio has changed and is changing, a play is very often piped straight to a listener's ears
- The third, and most significant, reason is that there are more gaps and blanks for a listener to fill. The writer hints at a picture, the listener completes it. (See **Visuals**, below.) The listener is, in a sense, a joint-creator of the play

This last reason makes radio the most intimate of the dramatic media. The radio writer is like the Ancient Mariner, latching on to passers-by to whisper close, lips against ears. Sometimes you can go even closer than that; you can get inside someone's head. That can be frighteningly intimate – and exciting to write.

The First Voice in *Under Milk Wood* tells us about all the sleeping villagers of Llareggub.

'From where you are,' he says, 'you can hear their dreams.'

You can tell that people have a more personal relationship with the radio by their inclination to shout at it. The other day I realized a friend and I were both shouting at the radio at the same moment, and about the same item, but in different parts of town.

Sound and vision

So you're writing a play and you're sure it'll be a radio play. Or a TV play. (But not both.) You've given some thought to what that means. You've thought about the audience, about some of the strengths and weaknesses of your chosen medium. What else do you need to consider?

Well, drama is two things: it's both the sweep of the story you're telling and the presentation of moments along the way. Sometimes these moments are so small they're almost like still photographs or paintings. And they're presented through sounds (usually, though not always, through words) and pictures.

Visuals …

Television is a visual medium; radio is not. If you're writing for TV you're thinking about pictures. If you're writing for radio you're thinking about words.

That seems self-evident, doesn't it? And it is, broadly speaking, true, but so is the reverse.

If you're writing for TV you must think about words. If you're writing for radio you must think about pictures.

The chapter on dialogue in Part 3 will have more to say about the importance of words in television. Here I want to consider why radio is, in fact, a visual medium.

When I started writing for radio I was lucky enough to have John Tydeman direct one of my plays. John – a great maker of, and thinker about, radio – was then the Head of Radio Drama at the BBC. He told me two particular things about the visual aspect of radio that I've always found useful. We were in the cubicle, during recording at Broadcasting House, and he leaned across to make these two passing references to something in the script, on one occasion to point out something that worked well, and on the other to point out something that didn't.

The first was the description of a room. It was a school caretaker's room, where the boiler was kept. We hear one of the characters describe it as he walks in . . .

> 'A folding bed in the middle of the floor. The boy stretched out on it. . . . A chair by the bed. Marriott on the chair.'

The second was a paragraph of stage directions which indicated what the listener would be hearing at the start of a scene – the caretaker cleaning the corridor with mop and bucket; the clank of the bucket as he moved it; the mop swishing over the shiny floor. He's at the far end of the corridor and no one else is around. It shows us something of who this man is: dogged, lonely, isolated.

Which of these two bits of script worked well and which didn't?

The first – the description of the caretaker's room – worked well.

'Good radio,' John said. I was pleased and encouraged but puzzled. I thought I'd written no more than a simple description of what a character saw when stepping into a room. What I'd unintentionally stumbled on, though, was the effectiveness of simplicity on radio. The spareness of a description – 'A chair by the bed. Marriott on the chair' – that leaves something for the listener to do. Gaps to fill in.[4]

[4] Another example of the 'handover' Michael Tolkin was talking about.

Looking back, I suspect it was also a matter of timing. There was a sense of threat about that room so there wasn't time to hold up the storytelling while we looked around and took *everything* in.

So I think I got that right, though more by luck than judgement.

The second thing – the caretaker mopping the floor – I got wrong. 'Doesn't work,' John said. 'That's a TV image.'

Of course it is. It seems obvious now. I put it in as a sound effect, thinking we'd hear the sounds and then see the picture. But all we'd hear would be clank-slop, clank-slop in the distance, and the picture wouldn't have been at all clear. It needed words to place the caretaker in the listener's mind but there was no one there, no character present, to provide them. So the sound picture didn't work and we cut it.

I once heard a story that shows how words can make pictures. Some children were listening to a tale told by the storytellers Hugh Lupton and Daniel Morden. The story was from *The Iliad* and it tells how Hector, about to go into battle, is with his wife, Andromache, who holds their son, Astyanax, 'the darling of his eyes and radiant as a star', in her arms. This is a family saying goodbye before a battle. The warrior's bronze helmet frightens the little boy so Andromache asks Hector to take the helmet off. The children were captivated by the story and later, when Troy falls and Astyanax is thrown to his death from the walls, they were deeply shocked.

They were so shocked that, instinctively, some of them covered their eyes.

They covered their eyes, not their ears. And they did that because they didn't want to *see* the poor child's fall.

The story did what a good radio play does. It offered its listeners the *suggestion* of a picture and then encouraged them to fill out the rest in their imaginations. It invited them to make the picture their own.

Faces and hugs…

On television the pictures themselves can do a lot of the storytelling. Faces can tell stories. Here are two examples from classic nineteenth-century novels that were adapted for television.

In *Persuasion* – adapted by Nick Dear from Jane Austen's novel – Anne Elliot (played by Amanda Root) hears disturbing news about Captain Wentworth, the man she loves. She is devastated by what she hears but she says nothing. There's no one to tell, and anyway she won't speak to anyone about her sadness. All this can be seen in her face. It's a portrait, a painting – Young Woman Sitting at a Piano.

And in Andrew Davies' adaptation of George Eliot's *Middlemarch*, Dr Lydgate (Douglas Hodge) is reconciled with his wife after a bitter falling-out. He realizes that the price of this reconciliation is his ambition. He's a doctor and he wants to do something of value in the world. She's interested in wealth and fashion and those interests will stand in his way. As she witters on we close on his face and her words fade. The words in fact become a kind of sound effect. Lydgate's face tells the story of his weakness and the failure ahead of him.

It took at least three people to make these two scenes work: a brilliant actor, a director who was prepared to allow screen time when not much appears to be happening,[5] and a writer who knows when silence is more effective than speech.

Hugs are also useful story-telling aids. Once two people hug each loses sight of the other's face. But we, the viewers, don't. So …

Two people move in for a hug. Their faces say the hug will mean everything to them and all is, or will be, well with their relationship and the world in general.

In mid-hug, however, the first hugger's face is still saying 'this hug is important to me and I am very much reassured by it' whereas the second hugger's face switches to something else: worry ('I'm not sure everything is as good as I'm pretending it is') or malevolence ('I may in hugging you seem supportive but in fact I have more sinister plans').

Hugging is such a useful device it's become something of a visual cliché, though perhaps one that can still be made to work.

[5] Only appears, of course; in fact a great deal is happening.

EXERCISE

The more television drama you watch the more visual clichés you'll notice. You'll see, for example a character who, under terrible stress, suddenly sweeps things off a desk or shelf, or punches a door; or the character who moves the bathroom mirror and suddenly sees that someone's standing behind her (and then turns round to find there's no one there); or that difficult-to-write letter (or script) that's screwed and thrown on the floor or lobbed into a bin.

So watch, and make a note of others you notice. And then avoid them. If you can.

It's fair to say, though, that these are clichés because they help to tell the story in a vivid and economical way.[6] They worked once and maybe, if they were employed with a bit of variety or an imaginative twist, they might be made to work again. So, better than merely listing clichés, you might think of some new way of conveying the message.

A character under terrible stress sits at a desk. If he's not going to sweep everything off the desk, what *is* he going to do?

Sounds…

Words are the most important part of a radio play but the way an audience hears them, and the sounds that accompany them, make a difference to any impact they might have. If you're writing for radio you must pay particular attention to everything a listener hears – the immediate sound environment, the sound events that punctuate the story, the music and the pauses and silences.

[6] Don Draper in *Mad Men* has been seen sweeping things off his desk; so even Homer nods sometimes.

> **KATIE HIMS' TOP TIP**
>
> You should, if you can, love the sound of the world that you're writing in.

But I'll say more about those things in **Hearing their dreams – the nuts and bolts of radio** in Part 3, page 222.

Either or both?

Sue Teddern

Milk or dark chocolate? *The West Wing* or *The Wire*? Cappuccino or latte? Writing for TV or for radio? Must I choose? Can't I do both?

It still surprises me that some radio writers don't 'see' how visual their plays are. Or why so many wannabe TV scriptwriters keep knocking on the door of the soaps for that first commission when they might find the route to less tortuous via an original radio play.

We writers can be a funny lot, probably because of the erratic nature of this business. We find ourselves a cosy little niche and we stay there. We don't want to upset the apple cart or put ourselves up for rejection by trying new media. I certainly feel that way about theatre and poetry. Comfort zones are safe and maybe, as a result, our work becomes 'safe' too.

People often say to me: 'I wouldn't know where to start with a radio play' or 'I'm not sure my stuff would work on TV.' And I say to them, 'If you can write either, you can write both.'

So is it 'horses for courses', as the title of this chapter suggests? Are you better suited to radio or TV? I'm not saying you have to do both, but it may make you more versatile if you do. If radio is where you heart is, stick with it. If TV is your medium of choice, go for it. But if you're undecided, read on.

Here are my pros and cons of writing for TV and radio.

See what resonates with you.

If you choose radio …

Radio is so much cheaper to make than big bucks TV. So it's less risky to try out a new writer. In fact radio thrives on its development of new talent. Where better to finesse the craft than under the wing of an encouraging producer. You'll be involved in the recording, casting, even the choice of music. Because I attended the edit of the first series of *soloparentpals.com*, I was able to play producer David Hunter a track from my iPod and it became the theme tune.[7] It's *that* collaborative.

'Cheaper' is also a practical consideration. If you want to write something set on a Mars space station, in *fin de siècle* Paris or during a solo yacht race, it might be a tough sell to a TV producer, especially if you don't have a track record. All that CGI and blue screen, all those corsets and wigs, all that … sea. If you just want a short scene set at a zoo or in a traffic jam, it's a breeze on radio, but it's a major logistical exercise on TV.

These settings won't cost you a bean on radio because the listener is your set designer. Once the sound effects kick in, your audience will colour in that cranky giraffe or overheated taxi. Listeners do a brilliant job because they do it all the time.

By the same token, actors are happy to commit to a few days recording a 45-minute play or late-night comedy because it's a fun gig, they don't have to lose/gain weight, wear a corset or sail a yacht. *And* they don't have to learn their lines. So they'll recite what you wrote, not accidentally paraphrase your favourite line. Which means you may get a star-studded cast, because the recording process is swift and suits the in-demand actor who has a theatre role that night.

Radio is still the best place for self-contained stories. TV eats up returnable dramas so its default setting is series and serials … unless you're a big name writer like Stephen Poliakoff or Abi Morgan and can successfully pitch a one-off TV movie. So if your idea has a beginning, middle, end and can be told in forty-five minutes, radio is the place to go.

---

[7] *Goldwrap* by the Esbjorn Svendsson Trio.

Radio doesn't just do great period, sci-fi and man-in-a-yacht dramas, it's also perfect for internal thoughts (e.g. *Stop Start*), monologues (e.g. *Cigarettes and Chocolate*) and epistolary exchanges (e.g. *Ladies of Letters*, and my own 45-min play *In Mates*).

What can't you do on radio...or can you?

1. **Sight gags, body language, distinctive clothes and funny costumes**: This kind of information can be difficult, but not impossible, to impart. In an early radio play, *Remember This*, I had a character dressed in full clown costume, hired to entertain children during an air traffic controllers' strike. My audience couldn't see him, so somehow I had to hint at his outfit, which I did by having him boast about his special clown's shoes and how expensive they were to have made.
2. **Silence**: Impossible on radio? Actually it can be very powerful. Anthony Minghella's *Cigarettes and Chocolate* is a play built around the central character's desire to stop speaking. But scenes without dialogue are best avoided unless there's a crucial point to them and you can make this device work to your favour.
3. **Large casts**: Yes, *The Charge of the Light Brigade* can be produced for radio but, as the writer, you'll have to think of ways to tell the story without massed battalions of foot soldiers. Better to think small if it's your first radio play.
4. **Kissing, sex, fights and other physical stuff**: However good the acting, sex sounds silly on radio and fights sound staged. I made my eponymous heroine an amateur sleuth in a radio series called *Lucky Heather*; the only way I could indicate that she was following someone was by having her give a running commentary on her phone. In TV, no words are necessary.

If you choose TV...

Creativity-wise and slog-wise, I'd say there's little to choose between TV and radio. So what makes TV the first port of call for so many writers? Might it be the money? It has to be said, radio is the poor relation as far as earnings are concerned. If you get on to the team of a TV soap or have your own series made, you will be aghast at the riches that come your way.

But you will have to jump through countless hoops and write numerous drafts (twenty isn't unusual) before you see your script on screen. What might seem like a huge amount of money, when it plinks into your bank account, may have been earned a thousand times over through all those late nights at your laptop.

If you're reading this book because you're in it for the money, start with TV, not radio.

You may not be as involved in the production of your TV drama as you would be in radio, especially if you're on a team, writing something you didn't create. But if you do happen to go on set and watch from the wings, it's hard not to get a flutter in your chest at the thought that everyone present – the caterers, extras, boom operators, script supervisors and stars – they're all here because of you. God complex doesn't come close!

When I went on to the set of my TV series *Homefront*, I was amazed at the size of the circus that had come to town. They were filming an Army Fun Day, complete with comedy pig (don't ask!) and a huge cast of extras. I wanted to tell a bunch of over-excited kids that they should pipe down because they were only here because of me.

Of course, I didn't. But it was tempting.

Worth a thousand words?

How many times have you been told that your script should 'show, not tell'?

This is sound advice in any medium but it's particularly potent when you can actually show. On TV, we see how someone feels and reacts, how they live, walk, eat, wait at a bus stop or search for their keys. If this is how you like to tell a story, you may find TV the more satisfying medium.

In Part 3, I write about 'the visuals'. A lighting cameraman can create an eerie sense of menace, present a subdued palette of colours or give everything a bubble-gum bright look of Fifties Technicolor, just because your script requested it.

You can ask for rain or sun, make a street busy or deserted, dress your heroine to look like Marilyn Monroe or put her in faded overalls, if it's important to the piece. These visual decisions start with you. If you don't make it clear in your script, you could be in for a surprise when you see the rushes for the first time.

Ultimately, there's no pressure on you to decide: TV or radio. Why not do both, as Nick and I have done? But if you find, as your writing career develops, that TV is your medium of choice or it's radio that inspires you, then that's a useful discovery and you can stop wasting time on something that ultimately isn't for you.

I asked some writers if/why they prefer one medium over another. I got some interesting replies:

- I like writing for TV because your work will be seen by several million people. If it was a stage play and it had an audience like that, it could fill the Olivier Theatre every night for fifty years.
- While writing for the TV soaps, I found the most satisfying thing was how certain storylines were received. People would come up to me and say "You put my life on screen" or "I realised I wasn't alone".
- I believe that good TV writing seeps into our collective psyche in a way that radio can't.
- With TV, audiences choose to watch a particular TV drama. It's more accidental with radio – you'll find yourself getting caught up in an afternoon play when you're meant to be cooking or driving.
- It's simple. I like telling stories, as far as possible, with pictures instead of words.
- Although I write a fair bit of radio, I do worry about the middle class nature of its audience. So the freedom and respect I get from writing for radio is always in a "homemade bread-scented" vacuum for me.

EXERCISE

Find a story from today's newspaper that inspires you.

Make a list of ten reasons why it would work best on TV, and then ten more with radio in mind.

Think about:

- What limits each medium, with this particular idea in mind?
- Which medium offers the most possibilities for your idea?
- Which slot would it suit on radio...on TV?
- Who is your audience...on TV or on radio?
- Which medium excites you most, with this particular idea in mind?

Ten memorable TV and radio characters

Sue Teddern

> *The bottom line is when it comes to characters on a TV show, I want to care. The comedy's important, the jokes are important but, fundamentally you've got to care about these people or you're not going to watch past a few episodes.*
>
> David Crane, co-creator of *Friends*

Roseanne Conner

If *The Lucy Show* was the mother of all sitcoms and the inspiration for eponymous shows like *Rhoda* and *The Mary Tyler Moore Show*, then the genre surely peaked with *Roseanne*. Lucille Ball proved that a sitcom centred around a female character could be hugely popular and that she deserved a driving seat in the production, via her company, Desilu.

Roseanne also took control. If her sitcom was going to present a version of her life, then she was not going to tolerate any Hollywood soft focus or 'Hi honey, I'm home' cutesiness.

It's hard to separate Roseanne Conner, blue-collar white trash housewife, from Roseanne Barr, stand-up comedian and TV star. Both were/are tough-talking, cynical, slightly scary and totally uncompromising. Creating a sitcom around such an unlikely 'star' was a big risk but it paid off.

Like many stand-up comedians, Roseanne Barr was no actress, but she could act 'herself' better than anyone. She'd had a tough upbringing and left home at 18. By the time she was performing her routine in comedy clubs, she'd created a semi-autobiographical schtick about her life as a reluctant homemaker.

Her appearances on all the prestigious late-night talk shows gave Roseanne the profile she needed and a sitcom was created around her by TV company Carsey-Werner. It seems hard to believe but a blue-collar family, as exemplified by Roseanne and Dan Conner, was a fairly new concept to 80s America. Not only were they working class, they lived in Illinois, the part of America that most TV execs fly over, en route to LA or New York.

Roseannes Barr *and* Conner showed that 'ordinary' lives could be packed with story, wit and humanity. The tone is set in the pilot episode: after her three kids have left for school, Roseanne suggests to Dan that they change the locks. She acts like she really means it but you know she's just kidding around. This was revolutionary stuff in 1988!

Roseanne Conner makes the best of her life choices but it's obvious that if circumstances had been different, she could have been a Supreme Court Judge or CEO. That was the appeal. Roseanne didn't crave a shiny wax-free kitchen floor or first prize for her apple pie recipe, like the *Brady Bunch* mom. She got semi-edible food on the table, she still fancied Dan and she unconditionally adored her kids. If that meant wearing the same Walmart sweatshirt three days running, hey, go suck it up.

Roseanne Barr's desire to have complete control over her show was eventually its undoing. See how the opening credits change as she takes over the reins and how her schlumpy housewife appearance gradually becomes more 'Hollywood' through plastic surgery. From 1988 to 1997, her attitude-shifting sitcom ruled; but the final episode ended eccentrically, with more whimper than bang.

The key question is: would sitcom have been the same without Roseanne? The answer is a resounding 'no'.

Alan Partridge

Some classic comedy characters appear on our TV screens, fully formed in all their ghastly glory: *Ab Fab*'s Edina and Patsy; David Brent from *The Office* and his US equivalent, Michael Scott; Fathers Ted, Jack and Dougal; *Cheers* bar props Cliff and Norm. Their back stories are clear. We hit the ground running.

Alan Partridge crept up on us, courtesy of Steve Coogan; he co-created the character with Armando Ianucci for the BBC Radio 4 spoof news show *On The Hour* in 1991. Alan, the unworldly sports reporter who had a poor grasp of his subject and an aptitude for mixed metaphors, was just one of a uniformly funny ensemble of characters who appeared each week.

His trajectory from sports reporter to household name can't have been planned. He went on to have his own BBC Radio 4 radio chat show, *Knowing Me Knowing You*, which transferred to TV ... followed by *I'm Alan Partridge*, a series about his foiled career, failed marriage and semi-permanent residence in the Linton Travel Tavern motel, assisted by his loyal PA, Lynn.

Alan wore bad golfing sweaters, had a classic comb-over and was obsessed with the hits of Abba. No stock comedy caricature here, because of the deftness of Coogan's portrayal, his attention to detail and a forensic understanding of Alan's inner life. And yet, a number of sports reporters and local radio DJs have a touch of Partridge about them, which we might never have noticed without his insightful performance.

For a while, it seemed the Partridge persona, all bombast, self-belief, reactionary views and vulnerability, was going to be overshadowed by the arrival of Ricky Gervais's David Brent, who also inhabited this increasingly popular genre of faux documentary. But Brent and Partridge had different emotional journeys and story arcs. I only wish they'd met.

Meanwhile Steve Coogan's film career was taking off, with parts in Hollywood movies like *Ruby Sparks*, *What Maisie Knew* and the Oscar-nominated *Philomena*, which he co-wrote. These breaks have allowed Coogan to dip into Partridge whenever inspiration strikes, most recently in the film *Alan Partridge: Alpha Papa*, set in and around his much-mocked hometown of Norwich.

The success of Partridge stems from the richness of his back story and the depth of Coogan's characterization. If you see him interviewed as Alan, every response is filtered through his childlike, thwarted and dated world view. He is a man doomed to fail, who can't see it. And perhaps it's his ability to bounce back that means Alan Partridge will always be a part of the comedy landscape.

It's hard to do his persona justice. His self-belief, self-absorption and thick skin make him someone you might feel sorry for if he wasn't quite so offensive. And yet he is an utterly compelling character, representing the kind of out-of-time TV presenter, local radio DJ and author of soon-to-be remaindered coffee table books that we'd avoid like the plague in real life.

Yosser Hughes

If a fictional character's success can be judged by the familiarity of their catchphrase, Yosser Hughes is up there with the best. Catchphrases tend to be the stuff of comedy, with a few choice exceptions.[1]

But Yosser's 'Give us a job' and 'I can do that' were pure tragedy, with a dash of dark humour thrown in. He remains the standout character of Alan Bleasdale's seminal BBC drama series, *Boys from the Black Stuff*.

Bleasdale developed the story and characters just as Margaret Thatcher came to power in 1979. The six-episode series followed a single play, *Black Stuff*, about a group of disparate Liverpudlian labourers laying tarmac, and was broadcast in 1982, at a time when unemployment stood at three million and the North of England was particularly hard hit.

Yosser's Story, the penultimate episode in the series, showed a man in the throes of a nervous breakdown as work, marriage, kids and home are all taken from him. His manic mantra 'Give us a job' comes out of a desperation to hold everything together, and also reflects the culture of the man as breadwinner and sole provider.

So Yosser collars the guy painting white lines on a soccer pitch and the rent collector's beefy sidekick and says over and over again: 'Give us a job. I can do that.' His other habit is to headbutt; mostly himself against trees, the walls of a lift, the passenger seat of a police car – after headbutting the policeman first. It's as if, by thumping himself in the brain, he can clear the fog and find a solution. Either that or he's punishing himself for his failure as a husband and father.

[1] For example, Vito Corleone's 'I'm going to make him an offer he can't refuse.'

His three kids (played by Bleasdale's own children) trail after him loyally and he is grief-stricken when they are taken in to care; shades of *Cathy Come Home*[2] and equally powerful.

Yosser's tale is a litany of grimness. And yet, there's a gallows humour that comes from Bleasdale's pen and from the Scouser's sensibility. Would a Cockney, Cornish or Glaswegian Yosser have been so achingly funny and tragic? It's possible, but because of Bernard Hill's performance, it's also hard to imagine.

Yosser has one of the best lines of TV drama EVER. As his life unravels, he pours his heart out to a young priest through a confession curtain. He wails: 'I'm desperate.' The priest says: 'Call me Dan.' Yosser obeys: 'I'm desperate, Dan.' Some time later, Bleasdale confessed that he'd had that gag up his sleeve for years and just needed a good home for it.

In 2007, *Boys from the Blackstuff* came second to *The Sopranos* in a Channel 4 Top 50 countdown of the best TV dramas. Other characters were skilfully crafted by Bleasdale and consummately fleshed out by a cast including Michael Angelis, Julie Walters and Tom Georgeson.

But it's sad, desperate Yosser Hughes who stands out as the character of the series, of the Eighties and of British TV drama in general.

Saga Noren

Hans Rosenfeldt, co-creator of *The Bridge*, the crime series (literally!) spanning Sweden and Denmark, described in a BBC blog the process of creating the two central characters. Martin Rohde, the Danish detective, came easily: 'Someone who was curious about his colleagues and close to his emotions.'

The Swedish detective took longer. Then he had an idea. 'What if she was a woman with absolutely no social skills? Everything she can read, she'll learn, but when it comes to interaction with another person, she's totally lost. That was pretty much all we said about Saga Norén. The media and

[2] See 'Ten landmark TV dramas and comedies', Part 1, page 10.

the audience have decided that she has Asperger's, but we've actually never diagnosed her in the show.

'I understood and loved Saga from day one. That was not the case for everybody. Broadcasters, directors and even Sofia [Helin, who plays Saga] were a little worried. "Are we really going to like her?" It turned out we were.'

As a viewer who loves watching complex female characters on TV, I can't help wondering: would we have taken to Saga so universally without the grounding we gained from the women cops who came before her? Like *Prime Suspect*'s Jane Tennison (Jane Timoney in the US version) and *The Killing*'s Sarah Lund (Sarah Linden in the US version), not to mention Cagney and Lacey and Scott and Bailey. All are real women with Achilles heels, stop-start careers and messy love lives, apart from happily married Mary Beth Lacey, of course.

By the time Saga appeared on our TV screens in 2011, we were ready to be challenged. The woman cop didn't have to be the sidekick in stilettoes who needs rescuing by the macho-yet-flawed hero in the final climactic episode. Saga would do the rescuing. Saga would be the quick-witted, instinctive cop who would gnaw away at a crime, when 'normal' people went home to bed, until it was solved.

Her partner, Martin (played by Kim Bodnia), is also a refreshing take on the cop stereotype. But would he have been so interesting without Saga? Sofia Helin's performance brings a dignity and sensitivity to a character who might otherwise seem cold and emotionless. Saga is, of course, both those things on the surface, because she doesn't understand how relationships work. She's good, however, at picking up guys in bars and taking them home for a quick fuck. She asks: is that wrong?

Like Tennison and Lund before her, Saga was 'reformatted' as a French policewoman in *The Tunnel* and an American cop in *The Bridge USA*. In both cases, the detectives' poor people skills are attributed to Asperger's.

But the diagnosis seems superfluous to the original (and best) Saga. She just *is*. If she can't hang on to a live-in boyfriend or understand the complexities of Martin's screwed-up personal life, so what? She's a brilliant detective and, in her eyes, nothing else matters.

Eddie Grundy

The Archers is a British phenomenon and a national institution.[3] Who knows why it has lasted and what it tells us about rural Britain, then and now? And because I've been a loyal listener all my adult life, how can I ignore it? But who is the most memorable character? (Only yesterday a good friend declared, with some feeling, that I 'must' write about snobby Lynda Snell.)

The Archers are an extended family of relatively affluent farmers who live in the fictitious county of Borsetshire, somewhere in the Midlands. The Grundy family are the 'rude mechanicals' who, over the years, have doffed their caps to the Archers, the Aldridges, the Sterlings, the Snells... the toffs of Ambridge. There are other working-class families in *The Archers* but none with the same comedic potential as the Grundys in general and Eddie in particular.

I must confess here that I have another reason for giving Eddie 'memorable character' status. About thirty years ago, when as a journalist I visited 'Borsetshire' to write a magazine feature about *The Archers*, I attended an Eddie Grundy fan club gathering in a rural pub. The next day, I was driven round the country roads of Warwickshire by 'Eddie' actor Trevor Harrison. We even had tea with Norman 'Phil Archer' Painting.

Back then, the early 80s, Eddie had been granted near cult status by DJ John Peel and his producer John Walters because he was young and daft and he wore a cowboy hat, complete with horns, and sang Country and Western songs with the Dolly Parton-esque Jolene Rogers (later Jolene Perks-Archer). Eddie's fame gave *The Archers* a whole new fan base which has grown with him and, like him, now has families of its own.

With marriage to Clarrie Larkin and the birth of his two boys, William and Edward, Eddie was forced to grow up. But that never stopped him latching on to all manner of money-making scams. And his shady business operations have always been sanctioned by his equally devious dad, Joe.

Some see Eddie as an archetypal rural chav: lazy, lacking in taste and prone to dodgy deals. But unlike other working-class caricatures, Eddie usually

---

[3] See 'Ten landmark radio dramas and comedies', Part 1, page 17.

comes good in the end, either because Clarrie nips his latest enterprise in the bud or because he sees the error of his ways in the nick of time

He has also becomes a slightly more thoughtful and three-dimensional character because of his sons. Will and Ed, both now husbands and fathers, are fuelled by an ongoing feud that has torn the Grundy clan apart. And all because they loved the same woman, manipulative Emma Carter. In dealing with the fallout of this sibling rivalry, Eddie has had to be sensible, sensitive, conflicted and resigned. And you can't do that in a ridiculous cowboy hat with horns.

He may have matured into a caring father and loving granddad but listeners would hate him to grow up too much. *The Archers* requires comedy and tragedy in equal measure. Eddie has had his fair share of tragedy but the comedy will always come through because, along with Lynda Snell, that's what he's there for.

Nick Warburton

Think of the five most memorable characters you've seen on television, or heard on radio, and ask yourself why you remember them. What makes them different? Here are five that impressed me.

Three particular things about these characters help them to lodge in my memory. The first two are their simplicity and the fact that they stand slightly apart from those around them. They seem to be familiar *and* different at the same time. The third thing is that, with one exception, they talk well.

When I say they're simple I don't mean that they're straightforward. I mean they have a kind of clarity that makes them *immediately* known. They're recognizable. I've met people like them; I may even see aspects of myself in them. This immediacy, though, doesn't stop them being complex and capable of springing surprises.

These five characters are all in some way outsiders and there's something about outsiders that appeals to all of us. (The Ugly Duckling, Hamlet and Tony Soprano are all outsiders.) There's a distance, a vulnerability, about outsiders, even strong and capable ones like Fletcher or Meyer, that audiences like.

And they all, with that one obvious exception, have a way with words, a clear and individual voice by which we come to know them.

The philosophy of Norman Stanley Fletcher

Fletcher first appeared in the BBC sitcom *Porridge*, written by Dick Clement and Ian La Frenais. The pilot – *Prisoner and Escort* – was broadcast in 1973 and *Porridge* then ran for three series.

Fletcher is a career criminal, trying to survive a stretch in Slade Prison. He was played, brilliantly, by Ronnie Barker in a performance full of detailed observation and precise timing. Barker said there was a lot of himself, and his father, in Fletcher. Most of the characters on this list are a combination of good writing and good acting. When the match is as good as it is here, with Fletcher and Barker, the result is always greater than the sum of its parts.

Fletcher wants to do his time without falling foul of either the authorities or the more sinister inmates of Slade Prison, but at the same time he keeps a sharp eye open for any chance to improve his lot. Like Autolycus he's a snapper-up of unconsidered trifles and he comes from a long line of literary self-serving chancers, from Falstaff to Del Boy Trotter via the Artful Dodger, Sergeant Bilko and Arthur Daley. All these characters work, more or less, outside the law, but manage to escape our condemnation because they all have a rough charm. And they're funny.

Fletcher's also a philosopher. Life for him is a series of small battles in confined spaces with the odds stacked against him. All he has to help him are experience, cunning and a stoic determination not to be beaten. Even when the battles are lost, he still manages to survive through a pragmatic, laid-back wisdom. He speaks working-class London with a flat, throwaway delivery and a keen sense of irony perfectly suited to this philosophy.

The enigma of Anton Meyer

Anton Meyer was a brilliant cardio-thoracic surgeon in the long-running medical drama *Holby City*. He was created by Tony McHale and Mal Young and developed by several hands thereafter. He was called Meyer, or Mr Meyer, very rarely Anton.

What sets Meyer apart is ice and enigma.

The iciness can be seen in his implacable and lucid thought processes. He's cool and detached to the point of ruthlessness. And he's driven by professionalism. People who have anything to do with him – his patients and their relatives, his doctors and nurses – often find him unsympathetic and lacking in feeling. But they still want Meyer on their case because Meyer always knows what needs to be done and he never lets anything get in his way. There's always the hint – maybe less of a hint and more of a suspicion – that he really does care. He clearly cares about something – doing a good job – so maybe he cares about people too. Maybe there's a heart beating somewhere beneath the cool green gown.

We all love a hint of pity in the apparently pitiless. Or a touch of wickedness in the apparently saintly.

Meyer's language reflects all this. He has no small talk and what he does say is always measured, professional and precise. He uses words to say exactly what he means and to hide what, if anything, he's feeling.

The enigma of Meyer comes partly from a suggestion that his background is exotic – there's something foreign and mysterious about him – but more from the fact that so little is known about him. As soon as there are unanswered questions about someone, we speculate and try to fill in the gaps, and in the process we become fascinated. Sometimes the less you say about a character the more powerful he or she appears to be.

I almost ran into Mr Meyer once when I was working on *Holby City*. I'd gone to Elstree for a script meeting and I saw him at the far end of a corridor, sweeping towards me from the production offices, gowned and ready for theatre with a team of lesser medics in his wake. What I saw, of course, was the actor (George Irving) heading not for theatre but for the studios, but I still stepped aside to let him pass. There was something about Mr Meyer that made you step aside.

The aspiration of Harold Steptoe

Harold Steptoe appeared in *Steptoe and Son*, a BBC sitcom written by Alan Simpson and Ray Galton. It ran for eight series from 1962 to 1974 and later crossed the Atlantic to become *Sanford and Son*. It centred on two rag-and-bone men, junk dealers, a father and his thirty-something son. Harold, the son, was played by Harry H. Corbett and his father, Albert, by Wilfred Brambell. It was a wonderful double act, at its best when there were just the two of them on screen.

Like Norman Fletcher, Harold is a working-class Londoner. Unlike Fletcher, he isn't content with his lot. He's always dreaming of a better life, a life less lonely or more culturally fulfilling, and far away from the claustrophobic surroundings of Oil Drum Lane and the junkyard. He could achieve it too – he has wit, intelligence and imagination – but he also has Albert.

Albert is shackled to Harold. Much as his father appals him, much as he drives him to distraction with his disgusting habits and his constant tendency to humiliate, Harold is bound to Albert by filial duty and love.

They snipe at each other and bicker all day long, but when Harold is stood up by one of the few girls he manages to persuade over the threshold at Oil Drum Lane, Albert's relief is almost palpable. At the end of that episode, the romantic supper prepared for the girl – fish and chips – is shared by father and son.

Albert's and Harold's sparring is funny and sometimes cruel. They're Vladimir and Estragon, doomed to stay together and wait hopelessly for something to happen. Their story revolves around frustration, sacrifice and resentment. It's also about their poignant inter-dependence.

Something else Harold has in common with Norman Fletcher is his use of colloquial London English. The difference is that, while Fletcher's language inclines to undercutting and bathos, Harold's tends to become flamboyant and pretentious. This is particularly so when he is with people he wants to impress – the middle class, artists and women.

When Albert reminisces about the girls he used to bring back to the junkyard, Harold scoffs at the romantic image of the junkyard by moonlight. He contrasts this with the world of Antony and Cleopatra: on the one hand the pyramids of Egypt, on the other a 'pile of old ballcocks and gas stoves'.

After its successful run on television, *Steptoe and Son* was adapted for radio. It works particularly well in that medium, especially when Albert and Harold are trapped in their junk-filled room with only each other for company.

The silence of Bessie Bighead

Bessie Bighead is the odd one out in this list, because she's not part of a series. She appears, only briefly, in a single radio play, and she has hardly anything to say. She's one of the huge parade of characters – more than sixty – in Dylan Thomas's *Under Milk Wood*. When Bessie does speak she seems to say nothing of any consequence: she merely recites a list of cows' names as she brings them in for milking at the end of the day.

In spite of the brevity of her appearance, we do get to know her and she makes a lasting impression. Thomas's First Voice tells us about her: 'Conceived in Milk Wood, born in a barn, wrapped in paper, left on a doorstep.' He tells the story of how she was kissed, once, by Gomer Owen who has long since died, and how she looks to be kissed again but never will be. It gives her life a Chekhovian sense of poignancy.

I've chosen Bessie because I find Thomas's tender concern for her so touching, and because she shows what can be done in a few brief images, and how an almost silent character can be so memorable.

Bessie is the humblest of all the characters in *Under Milk Wood*, but she has her moment. Everything stops when she greets the cows and all attention is on her. When she says their names, the cows bow their heads.

The progress of Peggy Olson

Peggy Olson (Elizabeth Moss) is a character in *Mad Men*, the long-running television drama series about an advertising agency, Sterling Cooper, on Madison Avenue, New York. She's a kind of Cinderella, an outsider unappreciated, threatened by the system but (so far) undefeated by it.

Mad Men, created by Matthew Weiner in 2007, begins in the 1960s and moves towards us through the decades. Most TV drama series have a sort of *internal* history and geography: they're set in a recognizable world during an identifiable period of time – a 'now' or a 'then' or a 'time to come' – and their main characters have their own, usually consistent pasts. Peggy Olson, and the other *Mad Men* characters, work in an identifiable place, but they move and change with the times.

Peggy gets hurt, learns, adapts and progresses, and she does this in a ruthlessly misogynistic environment in which women aren't expected to progress.

She first appears in series one as the unassuming, slightly awkward secretary of the Byronic advertising genius Don Draper. She's quiet and watchful, often put-upon and frequently bewildered, but she won't accept the status quo and she will ask questions. Don isn't easy to work for. He's enigmatic (another one) and self-destructive. Most of the other characters bend over backwards to impress him but Peggy doesn't play that game. She does, however, understand him in a way that almost no one else does.

It's clear from the start of the series that Peggy is an outsider. All the other women in the office know they must dress to impress, keep the drinks cabinet filled and learn to play a game devised by men. The most 'successful' of these women is office manager Joan. Joan is super-efficient, wise and beautiful. She succeeds because she has a complete understanding of the business and the rules that govern it. But success for these women is no more than being the office manager, a kind of super secretary. They can't go beyond that. Peggy isn't even sure what the rules are – she sometimes breaks them by accident – but she can and does go beyond.

How to make your own memorable characters

It seems quite straightforward. Put together some combination of outsider, enigma, philosopher and/or wit. Throw in some flaws and find their voice. Then get a brilliant, perfectly suited actor to play the part.

It might just work – but there's no guarantee.

Notes on notes: Dealing with feedback

Sue Teddern

> *I owe my success to having listened respectfully to the very best advice and then going away and doing the exact opposite.*
>
> G. K. Chesterton

> *Remember, when people tell you something's wrong or doesn't work for them, they are almost always right. When they tell you exactly what they think is wrong and how to fix it, they are almost always wrong.'*
>
> Neil Gaiman

> *Nobody knows anything.*
>
> William Goldman, *Adventures in the Screen Trade*

If we only had to write for ourselves, our family and friends, there'd be no need for feedback; just a cosy excess of back-slapping on the brilliance of our bon mots. But that would only work for so long. Writing for yourself is not why you're reading this book; your aim is to write for TV and Radio. And with that, comes the joy and despair that is feedback.

Sometimes a first draft practically writes itself. You feel giddy from the adrenalin rush of filling page after page. You send your script off to the person whose approval you seek and you anticipate a medal for crossing the finishing line. You did it!

Then, swiftly or slowly, comes the response. Sometimes it's helpful and encouraging, sometimes it's so destructive, vague or irrelevant that you sink into a fug of confusion. You might punch the wall or curl up in the foetal position with your thumb in your mouth. Effective in the short term but it won't get you back on the horse.

Feedback comes in many forms so it might help to break it down into sub-sections.

The scriptwriting competition

If you need a deadline, writing competitions can be extremely helpful. Nothing concentrates the mind better than a fast-approaching date in your diary.

But you have to remember that you will be in 'competition' with a vast number of other entrants. That's bound to stack the odds against you, even if yours is a real page-turner. Your script will be assessed by the legion of unsung hero(in)es of script competitions – I have been one myself – for the long list and, ultimately, the shortlist.

If your script reaches the final ten but doesn't win, you'll probably get some very helpful and encouraging feedback. Second and third prize-winners sometimes get a commission.

If it falls at the very first hurdle, you'll receive an anodyne standard letter, thanking you for your interest but not telling you why your script didn't tick sufficient boxes. Discouraging, to say the least. If you aren't told where you went wrong, how can you fix it in your next script? Dare you show it to an honest friend or partner? Will they stroke your ego or make you feel worse?

Your best bet is to read it through some time later, when the hurt has gone away. Pretend you're one of the judges. Read it through their eyes. What didn't work for them? What would you do differently?

Of course, if you can see nothing wrong with your script, it could just be that the sheer volume of numbers was against you or something similar beat you by a head. Or it just wasn't good enough. Don't be discouraged. Back to the blank page and start again.

Submitting a script

Let's assume you sent a script of an original piece of work to a specific producer or development person. It could be a while before you hear anything. If they like what they read, they'll probably invite you in for a meeting. Don't crack open the vintage Moet just yet but you can treat yourself to a celebratory glass of supermarket Merlot.

What if they don't like it? You have to hope their comments will be constructive and of value.

Here's a recent rejection of something I wrote, which my agent passed on to me.

> 'I'm so sorry for the long delay in getting back to you. The reason for this is that I wanted to share the script with the others here. This only happens rarely, when something has potential!
>
> Unfortunately, however, I don't think it's one for us. We enjoyed the warmth and the lightness of touch, and the writing felt truthful and real. There's very much a market for a lighter, relationship-based series right now. That said, we felt that ultimately the characters didn't quite punch through enough to really make this a standout commission.
>
> I'm really sorry not to come back with a more enthusiastic response! We thought it had lots of potential, but not quite enough to warrant putting it into development.'

So it's a no. But it's a fairly positive one. Generally, this kind of feedback will be gentle, to the point of bland, and won't have you bawling your eyes out or kicking the cat. Even if something's really not their cup of tea, they'll say so nicely; the kind of polite brush-off you would give someone after a first date. Why stick the knife in?

Hey-ho, onward and upward...

> **SAM BAIN TOP TIP**
>
> Try not to treat every note as if it was an arrow aimed by an assassin straight for your heart. If you can find even one thing in any given set of notes which helps you improve your script, they were worth receiving.

> Have compassion for the note-giver. Like the wolf in the forest, they are just as scared of you as you are of them. They are probably frustrated writers at heart, who envy your good looks and your prodigious talent.

As Sam says in his excellent essay, Notiquette,[1] this process shouldn't have to be unpleasant. I reckon velvet gloves are worn more often in radio than TV. Because of the fast turnaround of TV scripts and the pressure producers are under, they can often forget to sugar the pill. Some go for the jugular because they like to show who's in charge.

Having been a script editor myself, I know the frustration of passing on gently phrased feedback and not seeing any attempt by the writer to address the problem in subsequent drafts. This is frustrating.

But just as script editors need to be diplomatic and encouraging, so writers have to listen and take criticism on board. If it's possible, change the things that don't matter and dig your heels in about the things that do. You will know the time to fight and the time to roll over.

Feedback can also be contrary. In draft two, you are told to make Sarah a hypochondriac. So reluctantly you do and, hey, it works brilliantly. In draft three, someone higher up the food chain says: 'Why the hell is Sarah a hypochondriac?' And you want to shout: 'Because that's what I was told to do!' But you bite your tongue and change it back to how it was ... or young sexy Sarah becomes anxious OAP Elsie ... or Sarah is a kleptomaniac, not a hypochondriac ... or Sarah is cut from the episode altogether.

Or you're sacked and who cares about Sarah!

Reviews from critics

I've had some lovely previews and reviews for my radio dramas, from my very first play onwards. TV critics tend to be more brutal. Or

---

[1] See Part 2, page 85.

maybe I've been unlucky. Or what I wrote deserved the harsh criticism it got. (Surely not ...)

Some actors refuse to read reviews in case it puts them off their stride. They have a point. It seems these days that TV reviewing is a glorified license to go for the jugular. Reviews like this are fun to write but hurtful to read, especially when you know how much blood, sweat and tears has gone into a production.

A famously acerbic TV reviewer recently listed some dramas that didn't work for her.

- '[The heroine] danced wildly in her flat, she sang along to the radio in her car. I hated her with every fibre of my being.'
- 'The dullest drama in recent years ... It was very brown.'
- 'Maundering, pretentious, mannered drama.'
- 'Xxxxx is a workaday, clichéd, lazy drama which isn't on nodding terms with even the teensiest bit of true emotion or authentic police procedure. It can hang off that cliff until its fingers bleed, it can fall down a mineshaft, my sleep won't be troubled.'

I must confess that some of these dramas didn't work for me either and yes, doesn't this critic have a witty, biting turn of phrase? But when reviews are so harsh, destructive and point-scoring, it makes good emotional sense not to take them too seriously.

Good notes v. bad notes

I asked some very experienced writers to nominate the best and worst feedback they've ever received from script editors and producers.

The negative comments demonstrate the importance of having a double-density rhino skin. The positive comments show how a simple word of encouragement can send you off to write that next draft with a spring in your step and an urgency in your typing fingers.

Bad notes top ten

1. 'We need to sympathise with the child more. Can you give him Down's Syndrome?'
2. 'It's a really glossy, sexy glamorous show set in London. So we want writers who can nail that. Obviously you are Welsh. I don't mean that's a problem but you do live in Cardiff.'
3. 'We probably had it right three drafts ago.'
4. Worst note I observed being given to another writer at a script meeting. He just turned page after page of the script saying: 'shite, shite, shite, shite, shite ...'
5. 'It's as bad as it could possibly be' left as a voicemail.
6. 'It's missing the X Factor.' I asked if he could explain exactly what he meant by that. The reply: 'You're the writer. Figure it out.'
7. 'Your scenes have no sense of mission, conflict, purpose or drama.' Still brings me out in a cold sweat when I remember it. The radio play was broadcast and was pretty successful.
8. 'I can tell it's well written but I don't like any of the characters, the era it's set in or the story.'
9. From a famous actor: 'This script is whippet shit!'
10. A relatively inexperienced script editor made a weighing motion with her hands, then said disapprovingly: 'Your script's heavier than Kate's.'

Good notes top ten

1. 'So many people in the office are choked up reading this last draft.'
2. I worked with a script editor who could ask for a total rewrite, yet somehow leave the writer feeling good about him/herself and enthused about the next draft. Genius!
3. 'Go home, have a big glass of wine and then write that scene again.'
4. The best note I ever got: 'When you finish a draft, make notes on each scene: what's in it, what the characters are doing, use of subtext.' You'd be surprised how many duplicate scenes you've written that can be cut.

5. There's a difference between someone saying something nice about what you wrote and being given a good note. Often, in telly writing, just the fact that the producer or script editor is turning page after page without saying anything has to be taken as positive approval.
6. This from a radio producer about a treatment for a play. 'Less *Archers*, more Pinter.' It worked for me. The play was a huge success.
7. I forgot my copy of the script at a meeting. The producer gave me her marked-up copy, warning me I'd need a thick skin. Reading her notes was an education. Full of swearing and exclamation marks. And this on a script she liked! Really helpful though to see it from her side of the desk.
8. One of my best notes came from an actress. She said: 'I missed that there wasn't a scene between the mother and the youngest son.' She was spot-on. I went away and wrote what became the most powerful scene in the piece.
9. 'Why is this character speaking? We could have an explosion instead.' A great note. I like to think I have never written a superfluous character since.
10. A script editor sent me a one-line note: 'Think *Brief Encounter*'. He was giving me permission to have fun with the script. And it worked!

Coping with the meddling

Nick Warburton

You are the writer, so you're responsible for every line of dialogue, every move an actor makes, every change in lighting, sound or location in your script. And yet, if that script is to reach an audience, if it's to be broadcast, other people will have their say about what you've written, and sometimes that say will outweigh yours. If those other people have put up the money or if they hold the purse strings, their opinion will certainly have more weight.

'I cannot endure another person to meddle with my sentences,' said Ada Lovelace[2] and most writers will know exactly what she meant.

---

[2] Ada Lovelace was Lord Byron's daughter. She was an exceptional mathematician and a gifted writer.

Learning to write drama means learning how to cope with meddling. You'll have to identify the boundary between what it's reasonable for you to accept ('We think it might work for us if you relocated this to Wolverhampton') and what you consider unacceptable ('We think the whole thing might be improved if your central character were a vampire'). You must decide where to draw the line. Different people draw the line in different places, but you should know that it's not a good idea to draw it thickly round your script like some sort of barricade to keep out anyone who attempts to come near. Writing for TV and radio (and stage) is a collaborative business. And a lot of the time – though not always – that's part of the pleasure of it.

I once worked on a series where a senior executive would come in at a late stage to make script changes. He (or was it she?) went through everyone's script and tweaked the dialogue. Ada would have hated that, and she would have been right. I should have objected to it and drawn the line. But I didn't. (I'm not sure if anyone ever did.) The result of this interference was, predictably, that the dialogue was homogenized to such an extent that almost all the characters sounded like the executive producer.

There are several groups who might see your script and have opinions about it and you'll probably react to each group in a different way. In fact, it wouldn't be appropriate to have the same reaction to them all.

Friends and family

If you've finished a script and consider showing it to a friend or a family member, the best thing you can do is change your mind. After all, what can you possibly gain from doing such a thing? Either you'll be pointlessly and meaninglessly flattered or you'll risk damaging a precious relationship. You might make an exception to this rule if you have one true friend or family member who's not afraid to tell you what he or she thinks, who can express that opinion in a way that's not cutting or destructive, and whose knowledge about and experience of writing for TV or radio you really respect. Do you have such an aunt, uncle, friend? If you do, go ahead and ask.

The alternative is to learn to do the job yourself, to learn the trick of self-criticism.[3] But it's not easy to be properly objective. Either you'll be tempted to be too soft on yourself ('Brilliant; this is exactly what the world's been waiting for!') or too hard ('It's complete rubbish! Give up now!'), which is just as pointless.

Something else to avoid is sending your script to a friend of a friend who happens to have some connection with the business. ('I just love your work. I wonder if you might give me a few pointers …') It's a very big favour to ask. Remember the scene in *Shakespeare in Love* when the man who rows Shakespeare up and down the river tells him, 'I'm a bit of a writer myself'? There are agencies who'll give your script a critical reading for you and, quite rightly, they'll charge a proper fee.[4]

You could take your script to a local writers' group who might workshop it and tell you what they think. But the friends and family rule applies here, too. If they know what they're talking about and can strike a balance between honesty and encouragement, listen to them and take notes. But often they'll try to be kind, and kindness – though it's always welcome – will not teach you to improve. And anyway praising a script which has no pulse is not kindness.

Script editors

If you're working in radio your director will probably be your script editor. It's likely, too, that he or she will also be your producer. This makes communication much easier and the whole process much quicker. In television your script editor should be your link with the rest of the team. They will also give you notes on your script. I mention this in more detail in chapter seven of section three because notes from script editors and producers might be considered part of the rewriting process.

A friend of mine says the ideal script editor is a grizzled sixty-plus writer who's been through the mill a few times and therefore knows not only what needs to be said about a script but also when it's best to

3 For how to become your own critic see Part 3, page 260, on rewriting.

4 See our reading, viewing and listening list in Part 3, page 284.

say little or nothing. It's rarely the case in TV that script editors are this old and experienced, though. They're usually young things and learning the business as they go. In my experience most of them are charming and talented, but they don't always have an understanding – and how could they? – of the writing process.

Producers

See above. Script editors are often the messengers who bring pronouncements from Olympus where the producers take their coffee. In television there's a hierarchy of producers and executives. As time rolls by and you get nearer to studio dates, you also get closer to Zeus; the biggest and the most influential member of that hierarchy moves in to have his or her say. On a well-run show, what they say will not come as a surprise because they will have made their feelings clear at the start of the process. They will have agreed the stories you're trying to tell.

But this doesn't always happen. You still get some who want to meddle with your sentences.

Tom Stoppard, in his introduction to the published script of *Parade's End* (his 2012 five-part adaptation of Ford Maddox Ford's novel) is very good on notes from producers and executives. He makes two important points. One is that the writer's immediate reaction to criticism is likely to be defensive. The other is that these notes from on high sometimes come with brilliant insights.

Directors

A director will have to realize your drama, change it from words on a page to sounds and/or pictures. And, if they're properly engaged in the process, directors will have ideas about how to do this.

In television you might not meet the director until quite late in the process. This always seemed to me a pity because my script might have been improved by hearing what a director had to say about it. Of course, it's usually the budget that decides when the director joins the production. Lots of money and the director can sit down with the writer right at the beginning. In radio you will probably have been talking to the director for some time.

The director's realm is the studio – or the set or location – and there may well be moments during recording when the sheer practicality of putting a script on its feet will suggest changes. ('We don't have to know that Herbert's left at this point: it might be more effective if Harriet turns and finds, exactly when we do, that he's not there.') If it's a brilliant idea there's no good reason to reject it. The trick is knowing – on the spur of the moment – whether it is or isn't brilliant.

Actors

Actors will also have opinions. It's worth listening to them. See Part 3, **The finishing line** for more on talking and listening to actors.

> **Actors**. Create lively, juicy, unexpected characters for actors to play and most will do you proud.
>
> *Marcy Kahan*

Audiences

It's in the nature of TV and radio that you're cut off from your audience. Hundreds of thousands of people may have heard or seen your work but you won't necessarily know that they have, or what their response was. If you do get some indication of what an audience thinks, you'll have to judge whether or not you agree with them. If a vociferous minority of people were confused by your script you might be justified in asking them to go back and look again, or to pay more attention next time. If nobody at all understands what you've written maybe you're the one who ought to think again.

This doesn't mean that you should underestimate, or patronize, the audience. To do so is almost always a mistake. Most audiences have a practised ability to follow complex storylines and cope with layers of meaning. And most good drama takes that into consideration.

Critics

Whether or not you pay any attention to what the critics say is up to you. I usually intend not to but sometimes break that rule, spontaneously and for no obvious reason. If you do read them – and if there are any reviews out there to read – it's likely that you'll take the good ones with a grain of salt and the bad ones will be branded on your memory. It's worth noting, though, that not all TV and radio critics are critics in the proper sense of the word. They don't all have an interest in the medium they're writing about. Many of them write entertaining and amusing columns which happen to be hung on what they've seen on TV or heard on radio. Radio critics like Gillian Reynolds (of *The Daily Telegraph*) and Kate Chisholm (of *The Spectator*), who both know and care about radio, are the exception.

Having a laugh: Writing comedy

Sue Teddern

Funny for money

We've all been at a wedding where the best man's speech is bum-clenchingly lame. Or the kiddie's party where the entertainer recites a bunch of creaky old gags to a screaming horde who'd rather be eating crisps and hitting each other. Or listened to the friend who thinks stand-up's simply a question of rattling off a string of second-hand sexist one-liners.

Are you funny enough to make a living from it?

> Ask yourself:
>
> - Do you think you're funny?
> - Do your friends think you're funny?
> - Do people often comment on the wittiness of your emails and Tweets?
> - When you try to write something serious, does it come out funny?

If you see your future in TV and radio, thinking you're funny may not be enough. Writing a script that's structurally sound, stuffed with great characters *and* LOL hilarious might just be too tall a mountain to climb. Getting it right and getting it funny is a bit like rubbing your tummy and patting your head at the same time.

And how many of us can do that?

Anyway, what's 'funny'? Out there at any one time, we have fifty shades of 'funny': from slapstick and banana skins, mistaken identity and double entendre to dry-as-a-bone satire, mockumentaries and gallows humour.

It may help to tell you the route I took.

'I could write rubbish like that!'

I'd written stacks of funny articles for teen magazines and they were hard to get right because the young female readership was unbelievably discerning. Good training for my future career, although I didn't know it at the time.

As a freelance journalist, I'd interviewed many of the comedy greats: Victoria Wood, French and Saunders, Bob Monkhouse, Ken Dodd, Larry Grayson, Paul Jackson, Stephen Fry and Hugh Laurie.

Maybe subconsciously I was embedding myself in this world so that I'd know what it looked like when the time came to craft my first sitcom.

I loved comedy and I wanted to be a writer. I'd watched a lot of bad sitcoms over the years and thought, as we all have: I can write rubbish like that!

TOP TIP

If you don't respect the genre, your script will be rubbish, you will be found out and you may even consider giving up on your ambition forever because of that growing stack of rejection letters in your desk drawer.

And if you're destined to write the next big award-winning hit, that would be a shame.

Lesson #1: Don't write anything you wouldn't watch/listen to.

During this period, I took what's known as the 'Yellow Pages' approach, finding instant inspiration for the 'situation' element of sitcom by flicking through this hefty directory.[1]

---

[1] For younger readers, Yellow Pages is a telephone directory, fashioned from paper and yellow in hue, much favoured by one J. R. Hartley, which, pre- Google and Mozilla Firefox, was used to locate local plumbers, party planners, catteries, carpet shops, you name it. Ask your grandmother.

'Hey, why don't I write a comedy series set in, um, let's see, a gas canister supply warehouse!'

My early sitcom ideas were not literally found via Yellow Pages. But almost: nannies, a second-hand dress shop, a trendy Soho restaurant, a one-woman catering company. This one was called *Sausage on a Stick*.

I used a writing technique much favoured by naïve newbies, which involved churning the script out in a couple of days, with no thought for characterization, structure, consistency of tone or plot. I was not very discerning about what went on the page and, consequently, I could get a script written really fast. Hey, this sitcom lark's a piece of cake. Bring on the BAFTA.

And yet there must have been something there, amongst all the hastily bashed-out dross. I got a lovely letter back about my nannies script from a TV director called Mandie Fletcher. She was supportive and sisterly. She liked my script, just not enough to take it any further. I was left with some useful, no-holds-barred feedback and a sense that I wasn't wasting my time.

This was the late 80s. Few women were getting their scripts on TV, apart from writer-performers like Victoria Wood and French & Saunders, and so various organizations set up workshops to encourage us. This is where I met a bunch of like-minded, funny women who became, and still are, some of my closest friends. We called ourselves Material Girls and we still do.

No, but seriously...

Being taken seriously by Mandie spurred me on. I edited my scripts more judiciously before sending them. Just because there was rubbish on the telly didn't mean I had to generate any more of it.

I find it hard now to remember this stroppy, motivated, driven, young(ish) woman who was me. I'm still all those things – except the young bit. What made me attend every workshop, enter every competition, follow up every initiative? What made me think I could do this?

And then, one of the doors I wedged my foot in suddenly opened wide. I attended the 1989 Edinburgh Television Festival as part of their Newcomers scheme. This gave me a free delegate's ticket to listen to the best practitioners in the business talking about their craft.

One session was an audience with writers Laurence Marks and Maurice Gran, who were talking about their new BBC One sitcom, *Birds of a Feather*. They'd written the first series themselves and intended to gather around them a writing team, to take on series two. A team-written sitcom about three women?

To quote Yosser Hughes:[2] 'I could do that!'

At the end of the session, a crowd of wannabes clustered around 'Lo and Mo' to express an interest in being on the team. I wasn't going to get a look-in. Yet.

Back in London, I wangled a commission from the *Guardian* to interview Marks and Gran about *Birds of a Feather*. After the feature was published, I sent them a cassette of my second radio play to show them what I could do.

Lo and Mo could see that it made sense to have a woman on a team writing a sitcom about women. I was the 'token' but I didn't care. Of the 100-plus episodes of the successful sitcom in its Nineties version,[3] I wrote thirteen. (Or maybe twelve. Or fourteen. I'm not entirely sure now …)

It was a baptism by fire. I was the last-minute addition to an established team, several of them pairs of young gung-ho guys who'd been writing together for years. Not only did I have to fit in with them, keep up with them and shout above them, I had to be funny too. And as 90 per cent of the time I was the only woman writer, I had to be 120 per cent funny 100 per cent of the time if I wanted to keep my place at the table. I didn't always manage it, but I gave it my best shot.

My first episode, *Keep off the Grass*, was recorded in front of an enthusiastic studio audience who laughed in all the right places. The BBC decided they wanted a longer run of series two. So, almost instantly, I got a commission to write a further episode, *Jobs for the Girls*. I also got an agent. It was official. My sitcom career had begun.

If comedy is about truth, I felt I had a big advantage over the guys on the *Birds* team. What they had in previous sitcom experience, I had in being a

---

[2] See 'Ten memorable TV and radio characters', page 47.

[3] *Birds of a Feather* returned on a different channel (ITV) in 2013.

woman. So when we discussed an episode about Sharon going on a diet, I made sure I was the one wrote it. Because I'd been there, done that, got the size 16 T-shirt. As a comedy apprenticeship, I sometimes felt I'd gone from nursery slope to ski jump with nothing in-between. But it was a brilliant experience and I'm very proud of my *Birds* episodes.

What kind of ha-ha?

Over the years, I've written numerous comedy scripts for TV and radio; some have been out-and-out sitcoms, some comedy-dramas. And with every script, I knew long before I wrote the very first line of dialogue the kind of ha-ha I was after... from belly laugh to wry smile, from surreal imagery to warts-and-all reality. Like I said, fifty shades of funny.

If you feel this is your world, that you can be funny for money, bear in mind that you might be choosing one of the hardest forms of writing there is. I would say that, wouldn't I. But it's true.

When you write straight drama, you have to work on structure, characters, dialogue, subtext, plot and subplots, themes, authenticity, marketability, length, story arcs, series arcs and should your heroine be Kayleigh, Kylie, Carli or Keeley?

When you write comedy, you have to do all the above *and* be funny. If that scares you, it's meant to. If you think it's too difficult, forget 'funny'. Be serious. Or try comedy-drama, where the comedy is an added extra, not the main ingredient. It's not an admission of guilt to steer clear of comedy, it's simply a question of knowing your strengths as a writer – what you do best.

Four laughs a page

A successful sitcom requires a minimum of four laughs per page. And I mean 'laughs', not silent titters or ironically raised eyebrows. Three laughs per page used to be the industry standard. I'm not sure at what point the extra laugh became de rigueur. If you talk to any comedy producer about how they read scripts, they'll tell you that they tick every potential laugh.

Two or three silent chuckles per page just won't cut it.

So. Can you do that?

- Be brave. Ask a friend whose taste you trust to go through one of your sitcom scripts and tick all the lines that made them laugh.
- Be *really* brave. Ask them to also put a cross beside the lines that didn't work.
- Now look through the script again with a clear dispassionate eye.
- Are they right?
- Or did you ask the wrong friend?

Seriously funny or funnily serious

Comedy doesn't always have to be funny but, in my book, it must be truthful. Gags shoehorned-in for the sake of an easy laugh will look out of place. There's nothing wrong with a dash of 'serious' if it's true to the tone and the characters.

Here's Christopher Lloyd talking about a serious scene in the sitcom pilot of *Frasier*:

> Towards the end of the second act of the pilot, Frasier and his father, Martin, finally have the confrontation that has been brewing since the start and it's a long, angry, mean and very true sounding fight. That doesn't happen in sitcoms very often. It happens in pilot scripts even less, the thinking presumably being that we are trying to get our audience to like these people and maybe having them say harsh hurtful things to each other for a long time isn't the best way to do that.
>
> But the scene played beautifully, and it taught us as writers that we never had to shy away from a dramatic scene – these actors would make such scenes compelling – even in the framework of a comedy. I think what the scene ultimately taught the audience was that this was a program which promised not just to be funny but also perhaps to be poignant and true.
>
> *The Best of Frasier*

I wrote a funny-serious moment in an episode of *Birds of a Feather* called *Baby Come Back*, when Dorien, the sex-crazed neighbour, suddenly gets uncharacteristically honest and talks about her decision not to have children.

> There comes a point where you have to choose: children or beige carpets. I opted for carpets.

Lesley Joseph delivers the line with an imperceptible flash of sadness which she almost instantly turns off again. A brilliant performance. Indeed when, years later, Lesley Joseph talked about Dorien in a BBC TV documentary,[4] she cited this scene as one that meant a lot to her, as it did to me.

I wrote that, I thought proudly to myself. Yes. Me. I did. Would a male writer have explored her vulnerability and sense of loss in the same way? Hmm, I wonder . . .

One idea, five formats

In Part 3 of this book, we'll provide the nuts, bolts, screws and hinges of writing for TV and radio. How to develop ideas, craft characters, embrace structure, finesse dialogue, reinvent that next draft.

But if you're still thinking 'funny', it's worth taking some time to look at your writing voice, your skills and your commitment to one long-term project. It's also vital to think about your ideal audience, slot and channel. Who will commission your sitcom? Who will watch it?

A poem exists as soon as it's written and recited. A song comes to life when it's sung. But a sitcom script for TV or radio only achieves its ambition when it's broadcast. If not, it's just a big wodge of paper in your desk drawer or 86.5 KB of memory on your hard drive. Making an audience hoot with laughter has to be your aim.

So. You have an idea. Let's say, for the sake of argument, it's about a quirky, eccentric family. What if they not only live together but work together? What if they run a café? Let's call it *Crunch Time*.

Now's the time to think about:

---

[4] *Sex and the Sitcom*, BBC Four.

- What direction should it go in?
- What makes it different?
- Who will commission it?
- Who will watch or listen to it?

Let's look at various genres of comedy and see whether *Crunch Time* would fit into each template.

The traditional sitcom

- TV examples: *Miranda, My Family, Mrs Brown's Boys, Fawlty Towers, Porridge, Friends, Absolutely Fabulous, Father Ted, The Big Bang Theory, Big School, Frasier, Red Dwarf, Birds of a Feather.*
- Radio examples: *Claire in the Community, Cabin Pressure, Old Harry's Game, The Clitheroe Kid, Bleak Expectations, Count Arthur's Radio Show.*

This category of comedy requires one essential ingredient: a studio audience. And to keep them laughing, you will need those four laugh-out-loud moments per page. At the very least. The audience has come along to a hot studio, expecting to be entertained. And their laughter – which is not 'canned' but may be 'tweaked' – is essential to their night out and to the sound of the show.

If it's a TV sitcom, it'll probably be set in a workplace (*Frasier, Miranda, Father Ted*) or a domestic setting (*Mrs Brown's Boys* and, again, *Miranda* and *Frasier*). There are two reasons for this. One is theoretical, one is practical.

The theoretical reason is that all classic sitcoms come out of captivity. *Gilligan's Island*, an American success of the 60s, was all about a group of people shipwrecked on an island. How captive can you get? *Hogan's Heroes*, about a POW camp, and *Porridge*, about prisoners, are two more examples.

Less literal models of captivity are 'work'- and 'home'-based sitcoms. In a two-star hotel in Devon, a friendly bar in Boston, a geeky flat share or daft priests' house, the characters are stuck with each other. Often the flat/workmates would love to be somewhere else but this is where they are right now. *Steptoe and Son*[5] is a perfect example: a father and son who can't live with each other and can't live without each other.

---

[5] Remade as *Sanford and Son* in the USA.

And the practical reason? If every week the story unfolds in the pub or around the kitchen table or on the flight deck of the spaceship; you can use the same studio set every week. And thus *Frasier*'s Café Nervosa, *Friends*' Central Perk, *Sharon* and Tracey's Chigwell kitchen and *Miranda*'s joke shop become familiar and recognizable, week after week after week. We like that. And the producers like it because it saves money!

Radio comedy doesn't need the same sets each week because the audience designs them while they listen. But a pilot's cabin, social workers' office or Hell can still provide that essential claustrophobia and mutual intolerance.

The other ingredient of the traditional sitcom is that our characters always return to the status quo. Yes, there may be long-term relationship arcs, as in *Friends* or *Claire in the Community*, but more often than not, the episodes of a traditional sitcom can be shown in any order because we always return to square one, with our characters none the wiser. We're back where we started twenty-five minutes ago.

So, the basic premise has to run and run, series after successful series, with enough characters to generate an almost infinite number of plots and subplots. *And* we need a central meeting place. *And* it needs to have an imperceptible pace of change. *And* we need it to be four-gags-a-page funny to make our audiences both in the studio and on the sofa laugh their socks off.

EXERCISE

Ask yourself:

- Could *Crunch Time*, set in a family-run café, work well as a traditional studio-based-audience sitcom?
- What kind of tone and humour is required to achieve a commission from one of the major broadcasters?
- Will you have enough ideas and plots for your setting and central characters for six episodes per series and, if you're lucky, a series that can return time after time?

The non-audience comedy

- TV examples: *The In-Betweeners, Gavin & Stacey, Episodes, Scrubs, Manchild, Boomers, Rev, Extras, The Detectorists, Marion and Geoff, How Do You Want Me?*
- Radio examples: *Fags, Mags and Bags, The Go-Betweenies, In and Out of the Kitchen, Ladies of Letters.*

The traditional sitcom went out of fashion for a while and was replaced by single-camera comedy, filmed away from the claustrophobia of the studio set and minus the tyranny of the laughter track.

Often it's because the comedy is gentler, aka 'bittersweet', as in *Getting On, Rev* and *Marion & Geoff. The In-Betweeners* certainly isn't gentle and it is full of big laughs. I suspect the creators and producers opted for a non-audience show because they wanted their characters' world to be larger, albeit the limited world of the late teen. Likewise *Gavin & Stacey* needed the freedom to hop between the couple's two home towns of Barry and Billericay.

Sometimes the difference in tone between a studio and non-studio sitcom is minimal, but for a writer the freedom not to have to be funny non-stop is very liberating.

EXERCISE

Ask yourself:

- What would you gain by making *Crunch Time* a gentler comedy-drama, without a studio audience?
- What would you lose?
- Which channel would commission it?
- What slot would it suit?

The spoof documentary

- TV examples: *The Office, Parks and Recreation, Twenty Twelve, Modern Family, Derek, Family Tree, Life's Too Short, People Like Us, W1A.*
- Radio examples: *People Like Us.*

The mockumentary genre was perfected by Christopher Guest and Michael McKean in their movies *Spinal Tap*, *Best in Show* and *A Mighty Wind*.

Three creative minds dominate the TV list: Ricky Gervais & Stephen Merchant and John Morton. Morton created the spoof documentary for BBC Radio 4, *People Like Us*, in 1999, in which reporter Roy Mallard (Chris Langham) profiled a different 'real person' each week: the estate agent, the photographer, the vicar. The series transferred, with some success, to BBC TV.

More recently, Morton's faux documentaries have looked at the build-up to London's Olympic Games with *Twenty Twelve* and the BBC itself with *W1A*. Morton's scripts thrive on a dysfunctional workplace, often staffed by yes-men, cliché spouters and idiots. There's always a plausibly over-wordy narration too; *Twenty Twelve*'s and *W1A*'s were supplied by David Tennant.

The template now set, Ricky Gervais and co-creator Stephen Merchant took the mockumentary and further explored its potential with *The Office*. Yes, another workplace setting, but by revisiting the Wernham Hogg paper company each week, we got to know the group dynamic: David Brent's misplaced self-belief, the bickering between cynical Tim and childlike Gareth, and Tim's secret love for Dawn.

The success of *The Office*, both in the UK and USA, gave Gervais and Merchant full rein to continue in this vein with *Life's Too Short* and *Derek*. And of course, *The Office* transferred seamlessly to the Dunder Mifflin paper company in Scranton, Pennsylvania and ran for nine seasons.

Like traditional sitcoms, mockumentaries are generally told in thirty-minute episodes. Look out for shaky hand-held single camera, pieces to camera where David Brent, Michael Scott, Siobhan Sharpe or Leslie Knope give their interpretation of what's going on, often at odds with what we see on screen. That's where the comedy comes from: people who are up against it or lacking self-awareness pretending everything's hunky-dory.

EXERCISE

Ask yourself:

- Could *Crunch Time* work in the mockumentary format?
- Would the café setting offer up enough plots?
- Is this a format and genre that's best left to experts like Gervais, Merchant and Morton?

The sketch show

- TV examples: *Harry and Paul, Little Britain, French and Saunders, Morecambe and Wise, Goodness Gracious Me, The Two Ronnies, Victoria Wood as seen on TV, Saturday Night Live, That Mitchell and Webb Look, Monty Python's Flying Circus.*
- Radio examples: *The Now Show, Goodness Gracious Me, Little Britain, Round the Horne, That Mitchell and Webb Sound.*

Many of the performers listed above learned their craft writing sketches for other people. It was a way to earn some dosh, get your material broadcast, get your name known, maybe even get an agent. There were and still are shows for TV and radio that eat up material and are always on the lookout for writers who can crank out sketch after sketch after sketch.

But there's also a common denominator to many of the shows I've listed, which is that sketch shows are often written by the performers themselves. So this is an excellent foot in the door if you're also a stand-up comedian or comic actor.

If you're not, you'll need to know through the grapevine which sketch shows are on the lookout for writers. And for every half-dozen sketches you write, maybe only one will make the grade. If that. I tried it when I was starting out and it wasn't for me. It's a tough way to earn a living but it can often open doors to bigger projects, as it has done for many of our best-known comedy writer-performers.

EXERCISE

Ask yourself:

- Could *Crunch Time* work as a sketch show set in a café?
- Would every sketch need to be catering related, themed around food, or featuring regular customers and cranky staff?
- Might this be too limiting for this format?

Single plays and films

By this, I mean the one-off radio play or made-for-TV movie. Radio is an excellent home for self-contained comedy plays. And they don't have the pressure of the studio audience and those dreaded four ticks a page. This is also the place for plots that don't run on, series after series, but have a nice neat beginning, middle and end. The 45-minute afternoon drama is a brilliant length for a play and it suits the three-act structure of good storytelling.

Made-for-TV one-off movies are only ever likely to be commissioned from established writers and, because of the cost, tend to be broadcast as and when, rather than in a regular slot. If you're the kind of writer who will get movies like this off the ground, I have one question: why are you reading this book?

But if you're starting out, just think of the filmic possibilities of slicing that 90-minute comedy film script into 45 minutes for radio, keeping all the locations and characters. If you write it for radio, you're more likely to get it made. And if it's a success, you can then turn it back into a movie.

EXERCISE

Ask yourself:

- Could *Crunch Time* work as a one-off comedy-drama for radio?
- Or might it expand into a 90-minute movie?
- Is there a strong narrative and a clear conclusion?
- How would the pace of change differ from that of a traditional sitcom?

Part 2

Tips and tales – guest contributors

The art of Notiquette

Sam Bain

Sam Bain met his writing partner Jesse Armstrong at Manchester University. Their TV credits include *Peep Show, Fresh Meat* and *Babylon.* Sam was script editor for series two of *Rev* and, with Jesse and Chris Morris, wrote the 2010 film *Four Lions.* Sam and Jesse have also written for David Mitchell and Robert Webb's TV and radio sketch shows.

'Notiquette' – the art of giving and receiving notes – is one of the least talked about but most vital parts of every screenwriter's life.

Being a member of a writing partnership makes Notiquette a constant part of my working life. Solo writers may have days, weeks or months of writing alone in their garret/penthouse (delete as applicable) before they send their masterpiece off and await the 'ping' of head-swelling praise or testicle/ovary-crushing criticism (delete as applicable), but a co-writer gets notes on a daily, hourly, minute-by-minute basis.

After fifteen years, I've learned what the tiniest muscle movement on my co-writer's face means with regard to the joke I've just pitched. Or what the tone of his voice on the other end of the phone says about the quality or otherwise of the scenes I've just emailed. And I'm pathetically grateful for his fake laughter at my substandard gag. I'd choose a genuine belly laugh every time, but I deeply appreciate what the fake laugh means; he's trying to deliver a negative note in the kindest possible way. Which is perhaps the essence of all good note giving.

Of course the basis of our note give-and-take is trust. We trust each other's judgement. We're patient with each other's foibles. It's a very different thing when we are faced with feedback from a producer or script editor whom we may not know very well, if at all. It's particularly hard when a writer is starting out. Everyone is a stranger. Am I a pawn in their weird mind-game or are they an angel sent to help me write a better script?

Here are some tips for note-givers.

NOTE DON'TS

- Don't rewrite the script and send it back to the writer. This has only happened to me once, and it was done by a producer/script editor who had come up with the concept of the show, but it is still a high-watermark of note-don'ts.
- Don't forward to the writer an uncensored email containing extensive, negative notes from a third party. The note-giving process has to occur within a 'circle of trust' and a note has value in proportion to the commitment of the person giving it. In other words, if you're not involved in the project and you don't even like it, please don't give me your notes. Rejection letters do occasionally contain worthwhile notes and if all the rejection letters you get contain the same note, it's probably worth taking.
- Don't take the piss. All writers get it wrong, but it is our right to fail (and know we've failed) without getting humiliated in the process.
- Don't give too many little notes at an early stage. We don't need to know if some jokes could be improved at Draft #1. We just want to know if the story's any good.
- Don't give notes based on how you'd write the script. If you want to write, there are plenty of blank pages still available.
- Avoid emotional/inflammatory language. Say there are problems, not that something is 'sloppy'. Say it could be funnier, not that it's schoolboy humour.

NOTE DO'S

- Please make suggestions and come up with ideas. A list of problems is depressing. A list of solutions is less depressing. Plus it shows you're making an effort and putting yourself on the line. It's a lot safer to be critical than it is to be creative. If even one of your ideas is worth including, we will be forever grateful. If all of your ideas are terrible, that will make us feel better about our half-decent ideas, although we may never take your notes seriously again. It's a risk worth taking.
- Do include relevant anecdotes from your life, the more embarrassing the better. They may not get into the script, but they make you more human and we are better able to accept you hitting us over the head with your notes as a result.

SOME TIPS FOR WRITERS

- Try not to treat every note as if it was an arrow aimed by an assassin straight for your heart. If you can find even one thing in any given set of notes which helps you improve your script, they were worth receiving.
- Have compassion for the note-giver. Like the wolf in the forest, they are just as scared of you as you are of them. They are probably frustrated writers at heart, who envy your good looks and your prodigious talent.
- Forgive them their confusion. They may not even know why they don't like something but if you can figure out why, you're halfway to solving it.
- If you find a note-giver whose judgement you respect, whose sense of humour you share, never let them go.

On research

Peter Bowker

Peter Bowker taught people with special needs before and after studying creative writing at the University of East Anglia. He wrote for *Casualty, Medics* and *Peak Practice*, followed by his own highly acclaimed dramas, including *Flesh and Blood, Blackpool, Occupation, Eric and Ernie* and *Marvellous*. He has won BAFTAs, Writers' Guild and Royal Television Society awards. He was nominated for a Golden Globe for *Blackpool* and was congratulated at the ceremony by his waiter for 'being the only guy in the room actually eating his food'.

Research rarely gives you what you want but it will often give you what you need. It will rarely give you plot – although it will often fool you by giving you anecdote, which isn't the same thing at all. It will, though, give you dialogue and sometimes, character.

I knew the story of my TV drama *Occupation* before I did any research. I knew that three soldiers had been to Iraq and were involved in a single incident. And I knew that they all went back: one for money, one for conscience and one for love. I didn't know any more than that. I didn't even know what the single incident might be.

I got Mike, my 'love' character, from a visit to the Ministry of Defence to meet a couple of members of the Royal Armoured Medical Corps. I met a Military Nurse, a Sergeant: neat, controlled, working class, defensive in a polite kind of way. I asked him what made him join the army in the first place and he said: 'It was the only way my family would accept me becoming a nurse.'

It occurred to me that a man not quite at home in his own family might well be a man who was not quite home in the Army either. A man who wanted to express his sensitive side and did so by joining an organization that, to do its job, needs to suppress any sensitivity. Mike wasn't the soldier I met, but my interpretation of that soldier became Mike.

The 'conscience' character came from a visit to Combat Stress, the charity that treats ex-servicemen suffering from post-traumatic stress. Again one sentence stood out in a fascinating hour: 'If you fight in an unpopular war, you're more likely to suffer mental illness than if you have fought in a popular war with a good outcome.'

So what if my character was going back to put things right, not because he had done something wrong, but because he couldn't help being tormented by the notion that the war hadn't turned out as he had hoped? In other words, he was attempting the impossible: to give the Iraq War a happy ending in order to assuage his own torment.

Finally, in order to nail my 'money' character, I spent a morning with an ex-soldier who had set up a private military contractor business in post-war Iraq and was reluctantly telling me about it. It wasn't a great meeting for either of us. He was understandably suspicious of me and I grew tired of his tales of derring-do from the Chris Ryan school of soldiering. We weren't rude to each other, we just didn't get on.

As I rose to leave, he told me about how, when his car was ambushed by insurgents, he had set about flagging down an American tank without first abandoning his Arab disguise. It was only when the American gun turret turned and aimed at him that he thought to start removing his headgear. It was an essentially comedic moment in the middle of a huge terrifying nightmare. It seemed to me to be closer to the stuff of war than anything else he had told me.

In imagining his vulnerability in that moment, I had my 'money' character. And more importantly, I had a character who had returned to Iraq to make money, but who we could nevertheless love.

Tracy and me

Elly Brewer

Elly Brewer started writing TV for young people in the mid-80s when she should have been writing sales promotion copy. Since then, she's written for everyone from *Postman Pat* to *Shaun the Sheep, Emu* and *Tracy Beaker*. And won a few gongs along the way.

Daydreaming: the best sort of creative spade work. Well, daydreaming and brainstorming. And I do a lot of both, though daydreaming mostly. (I went three Tube stops past the one I wanted yesterday. Sigh.)

I recently finished a six-year run as a Lead Writer, firstly on a TV series called *Tracy Beaker Returns*, which then became a series called *The Dumping Ground*. Both spin-offs of *The Story of Tracy Beaker*; an adaptation of a book by former Children's Laureate Jacqueline Wilson, about a young girl living in care.

I did the original development work on 'Story of' and was Lead Writer on the first series. So some eight years later, when the BBC wanted to bring the series back with Tracy as an adult, they asked if I'd like to be involved in reformatting. I brought my chum Ben Ward along for the ride (*Horrible Histories, MI High*). We were joint Lead Writers on Series one and two, and I carried on as Lead Writer on Series three and the first two series of *The Dumping Ground*.

Ben and I worked with the CBBC Drama Department and Jacqueline Wilson to put *Tracy Beaker Returns* together. That's format, characters and possible storylines. Ben and I then worked up the characters and devised some new ones. I devised any subsequent characters as they were needed, with loads of buffing and honing chats along the way with the Producer and Script Editor. It's a very collaborative process.

We had a team of writers. And we'd hold a storyline day at the start of each series, where we'd get together with the Producer, Exec Producer and Script Editor, to discuss what stories we'd like to tell. We wanted to be true to what it was really like, living in care. We also had a great researcher who helped us keep things accurate. Having said that, we had to occasionally use a bit of poetic licence because we were there to entertain.

The core audience is six- to twelve-year-olds. They have so many choices about how, when and where they watch TV that if you don't grab them from the off, they're gone. So pace is really important. Show, don't tell. Never patronize. And don't use hip language.

The Story of Tracy Beaker is still being repeated many, many years later, along with *Tracy Beaker Returns* and *The Dumping Ground*. What's 'street' today, looks very old fogey tomorrow.

By the end of our storyline days, we'd have allocated stories to specific writers and then everyone would go off to work up their ideas. I'd do two or three drafts of my storylines – having had notes each time, from the Script Editor. Once the storyline was approved, I'd work up my Scene by Scene breakdown. That's a prose version of a script, showing in detail what each scene will contain.

Some writers hate doing lengthy Scene by Scenes because they feel it stunts the creativity they'd rather put in to the actual script. I prefer it, because then I know where I'm going when I get to script. I'll often cut scenes that turn out to be unnecessary or repetitious but it's a good blueprint to work from. I might do two or three versions of a Scene by Scene before I'm given the go-ahead to script. But when it comes to telling you how many drafts of a script there'll be – who knows? Enough to get it right... in the Producer's opinion, not yours.

Over one year of development and five series, I wrote twenty half-hour episodes and one hour-long Christmas Special, and we picked up some wonderful awards along the way. But that's an awful lot of daydreaming about young people in care and, sad though I was to leave my characters behind, I felt it was time to move on and start daydreaming about something new.

How the NDA kept ZB DOA on the QT (spoiler alert!)

Laura Eason

Laura Eason played bass with an indie girl band, did circus tricks with Ringling Brothers and acted on Broadway before becoming a writer. She's now the author of twenty plays, original works and adaptations, a musical book writer and screenwriter. Her credits include the play *Sex with Strangers* and the Netflix drama *House of Cards*.

> In the first episode of season two, Francis Underwood will kill Zoe Barnes by pushing her in front of a Metro train.

This is what Beau Willimon, our visionary show runner and head writer, told us in the first hour on the first day on my first TV writing gig on the Netflix series *House of Cards*. This was late January 2013, a little over a week before the world would meet Frank and Claire Underwood, Doug Stamper, Zoe Barnes and all the scheming, ruthless, power hungry *HOC* characters who would captivate the popular imagination, as well as my own.

I was hired for season two and joined a whole new four-person writing team. Part of our prep work was bingeing the first season and we all knew it was something special. But it was also an experiment; a show created by incredible artists new to TV that wasn't actually on TV, where all thirteen episodes were available at once.

That *House of Cards* would be successful beyond anyone's expectations was ten days off. What we did know was that killing Zoe was a bold move, coming but midway through the first episode of season two. By the time *HOC* had become a certifiable pop culture phenomenon, we already knew that Zoe, the controversial young reporter, was doomed. Thus began the hardest part of being a member of the *HOC* inner circle.

When you have a cool job, you want to talk about it. When you have a fascinating day, meeting world-renowned experts who let you ask questions as they talk about their area of expertise, you want to talk about it. When the TV show you work on becomes a sensation and people grill you at cocktail parties about it, you want to talk about it. But no – I had signed an NDA (non-disclosure agreement).

This is nothing new for TV. You sign a binding agreement that you will disclose no details about the show. And for a show like *HOC*, where surprise is essential, this is more critical than most. Leaks could profoundly damage the show and so all of us on staff take them profoundly seriously. But this was new for me and the most unique challenge of being a *HOC* writer. I'd spent many years in the theatre as a playwright/director/actor. In the theatre world, you talk about your work all the time, in order to generate interest. What a shock to be on a show where I knew everything that was going to happen but couldn't say a word.

By the time season one debuted, major aspects of the season two story were falling into place. Zoe's death was just the beginning. As the interest in *HOC* grew, the process was more and more fascinating. Unlike a network show that rolls out a week at a time and allows some of the pressure to decrease, the gap between the launch of season one and the launch of season two was just shy of a year. I couldn't talk about anything for a year! I couldn't discuss the remarkable consultants we met. Nor could I talk about the incredible actors who came aboard for season two.

Hardest of all was having to keep mum about my first solo writing credit. Being on set, getting to see Robin Wright speak lines I wrote in that chilling, calculated style was a career highlight. But until season two debuted on 14 February 2014, we said nothing.

When asked – again and again by rabid fans when they learned I wrote on the show – I would say only that I was glad they loved the show. I was afraid if I shared even the smallest detail, I'd blow it. I would have one too many beers and spill the beans, or even one bean that would spoil everything. So I hid what books I was reading for research, putting paper covers on books when reading on the subway. Even the location of the writers' room in New York was kept secret and my husband didn't know the exact address of my office.

The best advice I can give is to pretend you're in the FBI, everything's top secret, lives depend on your discretion. In a way they do. *HOC* employs a lot of people who depend on everyone keeping things under wraps. So I revealed nothing. It was hard. But when that train hit Zoe and the internet lost its mind, it was worth it.

As I write this essay, I know everything that will happen in season three. I'm sitting on so much good stuff. But don't bother asking. You'll get nothing out of me.

The American writers' room – tips, insights and sweeping generalizations

Ellen Fairey

Ellen Fairey's play *Graceland* was produced as part of Lincoln Center Theatre's LCT3 program in 2010 and won a Joseph Jefferson award for Best New Work in Chicago. She is a writer/producer on Showtime's *Nurse Jackie* and is a graduate of the School of the Art Institute of Chicago.

1. Embrace insecurity. Sharing your ideas out loud with other writers, many of whom you will have no connection to, is nerve-racking to say the least. It's normal to have a low-grade feeling of 'do I suck?' for the first few weeks in a new room. Take comfort in the fact that every writer in the room, even the most experienced, probably feels the same way.
2. Listen. If it's your first week in a room, or worse your first job ever, don't try and prove yourself. Now is the time to hang back and see how things are going to be run. The showrunner sets the tone; maybe it's freewheeling and unstructured. I worked in a room where we once played Hearts for two hours then went back to breaking story. Or it may be a room that is rigid and controlled with directives such as 'no cross talk' and long discourses on narrative theory. Whatever it is, if you're a writer you're an observer. Observe and proceed accordingly.
3. Personalities. The writing is the easiest part of the job. It's the personalities that can be hard to manage. Some types:
   (a) The Constant Pitcher

This person thinks that quantity equals quality. They are constantly pitching ideas – good, bad and in-between. Often fans of 'focus-enhancing' drugs like Adderall or Provigil.

(b) The Mouse

This person says maybe one or two things a day, usually thoughtfully considered and often insightful. Probably doodles a lot. Apologetic.

(c) Angry and Bitter

This person has been on many shows and makes sure you know it. They have no problem bad-mouthing people they've worked with. Violently aware of everyone's pay grade and title. Tenacious, hostile, generally unpleasant.

(d) Academic

Educated, intellectual, articulate. Has no problem spending hours discussing theory, rather than breaking story. Often a playwright.

(e) The brand new staff writer

Terrified.

4. Don't re-pitch the same thing more than three times. If something you've pitched has been shot down, it's fine to try to find a different way in. If it's shot down a second time, it's probably best to let it go – even more so if it's the showrunner who's nixing your idea. There's a fine line between tenacity and driving everyone insane.
5. Find something good about a bad situation. Maybe you write nuanced family dramedies and suddenly find yourself staffed on a show about slutty alien vampires. Or you get staffed on a show with a bi-polar, weepy showrunner. Lay low, learn as much as you can, be helpful, be available and bide your time. A bad experience is a learning experience. It also helps to purchase something nice for yourself from the money you're making on the hateful show. Years later you can look at that guitar/motorcycle/Mini Cooper and realize that slutty alien vampires actually paid for that.
6. A word about food. If you're lucky you'll be on a show that has the budget to buy the writers lunch every day. Don't order the most expensive thing or worse, order multiple things and then pack away your leftovers to take home for later. You're getting paid more than you ever thought you would be in your life to sit around and come up with story ideas. Don't take advantage of the situation. And yes, American writers' rooms do order sushi.

Digging for drama

Nick Fisher

Nick Fisher has been an art dealer, journalist, TV presenter, commercial fisherman and agony uncle. His TV credits include creating *Manchild* and BAFTA award-winning children's comedy *The Giblet Boys*. He has written episodes of *New Tricks, Hustle, Casualty, EastEnders* and over thirty episodes of *Holby City*.

With my first *Holby City* payment, I bought a 1.5-tonne mini-digger off eBay. It's a real-life Tonka toy, has three buckets and is capable of excavating ponds, lakes, drains, ditches and pulling up tree stumps. I know, because I spend most mornings writing and most afternoons moving earth.

I was invited to write episodes of *Holby City* and later join the core team while I was in the dying throes of my own personal development hell. After creating two successful TV series, one that won a BAFTA, I struck-out on half a dozen development projects. Near misses, script commissions, a well-paid US pilot... but misses all the same.

In the space of three years, I had just one half-hour US pilot made. Which to be frank was mostly the work of hired-gun US team writers. And even though it cost over $5m, was directed by Stephen Gyllenhaal, starred Indie film guru Kevin Smith, was produced by *Sex and the City*'s Darren Starr and shot on Malibu Beach, it was still an unwatchable piece of misogynistic bollocks.

My other development projects – a commissioned 2 x 90-minute drama about the 1948 London Olympics and a cracking multi-cultural police drama about undercover informants – both died in eleventh-hour agonies.

I took my wounds to Holby City General Hospital. Where I discovered a TV-making machine the like of which I'd never encountered in a career of creating shows and 'guesting' episodes of *New Tricks, Hustle, Diamond Geezer* et al. Fifty-two weeks of the year, the modest team at *Holby City* produce an hour of prime-time drama, with an audience that hovers around five million. And what they require most are writers who are fast, flexible, imaginative and, well, fast.

I grew up writing features for magazines and newspapers. No deadline was more than forty-eight hours. We used to scoff at the glossies and their six-week lead times. I learnt to do 'fast' at *The Sun* where 600 words were needed in an hour's time. Thrilling work. Delicious. Frantic.

Working for *Holby City* and *Casualty*, and occasionally *EastEnders*, has two different time frames: the 'normal' twelve-week cycle to craft a script, and the panic stations: a script-has-just-died-at-third-draft-and-we-need-a-new-one-within-ten-days' scenario. It's these high-pressure, against-all-odds rewrites that I love most.

Being parachuted into a problem, where, with imagination, pre-dawn scribbling and speed, I can walk out of the rubble holding a ready-to-shoot script, is a buzz. The nearest a man who earns a living typing will ever get to being a hero. And something that is so totally absent from the deadline-less hell that is 'development'.

I like to see results. I like to be busy. Productive. Creative. It pours balm on my over-active Protestant work ethic to have in any one week a script being written, one being shot, one in edit and another being transmitted. Feeling that nauseous howling emptiness of fruitless development only sharpened my hunger for being busy.

I like to write every day. And I like as much as possible of what I write to be made. That is, after all, the whole point of writing scripts. They are manuals from which to make TV shows. If the shows don't get made, the manuals become just odd, interesting, but ultimately pointless things.

I love writing for continuing drama because I love to see results. It's like an afternoon operating a digger: you can make a big impression, move mounds, dig deep and see the results of your effort.

I'm not a cerebral writer. I don't write to amuse, entertain or edify myself. I write like I dig, so I can stand back at the end of the day and feel the warm glow of productivity.

A guide to slaying dragons

Phil Ford

Phil Ford always wanted to be a writer. He wasn't much good at anything else. His first *Doctor Who* script, *The Waters of Mars*, was his 150th

TV commission. He won a Writers' Guild Award for *The Sarah Jane Adventures* and co-created *Wizards vs Aliens* with Russell T. Davies.

G. K. Chesterton once said: 'Fairy tales don't tell children that dragons exist, children already know that dragons exist. Fairy tales tell children that dragons can be killed.'

And that is what makes writing good drama for children so important.

Not because every kid needs to learn a lesson in How to Slay Your Dragon, but because great storytelling can influence us all from the youngest age, teach us life lessons and maybe even swing the compass on an adventure that will last a whole lifetime.

We've been telling stories since humanity first found an ability to express itself; they were painted on cave walls and told around ancient campfires long before anyone learned how to write or tune a TV channel. And we've told children stories to prepare them for the wonders – and the dangers – of life.

Okay, so the last thing a ten-year-old kid is looking for after a hard day in class is a thirty-minute TV lesson on life. They want to be entertained, thrilled, maybe a little scared, and have a laugh. It's the same when a family comes together around the TV on a Saturday evening; they're not looking for a Public Information film – they want to have fun.

When I write an episode of *Wizards vs Aliens* or *Doctor Who*, I don't first consider, like some grand metaphysical tutor: 'What important lesson can I teach the young of the world today?' I just try to come up with a great story and a bunch of great characters to help me tell it.

But if I'm the slightest bit clever, I can make that story relatable for the kids who watch. And possibly they'll recognize things in it that maybe I never even intended. And they'll see that they can stand up to that monster (or bully) and they can work out the Electazine Equation (or just plain algebra).

Or maybe they'll be inspired by the show itself. Maybe that one episode of something you write will give someone a desire to one day write their own TV show, or novel or comic strip.

The day I first met Gerry Anderson, creator of *Thunderbirds*, *Stingray*, *Captain Scarlet*, *UFO* and so many other iconic shows of the 60s and 70s, it just happened to be his 70th birthday. We were at Pinewood Studios and a guy appeared with a bottle of champagne. He explained that he and Gerry had not met, but he wanted to thank him for all his sci-fi shows that inspired him as a kid to come into the movie industry.

Over the years, I've met so many people in the movie and TV industry with the same story. But I've also met people who became scientists, worked for NASA, became jet pilots, engineers, car designers ... all because they were inspired by a kids' show that Gerry Anderson made.

And that is the real value of writing good drama for kids. Those lines you bang out in Final Draft can really make a difference, not just for thirty or forty-five minutes, but for a lifetime.

The double story

Jeppe Gjervig Gram

Jeppe Gjervig Gram was headhunted by Danish broadcaster DR straight out of film school to work on the drama series, *Sommer*. He went on to co-create *Borgen* with Adam Price and wrote fourteen of the thirty episodes, for which he was awarded a BAFTA. Gram is showrunner on the DR series *Follow the Money*.

In 2000, the head of drama at Danish broadcaster/production house DR, Ingolf Gabold, formulated a series of fifteen dogmas for the production of future DR TV series. He had been inspired by Lars von Trier's Danish film movement DOGMA 95. The principles of these dogmas had already been the modus operandi for a few years at DR but Gabold redefined them and made them official guidelines for the production of long-running TV drama.

These guidelines are, in my view, absolutely crucial to the development of what some have labelled 'the golden age of Danish TV', particularly those relating to writing and to story. But then again, I am a writer.

The first dogma simply declares that 'at DR, the writer is king'. The second dogma states that a successful long-running series cannot be made as a result of compromise and input from numerous editors, but must always adhere to the head writer's vision.

These two principles are of little help when you are writing your script – unless of course you're working at DR! But a third dogma might be useful beyond the remit of Danish TV, because it's a working guideline for all writers. Gabold called this crucial dogma the 'Double Story'.

It goes something like this: a DR TV series may never have just one simple story: the entertaining, well-plotted storyline that thrills, excites and entertains an audience momentarily. A story with these qualities would be considered very attractive to broadcasters around the world.

But at DR, this is not enough.

So what's the other half of the Double Story? It's simple really: beneath the engaging and thrilling storyline, a bigger story must always be at work; a story that's not just about the character but about (Danish) society itself. The other half of the Double Story is the 'bigger picture', the socio-ethical connotations of the storyline. However good your story is, it's not good enough for the DR bosses without this second vital element.

Does that sound like the diktat of a state-funded broadcaster's public service obligations? Or like a well-meaning Movie-of-the-Week, dealing with 'important issues' of some sort? Executed poorly, it could easily end up looking like that. But executed well, it is in my view a very powerful tool. It engages your audience on a much deeper level and makes them eagerly anticipate next week's episode because every storyline in the series in some way resonates with themes in their own lives.

Two examples: *Forbrydelsen* (*The Killing*) is not just a whodunit – that would be the 'simple story'. It's about the way a murder affects the people connected by it. How a horrible crime links them and how it's reflected by our modern society. It is as much about the personal lives and relationships of the characters as it is about finding the murderer. Without that Double Story, the series might still be watchable and thrilling. But it would never feel so original or resonate so powerfully.

And, however tempting it might be, *Borgen*'s Double Story is not built around the banal fact that a political drama series, by definition, deals with society. That's no guarantee that these stories will feel relevant to a larger part of society. *Borgen* relates the underlying story of how we all try to tackle the tough dilemmas that arise with the implementation of gender equality.

Birgitte Nyborg is Denmark's first female prime minister and this makes an excellent platform for the dilemmas that arise out of being a woman with a (very!) important career, alongside her need to be a good wife and mother. This story is not only relevant to female prime ministers. It will resonate with every woman in the Western world. And with the men who deal with, live with, fall in love with women like Birgitte.

So, even though you're not pitching your drama to Ingolf Gabold or DR, give it a try. What is your Double Story? Make it relate to society today, something that affects or concerns if not all of us, then most of us. Delve into it, explore it.

Don't just seduce your viewers, but create a relationship with them through a second meaningful story that is close to their hearts.

Love the sound of the world

Katie Hims

Katie Hims' first radio play *The Earthquake Girl* won the Richard Imison Award. Recent work includes *Lost Property,* which won The BBC Audio Drama Award 2012. She was lead writer on the first two seasons of Radio 4's new First World War drama *Home Front* and her most recent stage play *Billy the Girl* was produced by Clean Break at Soho Theatre.

By happy accident – or perhaps it was a sort of beginner's luck – my first radio play *The Earthquake Girl* was set in only three very distinct acoustics. The central character, Edie, worked in a library. She also received regular phone calls from her irate sister-in-law Lila. She was also writing a novel, and all the characters in the novel spoke like Celia Johnson and Trevor Howard in *Brief Encounter.* Whenever Edie sat down to type – on a good old-fashioned typewriter of course – it began to rain. This was solely because I love writing when it's raining. When the sun is shining I feel like I should be outside living a sunnier, more part-of-the-world life. When it's raining I feel like writing is the most gorgeous job in the world. I'm digressing slightly now. But the point I'm trying to make is that you should, if you can, love the sound of the world that you're writing in. And a slightly magical surreal quality can suit a radio play very well. Therefore I could make it rain whenever I wanted to, unlike in real life. But by creating three set-ups that sounded so different, I avoided getting into a mess trying to explain that time had moved on, or that it was a different day. There was no need for music to bridge the gap or internal monologue. Of course music and internal monologue can be used to great effect in radio. But I think because they are there it's very tempting to use them before you've explored all your options.

Years after writing *The Earthquake Girl* I wrote a series for Woman's Hour called *The Kiss*, and the producer Jessica Dromgoole said 'I think we should have no narrator for this series.' We had done a couple of Woman's Hour series with a lot of narration and I was a bit taken aback. I'd got used to it being there, had in fact started to rely on it. But when I got started I really loved having no narration. There's something more mysterious about having no one to guide you through the story. There's less explaining to do somehow. The characters just say and do what they're doing without a narrator justifying or saying 'it's the next day now'… I love writing for radio. I love the scope and variety of stories you can tell. There's no committee process of creating the work. Just you and the producer. And then it gets made. It actually gets made.

The beginning in the end

Rachel Joyce

Rachel Joyce began writing for radio when she was pregnant with her first child. Since then she has had three more children and written thirty more plays. She has managed a few books as well, including the No 1 *Sunday Times* Best Seller, *The Unlikely Pilgrimage of Harold Fry*.

Years ago I was in *As You Like It*, with Niamh Cusack playing Rosalind. I used to watch from the wings every night as she took the stage, alone, after the final applause and began the epilogue. You could feel the audience's confusion. Hang on, you could feel them thinking, the play has just finished, hasn't it? With the most delicious smile she promised '*My way is to conjure you.*' And she did just that. She charmed the audience into giving us another curtain call.

I think radio drama is the same. It is a piece of magic. A spell. It can be gritty, it can take place in a police interview room, a shopping mall, a cul-de-sac house, but equally it can take place on a cloud, inside a head, on a trapeze wire. Create a world the listener believes in, and you can take that listener anywhere. *Yes, this is not real but come with me. I am going to tell you a story and you won't want to leave me until you know the end.* I remember Rosalind's words when I write a radio play. I think of it as a piece of seduction.

How I achieve that is of course not so simple. I have a few tricks, though, to help me, and here they are:

> Think carefully about how you begin. Do you want to shock someone into listening? Do you want to make them laugh? Or will you whisper a secret? The style of the beginning is how you take your listener by the hand. (NB, Remember not to whisper too quietly, if you go for that option. This is radio, after all.)
>
> I often write the end of my play soon after writing my beginning. Once I know where I am heading, I can have enormous fun getting there. Your characters and your play can take all sorts of wrong turnings, so long as the writer is in control of the final destination. Besides, as far as I am concerned, the end is always contained in the beginning, and vice versa. One is the answer to the other. (Bear in mind, though, that you must be prepared to amend both beginning and ending as your play takes shape. I never really settle on the beginning of my play until I have finished.)
>
> I think very hard about dialogue. Of course this is obvious, but what I mean is I make sure that my characters aren't all blessed with the same voice (i.e. mine). Listen to people talking. Listen to them in cafés and shops and on public transport. Listen to how we use assonance, alliteration, repetition, names; all those things. Listen to the poetry of everyday talk.
>
> If I have a monologue to write – especially one where someone reveals the truth – I try to say it first into my phone. (I used to use my children's yellow plastic tape recorder, but I have got more sophisticated.) It always surprises me how many words I use when I write a speech, whereas if I say it first, I find I get there very quickly. And I don't even mean that I say the obvious. In fact I normally end up saying the not-obvious.
>
> Which brings me to my last tip. And this I only mention because it is a favourite of mine. If there is a scene, or a speech, in which something needs to be said, try writing that scene without *the huge thing being actually spoken*. It's far more

moving to me (or funny or intriguing or unsettling, depending on the genre of the play) if a woman tries to tell a man she loves him and never manages to say the words 'I love you.' So – as an experiment – take one of your scenes where people state their objectives ('I want you', 'I need money', 'I am leaving') and re-write it so that the one thing they don't say is *that*.

More and more, I think of writing as playing. Remember how it was when you were a child and you kept playing the same game, slightly changing the rules to see where it went next? Keep playing.

A radio playwright's A–Z

Marcy Kahan

Marcy Kahan, born in Montreal, educated in Oxford and Paris, now lives in London. She wrote the BBC screenplay *Antonia & Jane*, a stage version of *When Harry Met Sally* (Theatre Royal, Haymarket), and for BBC Radio the romantic comedy series *Lunch* and a sextet of plays about the great Noel Coward.

Actors: Create lively, juicy, unexpected characters for actors to play and most will do you proud.

Books about Writing are like cookbooks. How many recipes in each of your cookbooks do you return to? Turn your notebooks into your private writing manuals.

The **Cubicle** is where the director will invite you to comment after each segment is recorded. You will have a lavish seventy-five seconds to respond [see **Studio**].

Deadlines are a playwright's best friend. Treat them with the respect and dread they deserve.

Editing and writing are two distinct processes. If you try to do both simultaneously, you may experience paralysis [see **Nervous Breakdown**].

First Drafts should be written rapidly, with great brio. Then shut in a drawer for a few days.

Grab your coat, **get** your hat, **go** for a walk. Observe the world. Eavesdrop.

Hard: Death is easy. Comedy is hard.

Internal Deadline: If your real deadline is Monday, tell yourself it's the preceding

Thursday. That gives you time to edit and polish, time to hear the play read aloud [see **Readings**].

Journey: What your characters – and audience – go on. They enter the Inmost Cave. They return home changed. Unless you're Samuel Beckett.

Keep in touch with the play. Even when life overwhelms you with responsibilities – or debauchery – find twenty minutes a day to ponder, tinker, scribble.

Listen to radio plays analytically.

Music: Compile a soundtrack for each play – music to get you going in the morning, music to inspire specific scenes, music you might want to use in the actual play.

Nervous Breakdown: Either a good sign that your creativity is kicking in and demanding more of you or a warning sign that you need a holiday.

Orchestrate the voices in your play: e.g. a violin, a woodwind, a trumpet, a bassoon. Think of the script as a musical score.

Process: You need to develop a repertoire of objectives for your writing sessions, a sense of what you should be doing and when. A play is created over time. Enjoy the process.

Questions: Interview your characters. Question your assumptions. Query each beat of each scene.

Readings: Invite actors to read your play aloud. Do not serve cheese; it clogs up the vocal chords.

Studio: The recording site. You meet and greet the actors on Monday and have the cast party on Tuesday. Be helpful. Incisive. Encouraging [see **Cubicle**].

Timing: Most radio drama is written for defined slots of fifteen, thirty, forty-five or sixty minutes. This will initially drive you crazy but you may eventually enjoy the constraint of exact timing.

Ukulele is a fine thing to strum when you're not writing.

Voice: How do you find your writing voice? Try writing. A lot.

Whiteboard: Useful for getting the play's structure onto a wall.

Xylophone [See **Ukulele**].

Yiddish Yoga Yoghurt and Yoruba are all potential subjects for radio plays.

Zeugma is a figure of speech in which several objects are governed by a single word, usually a verb. E.g. 'She broke his car and his heart.' A study of rhetoric is useful for dramatists, especially for political plays and courtroom dramas.

A dream cast

Rebecca Lenkiewicz

Rebecca Lenkiewicz studied acting and became a writer. She has written for many theatres including the National and the Arcola. She co-wrote the film *IDA* with Pawel Pawlikowski. She has loved the writing and recording of radio plays.

Writing drama for radio has one luxury for a writer that is very rare. One can propose a dream cast and actually achieve it. I wrote a play with Annette Crosbie and David Bradley's voices in my mind because I had enjoyed working with them so hugely on stage, where they played sparring in-laws. In my radio play *Sarah and Ken* they played foster siblings who were lovers in their youth. They broke my heart with their subtle and brilliant performances. Jessica Dromgoole directed it beautifully and the rest of the cast, including Jessica Raine, were equally superb. The result was the closest I have ever experienced to hearing the play I envisaged.

As a dramatist one accepts that the final work will inevitably be very different to the images and music in one's mind. But that rare thing of realizing the dream – radio drama can sometimes do that. I find that amazing and wonderful.

Life at the sausage factory

Jan McVerry

Jan McVerry got her first break into television after a fortuitous meeting with Jimmy McGovern in a pub. These days they'd call it stalking. Career low point: the *This Morning* Christmas Panto. Career high points: *Children's Ward, Clocking Off, The Forsyte Saga* and two BAFTAs for her writing on *Coronation Street*.

'Sit there, and don't speak for the first three months.' This was the considered advice given to me on my first day as a storyliner on The Nation's Favourite Soap, *Coronation Street*.

I was fresh off the *Brookside* production line, where democracy dictated that Jean and Rona from the canteen could chip in on plotlines when they were passing through with toast. So to tell me, a Scouser, to sit tight and keep my gob shut? I spoke. The sky didn't fall in. In fact, we got six weeks of story out of my one little suggestion. I carried on.

I've been writing soap, off and on, for over twenty years, most of them at *Coronation Street*. It's a very different place now from the straight, male-dominated show I joined in 1992. It runs like a perfectly calibrated machine. Except sometimes the wheels come off. Hardly surprising when you consider that we produce the equivalent of a Hollywood blockbuster – two and a half hours of drama – each week.

A Media Studies lecturer once invited me in to speak to his students, then proceeded to dismiss us as a sausage factory and to warn them of its perils. I won't deny, Continuous Drama can contort your writing muscles into interesting shapes.

Uncomfortable with dramatic irony? Learn to embrace it. Let coincidence be your friend. Plot your stories chronologically by all means, but learn to think laterally. The very best stories ripple out to as many surrounding characters as possible, like a pebble tossed into a pool. Know that you'll be expected to wring out every last permutation of every last emotion. On most dramas, people drink a cup of tea. In soap you have to show them buying the milk and boiling the kettle.

I like to point out to the disappointed and the bitter that a producer casts a writing team the way they cast a serial. Sometimes you get rejected not because you're crap but because you're too like someone else who got there first.

Once on the team, we might kid ourselves we're Renaissance men and women but some are inevitably stronger on plot than dialogue, others brilliant on the page but frightened rabbits round a thirty-strong Long Term Planning Conference table.

And performance around the table does count. I've heard the atmosphere described as 'robust', even 'gladiatorial'. It's also warm, witty and scabrous. Some days the inspiration flashes like lightning around the room and only the fastest brains can keep up; on bad days every second drags.

Occasionally, if you're really lucky, you'll see someone resign. I once saw a distinguished older writer throw a hissy fit and flounce out of the room on principle – but leave his briefcase on the chair. How we laughed.

Then there are the slower exits. The deaths by a thousand cuts. Sporadic commissions. Bowel-juddering calls late on Friday night demanding total rewrites by Monday. To survive, successful soap writers need to learn to be tough, pragmatic and constructive. They need to know when to lose the battle in order to win the war. They need to remember it's always a team game, with all the joys and frustrations that can bring.

Mostly, it's a privilege. You earn a familiarity with your audience, build a dialogue. Get it wrong and the world and his taxi driver will be quick to let you know. (Actually, that's a lie; taxi drivers prefer a nature documentary.) You have to remind yourself they're being critical because they care. People who don't love the genre like we do are dismissive of it and its fans.

On *Corry* we know our viewers are intelligent and literary and cultured. I've written heartbreak and snot in the fiftieth-anniversary live hour, sniffled to myself as I typed Hayley resolving to take her own life before the cancer took it first. My proudest moment? A protesting Emily Bishop up a tree shouting 'No Pasaran!' Only on *Coronation Street*.

They don't call it Development Hell for nothing. I know what it's like to be broken as two years of blood, sweat and tears are snuffed out in a cursory email from some big cheese or other. Writing's lonely by its very nature. Some people prefer it that way: the mavericks, the singular visionaries.

But if you don't, if you miss the banter, the office gossip, the occasional need to step out of your stained trackie bottoms into something resembling proper clothes; if you like knowing there's a safety net of soulmates you can email when you're stuck at 2 am, if you enjoy thinking up a story then watching it acted out for nine million viewers just three months down the line, then maybe the sausage factory is the place for you.

That fly under the lampshade

Jonathan Myerson

Jonathan Myerson is the Senior Lecturer on the MA in Creative Writing at City University London. His work for radio includes an acclaimed dramatization of Vasili Grossman's *Life and Fate* and five series of *Number 10*, which won the Writers' Guild Award for Best Radio Drama. His other writing ranges from screenplays to novels to TV series episodes, with one BAFTA and one Oscar Nomination along the way.

Every time I sit down to structure a new play, I come smack up against the biggest problem for radio writers: POV. All the other narrative art forms have their inbuilt ways of telling the audience where to look, where to invest sympathy and suspense. The novelist dictates it from the very first sentence, the film director can set up each shot exactly in order to channel it, and the theatre director can deploy lighting or costume, or even star-casting, to focus our attention. But the radio writer has none of these tricks, and if left to their own devices the audience can easily end up feeling like that fly buzzing around under the lampshade in the middle of the ceiling, zig-zagging mindlessly, wondering where to look and where on earth to go next. So how do you channel POV in a radio play? The easiest, the most effective and simultaneously the most damaging is the Voice Over, the Narration, the Interior Monologue. At a stroke it tells us who is central, whose story this is and what will be important in it. So it's very, very tempting. And as the writer, it's your chance to speak direct and unimpeded to the audience.

But let me warn you: it's a disaster. Because that very unimpededness, that very honesty, destroys any genuine suspense. At a stroke, you lose all self-unawareness of the central character, and the result is that we are left so much less to learn as audience members. A Voice Over is like a safety net under this central character: however badly things might turn out in the action of the play, he or she is still able to tell us about it all, can still enunciate and organize it. And that's my idea of boring. After my first few plays, which I came to realize were virtually single speeches occasionally interrupted by other characters, I swore an oath: never again will I use Interior Monologue. In subsequent plays, producers have both expected and begged me to do so, but an oath is an oath. So how have I solved this self-imposed stricture? The most effective is the simplest solution: plot your play so that you do not need any voice over. Tell everything that needs to be told in the action, in the dialogue. Because that's why we pay the price of admission: to watch characters conflict and collide and bang against each other. I don't switch on the radio to hear someone settle into the therapist's sofa. Then you can go one better: the most successful solution I have employed – but also the hardest – is to put the protagonist in every scene. Thus, the predicament of this one character inevitably rises to the surface, the audience cannot avoid it. It does make plotting a nightmare but the result is more than worthwhile. Every time one character holds centre stage, unopposed – whether it is Hamlet or the protagonist of your latest – the tension drops away. As listeners, we never want to be left as aimless as that fly, but the Interior Monologue is as deadening as a can of Raid.

Clarity is essential

Hattie Naylor

Hattie Naylor is an award-winning writer. Credits include: *Going Dark* (Sound&Fury, 2014), *Bluebeard* (Gallivant, 2013), *Piccard in Space* (libretto for Will Gregory's opera, 2012), *The Diaries of Samuel Pepys* (nominated Best Radio Drama 2012), and *Ivan and the Dogs* (nominated in the Olivier Awards and winner of the Tinniswood Award 2010).

When writing for radio, for the obvious reason that we cannot see anyone, clarity is essential. It is very easy to become lost within the storyline of a radio play. For this reason it is sometimes suggested that you should stick to the rule of no more than five characters. However, radio thrives on narration and the intimacy of the single voice, sometimes referred to as an internal monologue. There is no medium which naturally lends itself so completely to this form of narration. It is also a medium that can thrive on the epic: Hannibal, for example, coming over the mountains with a herd of elephants – easy to depict in radio, harder in any other medium; or a photon travelling through infinite space to land on the tip of my finger, easy in a moment of radio with the right wording and sound. Radio is arguably the most expansive canvas, as the landscape of the mind is bigger than anything depicted in film. Though an epic may have ten or even fifty characters, clever narration can guide us through each character and each twist and turn by the way in which we defy the five character rule.

Clarity is further enhanced by using a character who has their own storyline within the drama, and also by using accents that are not obvious, or not used extensively in radio. The Manchester accent, 'R.P.' (BBC English) and a generic Yorkshire prevail. When was the last time you heard the Wrexham accent or Black Country accent used in classic narration and not as some sort of joke? The choice of accent is political and can enhance your work further. It should be at the forefront of the choices a writer makes.

An oasis from the theatre

Richard Nelson

Richard Nelson, born in Chicago, has written numerous plays which have been produced in England and across America. Among his many awards are an Olivier for Best Play, a Tony Award, and two New York Drama Critics Awards. He is an Honorary Associate Artist of the Royal Shakespeare Company.

With the brief exception in the 1970s of something called *Earplay* (which was produced in Minnesota by a Brit, the now well-known film director, John Madden), serious original radio drama has long been an extinct species in my country. Occasionally theatre plays will be taped for the radio; but new original plays written just for the radio? They simply do not seem to exist.

When I graduated from college in the Seventies, my wife and I moved to England for a year, courtesy of a travel grant from an American foundation. We had no television (and no central heating – we put shillings into the meter) and no phone for the entire year. We did, however, have a small transistor radio; and it was out of this small black radio that I heard my first radio plays. I still remember sitting in our (very cold) kitchen listening to an extraordinary play by John Arden, and then the next week one by David Rudkin.

Now after over thirty years of working in the theatre, I have on six occasions found myself writing radio dramas for the BBC, each commissioned and produced by my friend, Ned Chaillet. And what an oasis from the theatre these have been. I say 'oasis' because the struggle of producing a radio play is far less than that of a play – the actors don't have to learn their lines, so from the get-go they are trying to act; the entire process usually takes only a couple of days, so you have a far greater chance of enticing your first choice of cast. You can edit out the bits you don't like; and as with film or television, the finished product remains the same no matter how many times you listen/watch it. And yet, as a writer, you are writing dialogue, creating people, working with live actors to create and build living worlds.

Among the various reactions and comments about my radio plays, the one I enjoyed the most came not from a review but rather from an editorial in *The Independent* about a much-beloved BBC Radio show, *A Book at Bedtime*:

> A hint of what the BBC felt was the true purpose of its nightly read-in came in Richard Nelson's play *Advice to Eastern Europe* ... the play's hero picks up a girl and takes her back to his flat. In order to convey aurally what ensued, the sound effects department eschewed the usual grunts and groans, and used instead silence, broken only by the squeaking of bed-springs and, in the background, the radio tuned to *A Book At Bedtime*.

Experience isn't wasted

Andrew Nickolds

Now principally known as one half of Radio 4's Ed Reardon, in a career (sic) spanning forty years Andrew Nickolds has put words into the mouths of Lenny Henry, Maureen Lipman, Frankie Howerd, Ned Sherrin, Arthur Daley, Rupert Bear and Dave Podmore, at least some of whom are fictional.

It was in 1973 that my name first appeared in the *Radio Times*. I'd hoped it might have been a few years earlier, when I submitted a script (a pun-laden Sherlock Holmes parody) to *I'm Sorry I'll Read That Again*, the 'water-cooler' radio show at that time, or in our case the drinking fountain in the school yard. I had some confidence in the script after obtaining a leaflet called 'How To Write For The BBC', which advised that submissions should be neatly typed and double-spaced. I did both; except – schoolboy error – I thought 'double-spaced' meant between the words not the lines, and so after laboriously hitting the space bar twice each time, I sent in a bizarre monstrosity which arrived after *ISIRTA*'s run had finished, so long had it taken to type.

I felt on safer ground with my appearance on *Start The Week*, despite a disconcerting first meeting with the producer, who during our conversation hurried out of his office to be (judging by the state of his tie when he came back in) sick. I was helping to put together an alternative football magazine called 'Foul' at the time, and my contribution was to be a light-hearted or rather 'sideways' look, as the current Radio 4 jargon had it, at the sporting press. Three tightly written minutes – and correctly spaced, therefore readable, too.

But my pre-recorded piece fell foul, appropriately enough, of the presenter, who had the air of taking an instant dislike to me and an enduring dislike to everybody else. He was sitting in for Richard Baker the regular host, so when he handed over to me I suggested in a light-hearted/sideways way that I say 'Thank you, Richard.' Despite the stony-faced reaction I said I'd try it anyway, to which he replied 'Then we'll take it out in the edit.' Duly encouraged, I stumbled through the piece, painfully aware as I heard myself during it that this was never going to be 'of broadcastable quality'; and that was that.

Almost. LBC (then called the London Broadcasting Company) was in its early months of getting stuff out on the air, to put it charitably. One admirable idea the sports editor had was recruiting the staff of *Foul* as football reporters, raucously different voices from the regular BBC pundits. I was among them, and that morning I went from Broadcasting House to LBC's studios in Gough Square, showed the sports editor my sweat-stained script, re-recorded it and for the next year turned in a sporting-pages round-up each Sunday morning. I got £1.50 a week and was introduced the first time as '*one* Andrew Nicholds', but never mind.

The point is that the material wasn't wasted, nor was the experience. I've incorporated radio station scenes or settings into at least half a dozen series, while in the wider field of career setbacks pretty well everything that's gone wrong since has found its way into the world of the hapless yet indomitable Ed Reardon. And if the last forty years have taught me anything, it's that revenge isn't just a dish best served cold. It can also be reheated and served again under a different name in a different eatery.

Throwing in an onion

Georgia Pritchett

Georgia Pritchett has written on shows such as *Have I Got News for You, Smack the Pony, Graham Norton, Not Going Out, The Thick of It, Miranda, Life of Riley, Quick Cuts* and *Veep*. She has worked on feature films including *Spiceworld* and *The Curse of the Wererabbit*. She continues to work with both real and plasticine people.

Working on *The Thick of It* has been one of my best writing experiences. It has also been my best team-writing experience. In fact, I would say that it is the most truly team-written show that I have ever been involved with.

Its creator, Armando Iannucci, used a very helpful analogy that made complete sense to me. He explained that we were making gravy. So you might throw in an onion or a carrot and then when you looked at the finished product, you might not recognize your onion or your carrot. But it had been a crucial part of the process.

A script gets passed round and round the team and you make suggestions and write lines and these will give the next writer ideas and they will make their suggestions and write their lines – and so on and so on. It's a bit like a game of Chinese whispers – you may have made a joke about a verruca, and it may end up as a joke about a giraffe – but the giraffe wouldn't exist without the verruca. Of course, this works best when you're working with a lovely, talented group of writers who have no egos and aren't precious about their lines or jokes.

There was one time when Armando told me a line I'd written was being taken out because it was 'too funny'. This may seem like an odd note to give a comedy writer but his point was that the character was absolutely furious and, in that moment, would not be able to come up with a great put-down. Armando felt it was much funnier to have them unable to come up with anything that was remotely funny or that even made sense. He was right.

It was this same team of people who then moved on to write the HBO series *Veep*. There are obvious differences between writing a BBC Four show in Britain and an HBO show in the States: the budget of course, the number of episodes and, crucially for me, the standard of on-set catering. Amazing. You haven't lived till you've had a breakfast burrito.

Now, don't tell anybody, but I know very little about American politics. Luckily for me, Armando knows everything and we had some excellent advisers. I actually had to look up who the Vice President was when I was offered the job, which shows (a) what an idiot I am but also (b) what a great idea for a show it is. The Vice President is theoretically the second most powerful person in the world, who has all of the trappings of power, without any actual power.

Writing a show about a system you don't entirely understand is a terrifying, thrilling, bewildering experience. But it has also made me truly understand that comedy really is all about character and although I can't name all the presidents of the United States, I can tell you how Selina Meyer would feel in any given situation.

And of course, it doesn't get better than writing for Julia Louis-Dreyfus, who is my absolute comedy hero.

The third act

Mike Walker

Mike Walker has written drama and adaptations for Radio 4, including series on the Caesars, the Plantagenets and the Stuarts; amongst his adaptations have been Dickens' *Our Mutual Friend, Dombey and Son*

and *Barnaby Rudge*, and Grossman's *Life and Fate*. He teaches Creative Writing at Morley College.

As a radio writer, as a sometime teacher of radio writing, as a listener and viewer of drama, the thing that, in my experience – which goes back a looooong way – disappoints most often is THE THIRD ACT!

OK, maybe it's really John Yorke's fifth act or whatever but it's the one where, after putting your protagonist in the tree – and then throwing stones at her – you have to get her down out of that tree. This is when you need to deliver on that promise to the audience: 'Hey, come along with me, give me your time and your attention, your heart and your hopes – and your money – and I PROMISE I will give you, in return, a climax that will ... (supply your own metaphor at this point).'

So does your ending deliver on the promise you sold to the audience?

Are the questions asked in the first and second acts answered: does Macbeth become King of Scotland? Does Michael Corleone become the true head of his Mafia family? It is amazing how often, in plays I've heard, the Big Mac buys into an *Irn Bru* franchise and Michael goes off to set up a celi – happier men, for sure, but drama?

Was the basic conflict between the most important characters resolved – between Macbeth and Macduff and Duncan and Mrs M? Does Michael reconcile his own family and his Mafia family? It is amazing how often the three jocks go off to the game together and Michael realizes that Fredo is really on the spectrum and deserves remedial help – *Guardian Society* would love it, but drama?

How has the hero changed as a result of what has happened? Does Macbeth prosper, does his marriage endure, what price does he pay? Does Michael retain the moral credibility and decency he has shown earlier in his life – does *his* marriage endure? It is amazing how often Mac realizes the throne is way above his pay grade and takes Mrs Mac off to Waitrose and Michael realizes that to save his marriage, he needs to give up this life of crime. Ahhhhhhh! But drama?

If your ending isn't doing its job, then one of the things you simply **can't do** is fix it by changing it. You can't have a man come through the door with a gun or a volcano erupting or Jupiter descending in a chariot to resolve the situation (Shakespeare could and did but only when he wanted to get out for a drink or the deadline was looming or he absolutely, positively had to buy another bed) because it looks like you don't know the rules, rather than that you are cleverly subverting them in your meta-drama. (Or that you think you're Shakespeare – which is a whole other sea of troubles.)

So what do you do if you need to fix the last act? The answer, reader, lies all around you …

The name's Bach. Johann Sebastian Bach

Stephen Wyatt

Stephen Wyatt is the only writer to have won the Tinniswood Award for Best Original Radio Drama Script twice. With the late Claire Grove, he has written *So You Want to Write Radio Drama?* published by Nick Hern Books.

I've written quite a few radio plays involving historical characters and events, ranging from the seventeenth century to the 1950s. Here are a few thoughts on the potential pitfalls.

Just because a character is called 'Isambard Kingdom Brunel' or 'Catherine the Great' does not make that character intrinsically interesting. If anything, you have to work harder to bring a historical character to life than one you've created yourself from scratch. One obvious pitfall is failing to transcend domestic banality ('You know, sometimes Fyodor/Leo/Virginia/Wolfgang, I think you care more about your work than about me') and another is overplaying the impending moment that will make this person famous ('WORDSWORTH: You know, Dorothy, when I see those daffodils over there, well, it just fills my heart with pleasure'). In my radio play *The Organist's Daughter*, both Handel and Bach turn up in Lübeck in search of a job. They were still only twenty so the challenge was to find a way of catching them before they turned into the iconic figures they later became. Bach was particularly interesting. He was in continuous dispute with his religious employers in Arnstadt and he'd bunked off for a far longer research and development time than agreed.

He'd also nearly had a punch-up in the town square in Arnstadt with a bassoonist whose playing he'd rubbished. For me, the young Bach was starting to become alive.

I've never forgotten the moment in a 1960s adaptation of *Hereward the Wake*, set in the eleventh century, when one of Hereward's men sidled up to a serving wench and enquired: 'Dost fancy me then?'

Or indeed a script submitted to the BBC Script Unit when I worked there in the 1970s which began:

> 'CABINET ROOM. DAY.
>
> PRIME MINISTER (to CABINET) Gentleman, as you know, Hitler is invading Poland . . .'

The hardest scene to write in my play about the Imperial War Graves Commission, *Memorials to the Missing*, was the one in which in the middle of World War One, Fabian Ware burst into the office of General Macready and explained the basic reasons why a proper commemoration of the dead was needed. It was rewritten and rewritten and a device was invented ('I can give you three minutes to explain your idea') to give it some tension. After that, the real emotional climaxes were comparatively easy.

And I do believe that there is no point in saying the past is exactly the same as the present, because there is then no obvious reason for setting plays in the past. This issue was very much in my mind when I wrote a play called *Gerontius*, set in the nineteenth century, which centred on the relationship between Cardinal Henry Newman and his acolyte Father Ambrose St John. When the Catholic Church proposed Newman for canonization prior to sainthood, the grave in which they had been buried together was dug up. This roused strong opinions from both the gay movement and the Catholic Church. I tried to represent their views in my play, but what I also tried to do was to be as honest as I could to the testimony of Newman's journals and letters. This was, I believe, a non-sexual but very intense relationship between two men and that was how they, alongside many Victorians, saw it. In the play, I tried to create a dialogue between what Newman and St John experienced and the varying modern interpretations of their relationship.

Some of the Catholic press accused me of showing Newman as 'a closet homosexual', which seems more their problem with history than mine. And the oldest surviving relative of Ambrose St John thanked me for the sensitivity with which I had treated her great uncle, having, she said, feared the worst. This in my view was a good result; but the balance of past and present, how they say things, how we see things, how they speak, how we perceive, is a perennial challenge.

To return briefly to my title. There's the problem of how to introduce famous historical figures ('Ah, Charles, come in. I don't believe you know William Makepeace Thackeray and Walter Savage Landor'). In *The Organist's Daughter*, Händel (as he still was) was introduced by someone else. But Bach had to introduce himself. So I'm afraid I opted for the knowing version above. 'Licensed to trill?' asked one of my friends.

Part 3

Write on – getting it right, getting it written

That's an idea: Tips and techniques to get you started

How to kick-start your creativity

Sue Teddern

The Big Question. The one all writers dread: 'Where do you get your ideas from?'

Sometimes you go to bed, convinced you'll never have an original thought again. Your writing career has come to an end and you'll have to get a job stacking shelves at Tesco. And then you wake up the next morning and from the depths of your subconscious, you've crafted a freshly minted, semi-workable idea. You're a writer again.

Then there are times when the ideas keep coming and if you don't write them down quickly, in your nearest notepad, they'll fly back into the ether for someone else to snap up.

> **JAN McVERRY'S TOP TIP**
>
> The very best stories ripple out to as many surrounding characters as possible, like a pebble tossed into a pool.

So how to come up with the solid-gold idea that will transport you, skipping and clapping with joy, to your computer screen every day? What will make it into the thing that excites, blocks and scares you – in a good way? The project that keeps you awake at night with all its pitfalls and possibilities?

A script for TV or radio can go in any number of directions. So it's vital to turn your idea into something concrete and marketable as soon as possible, while retaining the seed of enthusiasm that inspired you in the first place.

Wherever your script takes you, you must have what Ray Frensham, in his book *Screenwriting*, calls the BPF – the Burning Passion Factor. If you aren't fired up, it's back to the drawing board.

If you're going through a fallow, ideas-free period, there are ways to kick-start your creativity.

What if…?

'What if' is an excellent starting place. We do this all the time. We're constantly constructing back stories for that woman on the train not answering her phone, the man walking past carrying a table lamp, the guy who runs the junk shop with no customers.

What if: the woman on the train is having an affair; the man with the lamp has just murdered someone with it; the junk shop is full of family belongings that the guy can't part with.

EXERCISE

- Invent three options for the woman on the train, the man with the lamp and the guy with the junk shop.
- Do any of them inspire further thoughts and developments?
- Take five minutes to develop your best idea.
- What if you introduce one of the other characters?
- What is their relationship?
- Where could it go?

One of my favourite films is Billy Wilder's *The Apartment*. If you haven't seen it (see it now!), it's about an office worker who allows his home to be used by married colleagues for illicit assignations. Was this based on personal experience? Or an overheard conversation? No. The seed was sewn by another classic film and a truly inspired 'what if'.

Wilder was fascinated by an unseen character in David Lean's *Brief Encounter*. Celia Johnson and Trevor Howard conduct their chaste affair at a friend's house. Wilder wondered: Who is the friend and does he know what he's sanctioning?

Wilder (and his co-writer I. A. L. Diamond) had the bones of an idea but it was only half formed. Then he remembered a Hollywood scandal, in which an ambitious employee had provided his boss with a love-nest venue, in return for a bump up the career ladder.

What if *The Apartment* is about corporate America, the morals you lose along the way, culminating in the realization that it's better to be a good person than an unfeeling 'yes' man?

EXERCISE

- Think of a minor character in one of your favourite TV or radio shows. (e.g. Gunther in *Friends*' favourite café, Central Perk, or Jennifer Aldridge's kitchen fitter in *The Archers*.)
- Find an incidental aspect or habit of their life that might be the catalyst for a brand new idea.

EXERCISE

'What if' can work in smaller ways. You have the germ of an idea but it doesn't give you goosebumps or offer possibilities. Or it feels flat and dull.

What if:

- Your twenty-year-old hero *is* a forty-year-old heroine? Or sixty or eighty?
- The setting is urban, not rural?
- Or affluent, not underclass?

- It's a thriller, not a farce?
- It's rom-com, not *noir*?
- It's for radio, not TV? (or vice versa, obviously!)
- It's the 60s or the 80s or 2030?
- You change the point of view?
- Everything happens in real time or at night or in an alternative reality?
- That interesting minor character becomes the central narrator?

More often than not, this process reveals some exciting new possibilities. If it doesn't, it's proof that your original idea was heading in the right direction.

Write about what you know...

Sounds familiar? This is the first nugget of advice newbie writers are ever given. It makes sense. But it shouldn't freeze you into thinking you can only write about a 36-year-old call centre manager living in Dunfermline, if that's who you are.

TOP TIP

When we write about what we know, this can come in many forms: how to comfort a friend; how to house-train a pit bull terrier; how *not* to throw a surprise party; how to make the perfect moussaka. We all have life skills and emotional qualifications that don't appear on our CV or at a job interview.

In his foreword to the scripts for *Queer as Folk*, Russell T. Davies explains how the idea for his groundbreaking series came about. He wanted to write 'what he knew'. His instincts were spot on.

> No one at Channel 4 said 'Let's have a gay drama series'. Catriona McKenzie in the Drama Department just looked at my work, and I'd been putting gay sub-plots in everything I'd written. I am actually gay, did you know?
>
> It was just a natural development of my work. If I'd been a vicar, Channel 4 would have encouraged me to write about God. So off I went. And at first, I did feel this incredible pressure to be representative, to include every single angle of gay life. But no straight drama has that kind of remit.
>
> In the end, I realised I had to focus – to find good characters, good stories and to hell with representation.

Davies had paid his dues writing and storylining shows like *Children's Ward*, *The Grand* and *Springhill*. But when he wrote about 'what he knew', he made his name. And that gave him the kudos and cred to go on to reinvent *Doctor Who*. The rest, as they say, is history.

'What you know' can be big or small. A specific event in your own life can evolve into something else, as long as the emotions remain authentic. I have never been an Army wife, a lonely single dad, a 50s film star or a spoilt Scottish events organizer, even though these characters have all featured in my writing. But I can identify with some of the emotions they've experienced and I can walk a mile in their shoes. That's what writing's all about.

David Chase, creator of *The Sopranos*, always had a strong sense of his central character, Tony. He explains why:

> ... perhaps because I personally relate to his anger and anxiety. Other things in our lives are similar as well – we both have smart wives, difficult mothers, love history and old gangster films, have nightmares and often feel like outsiders.

How could Chase not fail to create such a classic drama series with self-knowledge like that?

Other people's lives

I was chatting to an acquaintance at a party. I hadn't seen him in years and, in the interim, his wife had been killed in a hit-and-run accident. Because my mother had recently died, I knew how cathartic it can be to talk about bereavement, rather than avoid it.

So I asked this quiet, self-effacing man about his recent loss and he opened up, just because I happened to ask at a time when he needed to unload.

This gave me an idea for a radio play. And a quandary. Can I take someone else's grief and make it into a story? Would my friend have kept quiet if he'd known I was listening with my writer's hat on?

Then the 'what if' process kicked in. What if it's a woman who is newly bereaved but none of her workmates can talk to her about what happened? What if the uncle of one of her husband's killers wants to apologize on behalf of his nephew? What if they become friends but their mutual support doesn't sit right with her workmates or with an ambitious local reporter?

Now I had a story and, instead of scavenging from someone else's sadness, my radio play, *Picking Up The Pieces*, became about how we deal with grief, loneliness, friendship, sympathy, empathy.

The 'other people' whose stories inspire us may be family or friends. But they can just as easily be someone we hear on the radio, or in a TV documentary about beekeeping or domestic abuse, or something we read in the papers or online.

We can lift an idea wholesale or we can fashion it into something else by dramatizing the interesting stuff, playing with timelines, abandoning the elements that don't fit the storyline and always asking 'what if…'.

As writers, we do this all the time, consciously and subconsciously. As long as we do it with sensitivity and respect, it's nothing to be ashamed of. It's all part of the process.

ELLEN FAIREY'S TOP TIP

Find something good about a bad situation. A bad experience is a learning experience.

EXERCISE

- Select three stories in today's newspaper.
- See how each of them might develop into a self-contained forty-five-minute radio play.
- Who would populate it in order to give it a voice and a tone?
- Use some of your 'what if' filters to add texture and layers.

What's in a name?

This is an exercise I used at Central School of Speech and Drama, where I taught the radio module of an MA in Writing for Stage and Broadcast Media. We came up with premises for forty-five-minute radio plays, inspired by song titles on the shuffle setting of my iPod.

Some worked better than others but they were all starting points for a number of interesting ideas.

I shall set my iPod to 'shuffle' now and see what presents itself, and I'll go with whatever thoughts come into my head, before they're refined and 'what-iffed' applied:

- *The Low Spark of High-Heeled Boys.* Something about transvestites or transsexuals.
- *My Funny Valentine.* Two stand-up comedians fall in love on the comedy circuit.
- *Owner of a Lonely Heart.* Someone has inherited an all-pervading pessimism about relationships from their widowed or divorced parent.

Even if you don't keep the title, it may be your way into a story you didn't know you wanted to tell. And these are just my thoughts. You may see these very same titles and come up with something completely different.

EXERCISE

Here are some song titles. How will they inspire *you*?

- *May You Never*
- *Your Town*
- *20 Million Things*
- *Meet on the Ledge*
- *Unfinished Sympathy*
- *The Time is Now*

I once came up with an idea for a radio play in a painfully slow fashion, until I got the title.

I wanted to write about a British woman who writes to a man on death row in the USA and somehow makes a difference in his life. I saw the play as epistolary in nature, inspired by Dennis Kelly's brilliant radio drama, *12 Shares*. But I was stuck.

What could she do that changes him? And how?

I knew this play was without substance or narrative until I thought of the title: *In Mates*. Then I realized – aha, she's agoraphobic, so they're *both* imprisoned! And it's *he* who makes a difference to *her* life by ultimately convincing her to leave the house.

I still get goosebumps thinking about the process and how it got me to precisely the right place to find my story.

TOP TIP

Train your brain to channel random thoughts into ideas by:

- Mind mapping and free association.
- Fleshing out an overheard snatch of dialogue.

- Giving a voice to a face in a photograph.
- Taking characters from two abandoned scripts and putting them in a room together.
- Imagining the story behind an unwanted item in a charity shop.
- Checking out someone's supermarket trolley contents: who/what are they shopping for and why are there so many eggs?

Ideas checklist

Ask yourself:

- What is my story about? In other words, what happens?
- Can I answer in one succinct sentence?
- What is it really about? What are the underlying themes? What's the grit that makes the pearl?
- Do I have subplots which will contradict/complement/contrast with the main plot?
- Is it for radio or TV?
- Is it a one-off, a series or a serial?
- Is it funny, sad, silly, scary, high-concept, low-concept?
- If it's a series idea, are there six, twelve, eighteen, twenty-four episodes *and* a Christmas Special in it?
- Is it the kind of script I want to write?
- Is it the kind of script I am able to write?
- Would I watch/listen to this if it was on TV/radio? If not why not?
- Who is its audience? Will they care?
- What makes it original and surprising?
- Do I know how it will end?
- Is it really a script? Or might the plot unfold more successfully as a short story or novel?
- Am I excited by this idea? Will I still be excited in six months' time?

EXERCISE

- Pick two characters from column one below, a genre from column two and a situation from column three.
- Make these ingredients the starting point for a TV or radio series or single play. If they don't work the first time, change one element.
- Or create three columns of your own which include characters, genres and situations that inspire you.

Character	*Genre*	*Situation*
Hannah (36), widowed bus driver	rom-com	interview
Robert (71), failed local politician	sci-fi/fantasy	competition
Lorraine (46), 'Stepford Wife'	satire	ceremony
Nathan (17), computer games inventor	crime thriller	reunion
Ruby (23), unemployed graduate	sitcom	departure
Jonathan (33), soldier with PTSD	medical drama	fresh start
Iris (69), political activist	noir	accident
Geoff (40), middle manager	ghost story	lost

The Old Lemon[1] *– or where ideas come from*

Nick Warburton

Unconsidered trifles

Most writers are, like Autolycus (and Norman Stanley Fletcher), snappers-up of unconsidered trifles. They are collectors of disconnected fragments that will

[1] "The old lemon throbbed fiercely. I got an idea." (P. G. Wodehouse).

sometimes lead to something – in our case plays, scripts and storylines – but more often won't. There's little correlation between how good an idea seems when it's first snapped up and how good the finished script will be. Ideas in their nascent form are often unpredictable. The least-promising trifle can develop into the most satisfying story.

So collect things that catch your eye (or ear). The fact that they've caught your eye (or ear) is a good enough reason to pick them up. Don't reject them simply because you can't see what they might become. If you can't see it now, you might later.

There's a difference between an idea and a story. An idea can be as simple as 'a room glimpsed from the top of a bus in which you see three people standing round an ironing board' or a sudden 'what if' thought ('what if the bears took over?'). They are potentially good starts to a story but they're not stories in themselves. An idea is the seed of a story. When you first pick it up you don't need to know what it'll become.

Writers differ in the way they collect ideas. They'll store them in the memory (an unreliable method, I think) or secure them in some electronic device or write them down in a notebook. I favour notebooks: I like the idea of ideas on paper, and the possibility of sketches, diagrams, arrows and underlining to add some flourish. Some of my notebooks are dedicated to a single project – the Barchester notebooks, for example, for all thoughts and ideas about Trollope's novels – but some are specifically for those unconsidered trifles, the things that *might* become something, the curiosities that aren't yet stories.

I used to think ideas were rare and precious things. They're not. You can find them all over the place. Wherever you direct your gaze, there you'll see ideas. It's the good ideas that are rare and precious. The great American chemist Linus Pauling was once asked how he came up with so many good ideas. He said he did it by having a lot of ideas and then throwing away the bad ones.

Where to find them

You can wait for ideas to hit you out of a clear blue sky, or you can go hunting for them. Here are six possible hunting grounds. They're in the form of brief exercises to bring about some beginnings, to uncover a few narrative possibilities. They're ways of gathering ideas that might become stories.

A few guiding principles

- Write quickly and don't censor yourself. ('No, I can't put that… that would never work… I'd never get away with it…')
- Be aware of *possibility*. Sometimes it's good to think small and look for the odd, unpromising scrap; consider the unconsidered.
- Develop a habit of questioning. (I'll say more about this under *interrogating the idea.*)
- Your first thoughts might be quite good; your second or third thought might be brilliant. So don't stop at first thoughts; collect as much raw material as you can.

When you've collected a bagful of ideas, take a look in the bag and pull out the ones that most appeal to you.

TOP TIP

Juxtaposition

- Juxtaposition is putting one thing with another. It's what writers do all the time.
- One character against another (Holmes and Watson).
- One story with or within another (the King Lear story and the Gloucester story).
- One idea next to another (broken refrigerators and broken dreams[2])
- At the most basic level, putting words together (metaphor is juxtaposition).
- Then see what happens. Will the ideas clash or resonate? Will the characters blossom or be crushed? Will the subplot (or B story, if you prefer,) throw any light on the main plot (or A story)?

[2] In Arthur Miller's *Death of a Salesman.*

- A writer can either manage and control these juxtapositions – *decide* which elements to put next to each other – or allow serendipity to play its part. I remember talking to a student who was having trouble with an argument between two of his characters. However he set about it, the argument always seemed laboured and predictable. It wouldn't ignite. I suggested he might throw in a random object and make his characters argue about that. Try including a bird in a cage. The juxtaposition of this random object with his characters brought a fresh and unexpected animation to their dispute. On the surface they were arguing about the bird, but the argument was coloured by years of resentment and difference.

EXERCISE

Below is a list of nouns. Without giving the matter any thought, pick two numbers from the list. The two numbers will give you a random juxtaposition. Then ask yourself how you might link those two things and note it down, quickly.

Take the first thoughts that occur to you, even if they seem odd. Oddness can be useful. If, for example, your first word is 'goose' and your second 'phone' you might think: a goose swallows a mobile phone and flies away; or a goose dials a number and puts the girl who looks after the geese in touch with a stranger; or...

Don't ask yourself what happens next – where does the goose go, who is the stranger? – because that's not the point. The point is to link the two objects and make no more than a suggestion for a beginning. What happens next is for later in the process and doesn't concern us here.

It might be the beginnings of a story about love, revenge, desertion, exposure, sacrifice, loss, guilt or penance – but it is only the beginning.

1. Lawn	*2. Fridge*	*3. Knee*
4. Cow	*5. Collar*	*6. Greenhouse*
7. Hat	*8. Hedge*	*9. Cake*
10. Brick	*11. Portrait*	*12. Diary*
13. Slippers	*14. Deckchair*	*15. Brush*
16. Eel	*17. Ladder*	*18. Envelope*

Character

Once you create a character you have also created a whole series of story possibilities. We have more to say on creating character in the next section. Your characters should be rounded and complex.

SCOTT FITZGERALD'S TOP TIP

Character is plot, plot is character.

The following idea uses character to generate stories. We don't need to know much about these characters; we simply want to know what's going to happen to them.

EXERCISE

Find a picture of someone you don't know. Use photographs from magazines or the internet. You might even use someone you've just seen in the street. The important thing is that you don't know who this person is. (So don't choose a picture of someone famous.)

Now think about this stranger. Don't give him or her a lot of thought; we don't want a fully fleshed character study. Just note down a few key facts. Where exactly are they at the moment? What do they do? Give a hint perhaps of their state of mind. Maybe think about a voice. That's all you'll need.

Now consider...

They are one minute from a life-changing event. Something is about to happen to them. Or they are about to discover something. Maybe where they are, or what they do, is relevant to what will happen to them.

Note down, quickly and without much concern for polish, what happens and the difference it makes.

Memory

Memory is a rich ground for the growing of ideas. You can use your own experience, or your own memory of your own experience. What really happened all those years ago and what you remember about it won't necessarily agree. You can check your account against those of others who were around at the time, but you don't have to. If you're writing autobiography it's probably important to recall things accurately, but if you're trawling for ideas that might become scripts or storylines, false memory can be just as productive.

You can also play with memory by thinking of yourself in the third person. What happened didn't happen to you but to someone else. Instead of remembering the day you got lost, remember the day *that little girl* got lost. Or remember the time *that little boy* broke the vase. Thinking of yourself in the third person will help you see things objectively, with a cold eye, and avoid special pleading. Charles Dickens managed to tell (at least part) of his own story by calling himself David Copperfield and in the novel of that name he both is and isn't young David.

You might also try changing your memory in other ways.

I can remember the afternoon when as a boy of nine or ten I broke my nose playing cricket. I can relate that incident in different ways and each way will yield a different sort of story.

PLAYING WITH MEMORY

- When I was ten I broke my nose playing cricket. I can still recall the pain and humiliation of that moment.
- The boys' game was interrupted when one of their number had his nose broken. The match had been evenly balanced at that point.
- The elderly man dreamed of playing once again the game he loved in his youth; and then he broke his nose.
- During the game the girl's nose was broken. There was a moment of pain and then she thought, 'Was that really an accident?'

So see what you can find in your memory. Then see what happens to it when you play around with it.

EXERCISE

Recall an incident from your past, some moment when you were hurt, embarrassed or ashamed.

Make notes about it, in the first person and in the third person, changing gender and age.

Observation

You can make notes on the slightly strange things people do and say. You might hear a fragment of conversation, or catch sight of some odd or interesting piece of behaviour, and then wonder about it. Remember the room glimpsed from the top of the bus? Those three people standing round the ironing board? Wondering about that – who they are and why they're there – could be enough to start you thinking of stories, or the starts of stories.

Public transport is a good place to hear strange things and witness interesting behaviour. Years ago I saw a girl talking intimately to her boyfriend

(I assumed it was her boyfriend). I couldn't hear what she said but all the way from York to Peterborough she picked hairs and crumbs and tiny unseen things from his sweater. She hardly looked him in the eye. Did that somehow represent their relationship? Or was she trying to put off telling him that it was all over?

EXERCISE

In your mind's eye retrace your steps. Go back to this morning, or yesterday, or the beginning of the week. A time when you were walking down the street, or sitting on a bus, or taking the train, and you noticed…what?

Something that you saw or overheard, something that made you wonder. Write down, quickly, what it was and what it made you think.

Old stories

I once pitched the plot of *Measure for Measure* as a possible A story for the TV series I was working on. I didn't credit Shakespeare at the time, though perhaps I should've done. The idea went down well and we were going to do it. I can't remember why we didn't in the end; certainly not because the story wasn't good enough. At a later date on the same series I used the conspiracy plot from *Julius Caesar* and that one was made. And on that occasion I did give Shakespeare a namecheck, at least to the actor playing the Brutus character.

When you're looking for new stories, it can be a good idea to sift through a few old and well-tried ones – ancient myths and legends, fairy stories, classic films, novels, plays, even family anecdotes. They're told and retold because they work. They're good stories and each retelling will offer something new. All a writer has to do is rework them, update, relocate or spin them.

SPINNING GOLDILOCKS

- Goldilocks the crime drama – a girl (or a boy) breaks into remote homes; is there a pattern emerging?
- Goldilocks the psychological drama – the girl (or boy) seeking perfection; she (he) will risk anything to find it.
- Goldilocks the family saga – three bears (or family members) cope with adversity, personal rivalry and a threat from outside.

And so on.

EXERCISE

Choose an old story familiar to you.

Update it, relocate it. Turn it into something new.

Make a few quick notes on what it might become.

What ifs (revisited)

David Edgar in *How Plays Work* writes about the way drama can come from an implied 'but'. There is a proposal:

> 'This is what usually happens; this is the normal state of affairs.'

The proposal is then followed by a BUT.

> 'On this occasion, the time I'm telling you about, something else happened instead. There was a twist, something that ran counter to our expectations.'

You can see this at work in many well-known stories:

- A young man's wife dies. He has lost her forever... BUT there is a way he can get her back (the story of Orpheus).
- Life goes on and then you die... BUT a scientist discovers the secret of creating new life (Frankenstein).

What ifs are similar to this. What if normality suddenly changes in some way? What would happen if I (or he or she) suddenly became rich and powerful? What difference would it make if I (or he or she) found that a stranger was following me (or him or her)?

Or, as Vince Gilligan said about the creation of *Breaking Bad*, 'What if we take Mr Chips and turn him into Scarface?'

What ifs can be big (what if it was the end of the world as we know it) or small (what if I lost that picture). They all work on the same principle, though. What if not this but that?

A lot come from idle speculation or daydreaming. Although hard work is admirable and necessary, a writer shouldn't overlook the benefits of idleness and unfocussed daydreaming.[3]

Several of my plays were written as a result of daydreaming, or wondering what if:

- What would happen if a man discovered that his pet rabbit could read?
- What would happen if someone wanted to perfect his bowling action but had nowhere to practise?
- What would happen if you appointed a health and safety officer who turned out to be accident-prone?

EXERCISE

Give yourself some moments of indolence. Sit down for a while and allow your mind to wander. Or go for a walk. On your own. (There's something about the rhythm of walking that stimulates invention.) Or flick idly through today's paper.

Then write down three what ifs...

[3] You might look at Billy Collins' poem 'The Trouble With Poetry' in which the world gets on with its work while the poets are looking out of windows.

What to do with ideas once you've got them

Once you've collected a few ideas you can begin the process of turning some of them into stories. But first...

Allow your idea some time

In the first instance, ideas in this rough and embryonic form benefit from being abandoned for a while. So leave them in the notebook and do nothing with them. Allow them to germinate. Several times I've returned to ideas after months, or even years, and found that they've somehow developed, taken on a new life. I was thinking about them, somehow, without realizing that I was.

Ask what sort of idea it is

Ponder the idea as a whole. What should it become? How big or small is it? Should it be a play or script? A scene? A series? A thread in a larger story? Or is it, in fact, more than one idea? Or half an idea that needs something else to put with it? How serious (or light) is it?[4]

I suggested that the exercises would provide you with beginnings. But perhaps what you found was not the start of a story but its middle. Or perhaps you stumbled on one of those rarities, a good ending.

Even so, you may not know until you've worked at it – until, sometimes, you've got to the end of the first draft – whether your idea is a good or bad one. Or one that, with some attention, can be made to work.

MARCY KAHAN'S TOP TIP

Questions: interview your characters. Question your assumptions. Query each beat of each scene.

[4] See also Part 1, 'Horses for courses'.

TOP TIP

Interrogate the idea

- Give some thought to the details of the idea. At this stage it's probably malleable. It can change. Don't accept that it must stay as it was when you first wrote it down. You might be able to persuade it in several different directions.
- Develop the habit of questioning the idea. Go back to that room I imagined glimpsing from the top of that bus. The essence of that idea was the picture – three people standing round an ironing board. That was odd enough to note down, with a simple question at the back of my mind: what's going on here? When we revisit an idea like this we can interrogate it in more detail, in as much detail as we like. Who are those people? Do they know each other? Who's in charge? Are they planning something? If so, what is it? What's the ironing board got to do with it? And so on.
- At this stage you can also consider flipping some of the elements of your idea. There were two women and a man standing round that ironing board. What difference would it make if had been two men and a woman? Or three women? Should we change the ironing board to something else? A safe, perhaps? Or is the ironing board more interesting because it's less expected?

Reject the idea

Don't be afraid to throw out the original idea. Sometimes the thinking about it, the interrogation of it, will lead to more interesting ideas. It's tempting to cling on to the image or thought that started your thinking. That's how it all begins – three people standing round an ironing board – we have to keep that. But you don't. Your story has moved on. That ironing board is now in the way.

You can, and sometimes should, ditch the idea that gave rise to it.

Recycle the idea

If you think you've come up with a good idea but no one wants it, don't throw it out. Put it in store and revisit it later.

ANDREW NICKOLDS' TOP TIP

Revenge isn't just a dish best served cold. It can also be reheated and served again under a different name in a different eatery.

Strip the idea down to its essentials and rebuild it. Flip the elements. Relocate it. Change the date. Re-interrogate it and bring it out again.

If it's good.

If you were wrong about it in the first place, forget it.

Simplicity

One more thing to say about ideas.

It should be possible to express your idea in the most straightforward terms. 'This is the story of four young people who get lost in a magic wood. Each then falls in love with the wrong person.'[5] The best idea is the simple idea that's full of possibilities.

If what you end up with is bigger, deeper than any explanation of it, you've probably stumbled on a good idea.

The more I write the more I find that what I'm looking for is simplicity.

Profound simplicity. That's the aim.

[5] *A Midsummer Night's Dream.*

Characters: Making them memorable

'Who am I and why am I here?'

Sue Teddern

> *Every literary work grew from character, even if the author planned the action first. As soon as his characters were created, they took up precedence and the action had to be reshaped to suit them.*
>
> Lajos Egri, *The Art of Dramatic Writing*

Whenever I teach a session on character, I always start with this quote. Character is everything, from three-minute short to long-running soap. A strong character, full of nuances and flaws, will dictate the direction of a story, with the invaluable assistance of his/her creator.

You!

The structure of a script – whether it's a single play, series, serial or sitcom – is governed by the decisions made by your characters. If they are ciphers, stereotypes or tools, if they do not act both according to type *and* wildly out of character, you won't have a story of surprise and substance.

So structure is vital. But you can only begin to construct in earnest when you've found your characters and know the kind of emotional adventure you intend to take together.

Don't let this go to your head, but you are God. You are the all-powerful puppeteer, pulling the strings. Where your characters go, who they are and how they are is all down to you. In your hands is the secret of life and death, comedy and tragedy, snakes and ladders. You decide.

From Hyacinth Bouquet to Phoebe Buffet…

If we're talking sitcom, character always comes first. Forget about puns and pratfalls. And don't concern yourself – yet – with your setting. A classic situation comedy is better described a character comedy or 'charcom' but it's too late to change the name now.

TOP TIP

Producer John Lloyd puts sitcom ingredients in the following order of importance:

1. Character
2. Situation
3. Story
4. Dialogue

If you build your sitcom around one-dimensional characters, the edifice will collapse while you're still mixing the concrete. But if your script is populated with real, fully formed, living, breathing people, they'll help you to excavate for quirks and surprises. When you know your characters inside out, they will ensure that you fill those scary blank pages.

Here are some familiar names from sitcom world:

- Frasier and Niles
- Captain Mainwaring and Sergeant Wilson
- Edina and Patsy
- Fathers Ted, Dougal and Jack
- David Brent and Michael Scott
- Harold and Albert Steptoe
- Diane Chambers and Rebecca Howe
- Samantha, Charlotte, Miranda and Carrie.[1]

[1] Delete Carrie. I've always felt she's the least interesting character in *Sex & the City.*

Each name conjures up a distinctive, instantly recognizable character. You know them. You know their world. You can predict how each of them will react if they're at a party and they don't know anyone, or if their car breaks down on the motorway.

You know what their New Year's resolutions will be and how long they'll keep them, what makes them happy or sad, what's their Achilles heel, what wakes them at 4 am: anxiety, libido, guilt, heartburn.

You know all this because of the writer.

Long before Arthur Lowe, Ardal O'Hanlon or Kim Cattrall had their first read of the pilot, the writer had invested a huge amount of time into discovering who their characters were, how they relate to those around them and how they exist in their own worlds.

If you get it right, it can be the most satisfying part of the process. If you get it wrong, your characters will behave like sullen children who don't want to help you. They may even throw all of their toys out of the pram, to prove the point.

EXERCISE

Take three of your favourite TV or radio characters and ask yourself:

- How they would behave at a party where they don't know anyone?
- What would they do if their car broke down on the motorway?
- What's their Achilles heel?
- What makes them sit bolt upright in bed at 4 am?

How different are their responses? What does that tell you about them?

Animal, child or machine?

Many years ago, I went on a comedy writers' fact-finding trip to Hollywood. We had sessions with script gurus Christopher Vogler and Linda Seger, we sat in on table readings and rehearsals of *Grace Under Fire*, *Frasier* and *Seinfeld*.

One session was with script consultant John Truby. He expounded on his theory that sitcoms are often inhabited by the following three archetypes:

- The **animal** is either very sexually active and/or has an obsession with bodily functions.
- The **child** is naïve and childlike in their reactions, often with a side order of 'stupid'.
- The **machine** is sarcastic, ironic, deadpan, with a machine-like delivery.

This is not the only way of delineating sitcom characters, nor is this theory hard and fast. But if you take a range of classic comedies, you will often find all three. For example:

- *Birds of a Feather*: Dorien is the sexually voracious 'animal'; Tracey is the naïve, gullible 'child'; and Sharon is the rat-tat-tat 'machine'. But she can also be quite exercised with bodily functions.
- *Father Ted*: Father Jack is the swearing, drinking 'animal'; Father Dougal couldn't be more 'child'-like if you put him in Pampers; and although Father Ted isn't a 'machine' per se, he is quite driven and unfeeling. (See what I mean. It's not hard and fast.)
- *Sex and the City*: Samantha is the 'animal', all about sexual gratification; Charlotte is a 'child' in a glamorous thirty-something body; Miranda is the cynical, sarcastic 'machine', or likes to appear so. And Carrie is the device which brings them and their subplots together.

Other sitcoms featuring these archetypes: *The Golden Girls*, *Parks and Recreation*, *Dad's Army*, *The InBetweeners*. In *The Office* (UK) Tim is the machine and Gareth is the child, but David Brent is too insecure to be any kind of animal.

There are also fifty shades of stupid, from the boy Pike (*Dad's Army*) and adorable Woody (*Cheers*) through to dopey Dougal (*Father Ted*), horny/innocent Neil (*The InBetweeners*) and other-worldly Phoebe (*Friends*).

Friends is a tough one because they all have 'child' tendencies: Phoebe is pure child, Joey is child/animal and Chandler is child/machine. How would *you* categorize Ross, Rachel and Monica?

EXERCISE

Watch a TV sitcom and see if these animal/child/machine definitions fit the characters.

- If not, what is the character dynamic?
- Who are the allies and enemies?

Look at one of your own sitcoms.

- Can you identify any animals, children and machines?
- What is the dynamic between each character?
- Does the mix work?
- Are any characters surplus to requirements?
- Who are the allies and enemies?

As Barry White said: 'Don't go changing'

If you're aiming to write the next great sitcom, don't forget that, because of the nature of the genre, characters don't change. They rarely learn lessons because we, the audience, want them to be the same every week.

Miranda Hart pulled the plug on her successful eponymous sitcom because she didn't want her heroine to be forever falling over, irritating her mother and never getting her man. She went out on a high and her loyal audience loved her for it.

Often there is no series arc in a sitcom; in other words, the episodes can be shown in any order. So what happens to Mrs Brown or Albert Steptoe in episode three will have no effect on how they act in episode six. Filmed comedies tend to have more of a series arc. See how David Brent changed – for the better – over the duration of *The Office*.

The name game

> **TOP TIP**
>
> When you find the right name for a character, you're one step closer to knowing who they are. Even if they play a minor role, don't call someone 'Joe's mum' or 'Co-worker' or 'Neighbour'.
>
> As soon as they become Rowena or Asif or Mr Sillitoe, a human dimension is added.

It's tempting to go for clichés, like (dare I say it?) Sharon and Tracey in *Birds of a Feather*. An unexpected name might be more revealing. Would it have been character-forming for your adult hero to be 'Piers' in a class full of 'Calums' and 'Ryans' when he was twelve?

Writers often give older characters names like Edna, Wilf and Albert, forgetting that they're children of the Forties and Fifties and are more likely to be Linda, Keith and Derek.

Some thoughts on the subject from Alan Bennett:

> One of the ways the young think they are safeguarded against the fate and future of their grandparents is by their names: Sharons don't suffer from dementia or Damians from incontinence. And if the old ones can think at all, they must wonder if their names are part of the trouble. They've been called the wrong thing, that's what's the matter. With names like Frank or Norman, Ernest or Gilbert, they're already weighted in the direction of the grave. Jeremys don't fail as they have failed. Piss doesn't trickle unheeded down a Nicky's leg. And if a Darren dies, it's in a motorway pile-up, not in a sunshine home. But not for much longer.

> In a TV play of mine called *Rolling Home*, there is a scene in which the middle-aged children of a father dead in an old people's home are coming away, carrying his meagre possessions just as the matron is helping a new arrival, another old man, out of the ambulance. 'Hello,' she says brightly. 'Welcome; you're our first Kevin.'
>
> *A Strip of Blue*, from *Telling Tales*

Drama karma

Characters created for a drama need to be as carefully constructed as their comedy cousins; more so, because you can't hide any inconsistencies with a zinging one-liner or a carefully thrown custard pie.

Some script gurus advocate that you flesh out your character in the form of an extensive CV or biography: school, parents' names, political views. Far be it from me to disagree if it works for you.

But, as a prime exponent of the art of displacement activity, this would be my way of *not* getting started. So Katie hated hockey at school and Liam had a newspaper round. Why am I wasting time with ten-page CVs when I should be writing?

> I'm not a fan of over-characterization. When preparing a character, I would never list: 'Michael, red T-shirt, yellow boots.' I'd say: 'Michael, coolest kid in class.' It's about capturing the energy of the character, not every last detail.
>
> Abi Morgan

TOP TIP

Ask your proto-characters the kind of questions that will give an insight into who they are and what emotional baggage burdens them. For example:

- Does she or he snore?
- Is she or he ticklish?

- What would she or he do if they found £10 in the street?
- What would she or he do if they saw a couple fighting in the street?

Don't answer as yourself. It's all too easy to make your characters into versions of you.

As Charlie Moritz points out in his book *Scriptwriting for the Screen*, these are the three vital questions:

- What would **I** say or do now?
- What would *anyone* say or do now?
- What would *my character* say or do now?

EXAMPLE

There's a national chain of newsagents which has the annoying habit of trying to sell you half-price bars of chocolate when you're paying for your newspaper. I used this situation to illustrate my two central characters in *Fix You*, a TV comedy-drama version of my radio serial *soloparentpals.com*. Tom is easy-going and naïve (a child?) while Rosie is spikey and angry, with machine-like tendencies. So:

- **What would *I* say when offered a bar of half-price chocolate?**

I would make a jokey attempt to bond with the shop assistant by telling her about my ongoing diet and lack of willpower. I would ultimately decline and feel pleased with myself.

- **What would *anyone* say?**

  'No, thanks' or 'Yes, please'. End of story.
- **What would *Tom* say?**

> 'Oh, wow, thanks. Yeah, awesome. Thanks.'
>
> - **What would *Rosie* say?**
>
>   'No, I *don't* want any chocolate, thank you! Honestly, why does your shop persist in this tacky marketing trick? Oh, alright, I'll have three.'
>
> What would some of your characters-in-progress say or do in this situation?

Character entry points

There are many ways to find out how your character ticks and relates to those around them. Here are some favourites:

- If your setting is a workplace, get one character to write an email to the other(s). It will set the tone and establish the hierarchy. Who's in charge? Who's *really* in charge? The efficient PA or her lazy boss?
- If it's a two-hander, ask each character to write a short description of the other in the first person. You'll get a useful sense of their speech patterns *and* what they think of each other.
- Get each character to give a one-sentence soundbite of what they think of all the others. You may find some interesting imbalances, perhaps even a spot of URST (unresolved sexual tension).

> **TOP TIP**
>
> *'Every character wants something, even if it's only a glass of water.'*
>
> Kurt Vonnegut

- What are your characters' wants and needs? Often the 'want' offers a public face and the 'need' is a hidden guilty secret or big scary emotional challenge.
- For example, to her friends and colleagues, an ambitious teacher says she wants to be a deputy head by the time she's thirty. But secretly she needs to break off all contact with her wastrel sister. Why? Or to make contact after a ten-year rift. Why? Already you've come up with two interesting angles that could be developed further.

- Get your character to write a short lonely hearts ad, giving a sense of how they would describe themselves (lies and all!) to a potential partner.[2]
- Write a 100-word first-person account of something that happened to your character this morning. It can be mundane and ordinary or surreal and extraordinary. How did your character view it? Has she or he learned something from the experience? If so, what?
- What was your character like at the age of seven, twelve, sixteen, eighteen? Headstrong? Insecure? How did she or he change as they got older? What external forces influenced the person she or he has become?
- David Chase did this in his creation of one of TV's most compelling characters.

  'As a child, Tony Soprano was shaped by forces over which he had no control (his parents). He's now an adult and must struggle to take responsibility for who he is. He has to stop blaming his mother and own up to his actions. It is a very compressed version of what actually would be years of therapy.'
- What does your character want to change as a New Year dawns? Think of ten resolutions that reveal inner conflicts.

EXAMPLE

Here are single parents Tom's and Rosie's resolutions:

Tom's New Year's Resolutions

1. Get a life.
2. Eat more vegetables.
3. Wash up every other day.
4. Be pleased to see happy families in the supermarket.
5. Do something mad and wacky: stand-up comedy? Juggling? New glasses?
6. Stop slagging off (ex-wife) Ginny to (daughter) Lily. It isn't clever or funny.

---

[2] I used this exercise with some students and one of them threw down his pen. 'Can't you think of anything?' I asked. 'My character doesn't *need* to advertise!' he replied. A great answer, a useful insight.

7. Chat up the next woman you fancy, instead of throwing coffee down your trousers.
8. Make people laugh. And not by throwing coffee down your trousers.
9. Put off asking for Prozac until 1 March (NB: mark date in diary).
10. Look at this list again next year and laugh. Or take all the Prozac.

Rosie's New Year's Resolutions

1. Learn to drive.
2. Learn Spanish/join a choir/do watercolours… or whatever evening class is on a Wednesday!
3. Count to ten and smile when Dad says something stupid.
4. Count to ten and smile when (son) Calum says something stupid.
5. Count to ten when (ex-husband) Phil says something stupid. Then thump him!
6. Relax.
7. Either buy a load of lard-butt slacks or lose weight, you doughnut!
8. RELAX!!! I mean it!
9. Read a book a week… a proper book, not the latest Katie Price!
10. Find a boyfriend OR have a double choc chip cheesecake at weekends only.

EXERCISE

Complete this questionnaire on behalf of three of your least-developed characters. Some answers will surprise you.

1. Is xxx ticklish?
2. If xxx found £10 in the street, what would she or he do with it?
3. Would xxx do karaoke? Which song?
4. What's the biggest lie xxx has ever told?

5. What would xxx do if she or he saw a couple fighting in the street?
6. What's xxx's favourite sandwich?
7. Does xxx check the weather forecast before going out?
8. Has xxx ever had his or her heart broken?
9. Does xxx snore?
10. Has xxx ever shoplifted? If yes, what?
11. What does xxx wear in bed?
12. What kind of air traveller is xxx?
13. If you sat next to xxx on a train, would you enjoy his or her company?
14. Fish and chips, pizza, Chinese/Indian takeaway? Or ...
15. Favourite newspaper/magazine?

Convincing surprises

Nick Warburton

A peculiar heart ...

E. M. Forster said you might consider a character truly rounded if he or she were able to surprise us 'in a convincing way'. He was asking for characters who are realistic enough to be recognizable, but who are nevertheless unpredictable.

How do you do this?

For a start a writer of dramatic fiction needs a peculiar heart, made up of both fire and ice. On the one hand you need enough warmth in your heart to care about your characters and their world; on the other hand you need to be indifferent to what happens to them, to what you put them through.

You must prepare to make them suffer.

And you must not take sides.

In fact, writers do sometimes take sides but it's a risky strategy. If you're too sympathetic to your characters you may find yourself loading the dice in their favour. You may be tempted to distort the story so the 'good' are rewarded and the 'bad' punished. You may even be tempted to over-draw your 'bad' characters so that they really deserve the punishment you've got lined up for them. This may be good box office – audiences like a bit of spite and revenge – but it won't necessarily help you create real and believable characters.

So you should neither favour nor chastize your characters but you should understand them. And the more you understand them, the more real they'll seem.

Where did you go to school?

One way to understand your characters is to create a sort of biography or CV for them, to assemble a dossier of facts about their lives.

Consider for a moment Amanda Leigh. Who is Amanda Leigh? You've just made her up, or you're about to. Now fill in her CV.

AMANDA LEIGH'S CV

- Full name:
- Date of birth:
- Place of birth:
- Occupation:
- Name and occupation of parents:
- Siblings:
- Marital status:
- School attended:
- Friends:
- And so on ...

You can no doubt think of other facts to include in such a CV. What does Amanda look like? How does she dress? So you gradually assemble the facts and build a picture.

It makes a more interesting picture if some of the facts you assemble are about the psychology of Amanda Leigh. Is she, for example, quick-tempered? Timid? Resentful?

You could then write out all Amanda's qualities in prose, rather than in chart form.

In TV new characters are often introduced with a substantial CV like this in the hope that the more facts you gather the better you'll know this person. So ...

> Quick-tempered yet timid Amanda Leigh (34) was born in Leeds to parents Rodney and Carol who both worked in the geography department of the university. Always resentful of her piano-playing younger brother Jason (32), she left Leeds when she was 16 to try her luck in the jewellery business ...

It's a scatter-gun approach and it can work.

Up to a point.

And, to a certain extent, by chance. You might stumble on the detail that suddenly brings her to life, but sheer weight of facts is just as likely to leave quick-tempered Amanda, in her favourite bright yellow shawl, flat on the page, little more than an amalgam; sometimes little more than a harking back to other characters a bit like her.

It's probably better to leave room for growth and development. You can get to know your characters in the way you get to know your friends. You meet them and something about them appeals to you and you form an impression. Then you learn something else about them ('I didn't know you were fond of frogs') and that impression changes.

We really need to give Amanda a pulse and I think there's a shorter, more efficient way of doing that than filling in a chart. In fact, you'll have a more profound understanding of her if you know only a handful of things.

TOP TIP

QUESTIONS FOR YOUR CHARACTER

- What's her voice?
- What's her driving condition? (What's this? See below.)

- What's her secret?
- Have you got a snapshot from her past?

If you understand these few things about Amanda, you may find you can answer other questions anyway, even if you haven't thought about them before.

Where did she go to school?

Well, I know her voice ... so I can tell you it was a small private school in a wealthy Leeds suburb. Or she was taught at home on a remote farm in the Highlands of Scotland.

Voice

When you're working on dialogue (or direct address) you need to think about things like accents and rhythm and quirks of speech.[3] When you're trying to create a believable character you need to hear them speaking to you. People reveal things about themselves when they speak. They don't give away secrets – they can be very careful and guarded – but they do give away clues.

Consider Amanda Leigh again.

Now imagine seeing her in a coffee shop, at a nearby table, talking to a friend.

Or talking to a lover.

Or telling someone she's just met about the cat she had when she was a child.

She might be wearing her favourite yellow scarf. It doesn't matter. You're not interested in her scarf (although you might be later). From where you're sitting you can't see her or her scarf. You can only hear her voice.

Listen to her.

The tone of her voice. The way she expresses herself.

---

[3] Voice and Dialogue are considered more closely in 'A most delicate monster – voice' and 'The talky bit: dialogue'.

When Amanda's voice is familiar to you she'll have given you, quite without meaning to, a number of clues about herself. After a while you might even imagine talking to Amanda yourself, asking her questions.

When you hear her speaking you'll begin to understand her.

EXERCISE

Forget Amanda for a moment. Think of someone else. Tony Pool. About whom you know nothing.

You're in that coffee shop and he sits behind you with an almost silent friend. And he talks.

So listen to Tony talking for five minutes. And take notes – the things he talks about, the odd phrase here and there.

The driving condition

This is not the same as 'what your characters want' because sometimes your characters won't particularly want anything. This is about the inner engine that makes them behave the way they do.

The easiest way to explain what I mean is to give some examples.

A nice clear-cut case is Iago in *Othello*. What drives him is his deep resentment of others and, in particular, of Othello. As a result he tries to destroy Othello. This is not a matter of what he wants – although it does generate wanting in Iago – it's a matter of what the man is.

Peggy in *Mad Men* is driven by a combination of ambition and insecurity. Her desire to succeed, and her not quite knowing how to go about it, make her be what she is and do what she does.

Sometimes your characters won't know themselves well enough to be aware of the engine that drives them. Peggy, I suspect, does. In a short play of mine called *For Starters* the central character, a waitress called Daisy, doesn't.

Daisy has just started work at a rather refined hotel and she makes mistakes. She knows that she makes mistakes but she can't quite work out why. In fact, the reason is rather an innocent one. She's the sort of girl people talk to; they tell her things; they tell her things they may never have told anyone else. So the thing that's driving Daisy is something in her character that invites confidence – and she's unaware of it. Here she is talking to Roland, a rather secretive businessman who has a regular table in the restaurant.

EXAMPLE: DAISY'S DRIVING CONDITION

ROLAND: People tell you things anyway. I've noticed.

DAISY: Do they?

ROLAND: How do you get them to do that?

DAISY: I didn't know I was doing it.

ROLAND: Course you do. That wimp that was in the other day... he told you about himself ...

DAISY: Patrick? Well, I suppose so.

ROLAND: I've seen you – yacking away at the diners. And they all yack back. I could find that quite useful in my line of business.

DAISY: Really?

ROLAND: Certainly. I got a few people on my list who could do with loosening up.

DAISY: What is your line of business?

ROLAND: Depends when you're asking. I do different things different days.

DAISY: Today, then. What do you do today?

When I started the play all I knew about Daisy was that she was young, probably in her first job, and that there was something about her that drew secrets and confessions from people. Everything else came from knowing that.

In Alan Ayckbourn's play *Time and Time Again*[4] Leonard (Tom Courtenay) doesn't *want* anything. His driving condition is a kind of apathy, an almost

[4] The TV version was broadcast in 1976.

complete lack of interest in how things will turn out, for him or for the women who fall in love with him. In fact, 'driving' seems too engaged a word for Leonard. But a lot happens in the play and the source of it is its central character's passivity.

TOP TIP

Not all characters are defined by 'what they want' – but something will drive them.

EXERCISE

Think of two or three of your favourite characters and try to identify their driving condition.

Secrets

Characters are often brought to life by the secrets writers give them. They can have big secrets – the murder that enabled Amanda to inherit all her wealth – or small secrets – Tony's ambition to dress up and dance in public.

Both big and small secrets can also become part of the engine that drives the plot. In Amanda's case, for example, keeping the murder quiet may lead to further and more desperate crimes. And before Tony can achieve his place in the chorus line he may have to overcome any number of obstacles, from the prejudice of his best friend to his own innate clumsiness. The fact that the secrets themselves are grounded in character – Amanda the ruthless, Tony the shy dreamer – means that the plot will convince more than a series of events bolted together for effect. Remember Scott Fitzgerald's dictum: 'Character is plot, plot is character.'

SECRET PERMUTATIONS

Think about how your characters might have secrets from:

- the audience
- themselves

- all other characters
- some other characters
- combinations of the above (from us and from some other characters; from themselves and from all other characters; and so on.)

With some characters it might be enough for you, as the writer, to know their secrets. Merely knowing might bring them to life for you. If you're going to share their secrets, though, you'll have to consider with whom you share them, how (by confession or by detection, for example) and, crucially for your plotting, when.

EXERCISE

Here are four characters who know each other but about whom you know nothing: Lesley, Cora, Ravi and Carter. Two of them have what we might call Big Secrets; the other two have Small Secrets. What are they? And who knows about them?

A snapshot from the past

Picture yourself climbing into an old attic in search of that comprehensive dossier on the character you've just created. It'll give you all the answers to those questions about jobs and next of kin and taste in clothes. Instead of the dossier, though, you find nothing but a faded envelope with two old photographs in it.

But the photographs are revealing.

They show your character at two points in the past, years ago and maybe years apart. They show this person at school, on a picnic, with a brother or sister, in a boat. They also show them momentarily, possibly even *unexpectedly* happy. Or sad. Or unguarded.

Look at the imaginary pictures and learn something else about your characters.

EXERCISE

Now you know a little bit about Lesley (or Cora, or Ravi or Carter) imagine finding the envelope with the two photographs. What do you see in the pictures?

Consistency?

You may well be told that your characters must be consistent. And so they must. Consistency, however, isn't the same as predictability. That's partly what E. M. Forster was getting at. Your characters can and should do unpredictable things. But the impetus to spring that surprise must be found somewhere inside them.

Breaking Bad is built on surprise and unpredictability in its main character. Walter White is a respectable, dedicated, anxious and caring chemistry teacher, and he becomes a violent drug dealer. His journey into crime is unexpected but entirely consistent with his character. His anxiety and determination to care for his family are the very things that push him to criminal extremes.

Flatness

Not all your characters can be rounded and compelling. An audience won't have time to take in all that roundedness. Some characters will have to come in to move the furniture or supply the funds or carry the messages. They will have a job to do. They will appear, do what's required and then be seen no more. But that's no reason to make them nonentities. They can display a flash of eccentricity, perhaps hints of dark or light. You can leave us feeling that, if this person were to reappear, we'd get to know another fascinating, complex character. Because there's a hint of something about them.

When David Copperfield runs away from the misery of London, almost everything he has is stolen from him. He meets a violent man who steals his handkerchief and threatens him with worse. The man has a woman with him and she gives young David a secret look and mouths the word 'go' to him, for which kindness she is knocked down.

And David, as narrator, says he sees her, bloodied and sitting in the road, and he declares he'll never forget her.

Dickens provides a suggestion of depth in this nameless woman who plays so fleeting a part in the story.

Interrogating characters

In the first section of this Part, I suggested that, in order to develop your ideas, you might find it useful to interrogate them. You can do something similar when you're creating characters. Ask them questions, but don't ask them the questions they might expect.[5]

EXERCISE

Bring to mind one of those characters – Lesley, Cora, Ravi or Carter. Now you know a little bit about them, ask one of them these questions and write a sentence or two in answer. Write your answers in the voice of the character.

- What is your recurring dream? (You might not know what it means but write down what happens in the dream and what you see.)
- Where's the place you always long to be? (A place you often go to when you want to be alone, or a place you used to go to but can't now.)
- Who are you scared of? (A person you know, perhaps, or one you imagine.)

[5] This is an idea developed from an exercise suggested by the poet Gillian Allnutt.

The building blocks: Plot and structure

'But where are the bones?'

Sue Teddern

My agent rang with bad news. The plug had been pulled on my ITV sitcom pilot, *Mad and Sandie*. These things happen.

A few years later, I had an idea. What if my thirty-somethings became fifty-somethings? A sixty-minute bittersweet comedy-drama, rather than half an hour played for laughs, but with the central love triangle dynamic intact.

So, along with my producer, Sioned Wiliam, I went to ITV HQ to pitch the idea to the then Head of Drama, Nick Elliot. He listened to our presentation.

'That's the basic premise', Sioned concluded. 'If you're interested, we can put some flesh on the bones.'

He gave us the look of one who's heard a lifetime of pitches and said: 'It's all flesh and no bones.'

In other words, we were building a house on sand, without any foundations. It might function as a temporary shelter but it would inevitably collapse around our ears.

We went away and found the bones. We made a sixty-minute pilot called *Happy Together*, starring Sue Johnston and Lynda Bellingham, which was broadcast by ITV in 2001. It was, however, never commissioned as a series. These things happen.

That said, it was built around a strong structural 'skeleton', thanks to Nick's stern words.

Another analogy: our idea was all icing and no cake. And although icing gives you an instant sugar rush, it can't offer long-term sustenance. Writing sparky dialogue or a moving scene is hugely satisfying. But where will you go if you haven't put some work into the foundations beneath?

TOP TIP

Yes, nifty dialogue helps a lot. Sure, it's nice if you can bring your characters to life. But you can have terrific characters spouting just swell talk to each other, and if the structure is unsound, forget it.

William Goldman, *Adventures in the Screen Trade*

The decisions you make at the plotting stage will all be influenced by your end result: are you writing a fifteen-minute episode of a radio serial or a ninety-minute screenplay? Will you achieve closure or are you going for a climactic cliffhanger?

Whatever you choose to write, the principles of storytelling remain the same, as they have since the very first tale was told around a Neolithic campfire. It's no surprise that Christopher Vogler's seminal book, *The Writer's Journey: Mythic Structure for Storytellers and Screenwriters*, was inspired by Joseph Campbell's *The Hero with a Thousand Faces*. As he in turn was inspired by the structure and narrative drive of Greek myths. Story is story and good story is always in demand.

You may say: 'I'm not interested in Zeus and Aphrodite. I just want to write a quirky comedy where this guy stops being a doofus and falls in love.'

TOP TIP

Don't forget that you will have absorbed the rules of storytelling, since time immemorial, in every book, film, play or TV show you've ever seen. You may not be able to fully articulate them but you know them. Consciously or subconsciously, you can tell when stories work and when they don't.

How you adapt the rules to suit the genre, medium or slot of your choice comes with practice.

Once you trust your creative instincts, you may even bend or break the rules when they don't work for your story. But it's best to know what you're doing first. Picasso learned how to draw anatomically perfect bodies before he gave them one eye and no feet.

Permission to be a couch potato

Find the best example of the genre you aspire to and immerse yourself in it, from the comfort of your favourite sofa. Therefore, my first rule of structure is to 'watch, watch, watch'.

Or, in the case of radio, 'listen, listen, listen'.

TOP TIP

Select a TV or radio show and watch/listen the first time as a 'consumer'. Then revisit it as a writer and with the aid of your 'pause' button.

Break down the structure scene by scene. Make helpful lists and flow charts. Use highlighter pens for colour coding and cross-referencing, if it helps.

Here are some important elements to note:

- What is the main plot?
- What is/are the subplot(s)?
- How are the main plot and subplots interwoven?
- Where are the plot twists and turning points?
- How many scenes are there?
- Do they all move the story along?
- Are there any that you would cut?
- If the story unfolds effectively, can you work out why?
- If it doesn't, what went wrong?
- The million-dollar question: does it conform to a three-act structure?

A beginning, a muddle and an end

The three-act structure has long been the Hollywood model. You'll find it in 90 per cent of all the films you see. And the reason? It works. Here are two simple definitions:

- 'A beginning, a muddle and an end.'
- 'Get your hero up a tree, throw stones at him, then get him down again.'

This model works equally well for the self-contained radio play. Think of it, structurally, as a movie for your ears; forty-five minutes is an ideal length for a beginning, a muddle and an end.

When I teach sitcom, I use my very own acronym: SHIGWIGB. This translates into 'something happens, it gets worse, it gets better'. 'Better' is not literal. Things don't always work out perfectly in the final act, but some kind of resolution is found, even if it's bittersweet or open-ended.

It's better to arrive than to travel... hopefully!

I envy those confident folk who start to write with only the vaguest idea of what their story will be about, how it will unfold, who will be the unforgettable characters and how it will resolve.

Actually, that's not true. I envy them their confidence that they'll discover these things along the way. But what if they don't? What if their characters drag them down unhelpful cul-de-sacs or they lose the plot? I can't work like that. It's too scary.

A novelist may have the luxury of setting off on their writing adventure with no route planned, just an intriguing premise and strong sense of the world they wish to inhabit. Put ridiculously simply, a novel is as long as it is.

Movies too are a moveable feast. Yes, they have a standard length of about ninety minutes, but we've all sat through films that hurtle to the end credits in a mere hour-and-a-quarter and others that may take two or three hours. (*Once Upon a Time in Anatolia*, anyone?)

But a radio drama fills a 45-minute slot, an episode of *EastEnders* comes in at 27 minutes or so and most prime-time TV dramas start at 9 pm and finish at 10 pm. That won't change, however brilliant your script. You have a slot to fill. 'Too short' or 'too long' won't do.

Scriptwriters don't have the luxury of filling pages with random dialogue and pretty images while they wait for their characters to kick in or for their subplot to unfold. You need to have your journey mapped and to know your destination so that you can set your creative satnav and find your route.

TOP TIP

Everything in your script must be there to establish character and/or move the story along. If it doesn't, it's holding you up. Delete it!

Imagine your storyline is a car journey from London to Manchester. You programme your satnav to take you via the most efficient route. Whatever happens along the way – stopping for a snack, making a detour, getting lost – your final destination will not change. You need to arrive in Manchester because that's the point of the journey.

Likewise, while you're writing your script, you may have one of those wonderful light-bulb moments where a new plot point comes to you twenty pages in and you deviate from your storyline. Your instincts are right and this scene is now vital. But don't forget your destination.

Ultimately, you will find your own way of writing. If that involves an unplanned, organic, magical-mystery tour technique, with massive detours and an unknown destination AND if you're happy with the finished script, then go for it. Whatever gets you to your final page must ultimately become the way you work best.

To 'guru' or not to 'guru'

In my kitchen, I have the usual row of recipe books: Delia Smith, Elizabeth David, Nigel Slater. They are all stain free and pristine because they've barely been opened. I consult them for ideas, rather than recipes.

Likewise, the shelf in my study holds books by the screenwriting equivalents of Delia, Elizabeth and Nigel.

- *Story* by Robert McKee
- *The Writers' Journey* by Christopher Vogler
- *Making a Good Script Great* by Linda Seger
- *The Art of Dramatic Writing* by Lajos Egri
- *Screenplay – The Foundations of Screenwriting* by Syd Field

These books are often dipped into. But none have become my 'go-to' how-to book. I consult them for guidance, but I also trust my own storytelling instincts because I'm telling 'my' story. The experts do, however, know what they're talking about and they've made careers out of it.

Let's see how *they* encapsulate the art of structure and storytelling:

> Originality is the confluence of content and form – distinctive choices of subject plus a unique shaping of the telling. Content (setting, characters, ideas) and form (selection and arrangement of events) require, inspire and mutually influence one another.
>
> With content in one hand and a mastery of form in the other, a writer sculpts story. As you rework a story's substance, the telling reshapes itself. As you play with a story's shape, its intellectual and emotional spirit evolves.

Robert McKee, *Story*

The 'sculpting' metaphor resonates with me. I remember a talk given by the late Alan Plater[1] about a TV series he had written. He said finding your story is like sculpting an elephant out of marble. What you must do is chip away everything that isn't elephant.

For me, that process is at the planning stage. Otherwise I would end up with several badly sculpted elephants and a lot of leftover marble.

> The needs of the story dictate its structure. Form follows function. Your beliefs and priorities, along with the characters, themes, style, tone and mood you are trying to get across, will determine the shape and design of the plot. Structure will also be influenced by the audience, and the time and place in which the story is being told.

Christopher Vogler, *The Writer's Journey*

[1] One of the core writing team of *Z Cars*. See Part 1, page 8.

Christopher Vogler's twelve stages of the hero's journey (from *The Writer's Journey*)

1. Heroes are introduced to the ordinary world, where
2. they receive the call to adventure.
3. They are reluctant at first or refuse the call, but
4. are encouraged by a mentor to
5. cross the first threshold and enter the special world where
6. they encounter tests, allies and enemies.
7. They approach the inmost cave, crossing a second threshold
8. where they endure the supreme ordeal.
9. They take possession of their reward and
10. are pursued on the road back to the ordinary world.
11. They cross the third threshold, experience a resurrection, and are transformed by the experience.
12. They return with the elixir, a boon or treasure to benefit the ordinary world.

As a storytelling template, the twelve stages can be helpful. Vogler adds that 'this is not a cookbook recipe or a mathematical formula to be applied rigidly to every story ... to force a story to conform to a structure model is putting the cart before the horse'.

Whether you subscribe to this model or not, you will find much to draw from. Certainly the first three stages have always inspired me. At the beginning of your story, your hero(ine) is stuck in his or her ordinary world: a dull job, bad marriage, cosy rut, damaging addiction, tendency to compromise – take your pick.

When something happens to take them out of their comfort zone – the 'call to adventure' – they decline. 'No thanks, I'm fine where I am.' In other words, the refusal of the call.

But then an incident forces them to set off on their journey and a significant point is the first threshold. Vogler likens it to that moment in a Western where the wagon train crosses the fast-flowing river and only just makes it to the other side. Now there's no turning back.

Turning points, tests, ordeals and challenges fill the second act: the middle/muddle! The third act offers resolution of some kind: good, bad, both, neither . . .

'The return with the elixir' shouldn't be taken literally. It's the grain of self-knowledge that your hero didn't have at the beginning of the story.

A good movie example is *Up in the Air* (screenplay by Jason Reitman and Sheldon Turner) starring George Clooney as a slick, sexy redundancy consultant. His 'elixir', after his heart is broken, is that his very specific lifestyle choices can continue and hey, he's the same as he ever was. But we know he isn't! Deep down, he does too and he can't un-know the 'elixir'.

'Yes, but how do you *do it?'*

Quoting Hollywood script gurus is all very well, but let's cut to the chase. How do I structure and plot a radio play, sitcom episode or six-part TV series, these being the most frequent credits on my CV?

My own technique comes from years of trial and error and if I said I only ever do it this way, I'd be lying. But some elements of the process are transferable from genre to genre. Let's take them one by one.

A single play for radio

Let's assume you have a good sense of your story. You know your starting point, your destination, the tone of the world you wish to inhabit and your cast of characters. What next?

If you haven't used the following technique before, give it a go. If you have and it didn't work, maybe your story was missing a beat or your characters' journeys were too linear.

Write every pivotal scene on separate index cards or post-it notes, then spread them out and place them in some kind of order. This can take a while as you re-jig, rethink, delete and augment.

When you see the whole thing on a large surface, you can take in every element of your story in one widescreen gaze. You'll spot the holes, the clunky stuff and the repetitions. Ask yourself:

- Where are my three acts?
- What's working?
- What's missing?
- Where are the twists, turns and surprises?
- What must be added to establish back story?
- What has to go because it serves no purpose?
- How will my audience know that she's lying – or he's a drunk – or this bit's a flashback – or that bit's ironic?

The final part of the process is to stack your cards into order and write your storyline from them. It can be highly detailed or broad brushstrokes, as long as you know your intentions at script stage.

This method has practical advantages: it stops you writing unwanted chunks of 'elephant' and it also cements the story in your head because of the refining process you've been through.

EXERCISE

Act1: Two people are moving house.

Act 2: Removals day.

Act 3: They don't leave.
Think about who they are, why they are moving, and how you'd tell this story.

- Using six index cards per act, show how you'd develop this premise, revealing character and back story, showing turning points and revelations, reaching a rewarding conclusion.
- Reorder, replace, delete and create until you are happy with the finished eighteen cards.

- Is your structure sound? Would this make a good radio play?

Now use the same process on an old script of your own, maybe even something that was rejected. Can you fill eighteen index cards with a satisfying through-line? If not, can you see where you went wrong, what's missing, what needs reworking?

Plotting the sitcom

The following technique works well if you're creating a sitcom with a main plot, subplot and running gag. I'm assuming that you have your characters and their world mapped out.

Take a large piece of paper and make three columns, labelled A–C.

- The 'A' column signifies plots that affect your characters' world, e.g. their home or workplace.
- The 'B' column is for personal and emotional plots.
- The 'C' column is something small-scale that complicates/contrasts with the 'A' and 'B' plots.

Force your brain to fill each column with ten ideas. They can be half formed, clichéd, off-the-wall, dull, daft, desperate. Don't think, just write! The faster, the better.

Now look through your thirty ideas and link up one plot from each column to make a good episode.

For example, halfway down column 'A' you've written 'Jo must re-apply for her job.' At the top of column 'B', you have: 'Dave's mum Sally comes to stay.' And somewhere in column 'C', you've scrawled: 'New iPad???'

Can these three random thoughts work together to make one episode? Kick them around, see how they impact on each other. For example:

- Would Jo's inability to set up her new iPad foil her chances to reapply for the job?
- Might Sally, who claims she hates technology, become obsessed with Twitter or turn into an evil 'troll' on Jo's iPad? Could this affect the job plot somehow?

- How does Sally indulge or annoy Dave whenever she visits?
- Could Sally's presence distract Jo from preparing for her job interview in some way?
- How does the new iPad mess things up?

From your three columns of plots, you should be able to link together enough ideas to create several good episodes. You may even find that two As and a B will do it; or one B and two Cs. I use this technique myself and it always offers surprises.

Once you settle on your A, B and C plots, it helps to break each one down into three acts. Remember that you're looking for SHIGWIGB: something happens, it gets worse, it gets better. For example:

'A' plot: Job

Act 1: Jo learns from her boss that she must reapply for her job. She's horrified.

Act 2: Sally accidentally deletes Jo's all-important interview presentation from the new iPad.

Act 3: Jo's boss is arrested for fraud and Jo is off the hook. Phew!

'B' plot: Sally's visit

Act 1: Dave grudgingly invites Sally to stay.

Act 2: Tension, rows, resentment between mother and son. Jo bears the brunt.

Act 3: Sally and Dave pretend Jo is causing the tension, which gives Sally permission to go home.

'C' plot: New iPad

Act 1: Dave buys an iPad for Jo from his unreliable friend, Tim.

Act 2: The iPad was cheap for a reason! It has Polish spellcheck and no memory.

Act 3: Sally meets an online Lonely Heart from Warsaw. She buys the iPad from them.

Now arrange the plots into a cohesive episode. You might end up with something like this:

1. Dave grudgingly invites Sally to stay.
2. Jo learns from her boss that she must reapply for her job. She's horrified.
3. Dave buys an iPad for Jo from his unreliable friend, Tim.
4. The iPad was cheap for a reason! It has Polish spellcheck and no memory.
5. Sally accidentally deletes Jo's all-important interview presentation from the iPad.
6. Tension, rows, resentment between mother and son. Jo bears the brunt.
7. Sally and Dave pretend Jo is causing the tension, which gives Sally permission to go home.
8. Jo's boss is arrested for fraud and Jo is off the hook. Phew!
9. Sally meets an online Lonely Heart from Warsaw. She buys the iPad from them.

Your episode may still not be ready to write. But it's not far off and you now have a good sense of how each plot impacts on the other two, which will give you greater narrative drive and increased comedic possibilities.

The series

Plotting a series is usually a team effort, after the initial idea has been optioned and developed by a production company. So this may not be something you ever need to face on your own. The process is collaborative and exciting, as you pitch ideas with the other writers, script editor and producer.

You may blurt out something half-formed and ill-shaped which is then picked up by someone else who then bats it back to you for input. And suddenly it's turned into a proper plot or storyline. When you're all on the same wavelength and there's endless coffee to fuel your creativity, it has to be one of the best experiences in the business. When you're not in tune with one another, it can be a long, deadly day and you'll get a migraine from all that caffeine.

A TV series with an ensemble cast and multiple storylines, all vying for attention, can seem too daunting to get your head around. How do you pace the stories, build to ad breaks and cliffhangers? How do you ensure that your audience will come back week after week and be satisfied with your final episode?

Again, it all comes down to stationery: those much-used index cards, a wodge of Blu-Tack and a bunch of coloured pens. Someone's in charge of them, usually the script editor. You'll also need a big conference room wall. At this planning stage, you will all know what happens through the series, but not when and possibly not how. So …

Cards are numbered one to six (or however many episodes there are) and Blu-Tacked to the wall in a horizontal line. At right angles to episode one, in a vertical line, another set of cards are attached to the wall denoting all your characters.

You know that your central character, Luke, has a mass of events and experiences to go through in the series. Let his marriage fall apart in episode three. What if Maria steals the money in episode four, with repercussions in episodes five and six? Cards are filled in and moved around until every character has a throughline and every episode is well served with plot and subplot.

It's a technique you can try if you have an idea which will expand to several episodes and you want to be sure you have enough story.

Plus a big enough wall, plenty of plots and coffee on tap.

No place where it's not

Nick Warburton

> *Form… is everywhere you are and there is no place where it's not.*
>
> *John Cage*

A tree and a bowl …

Structure is like a tree.

What you see of a tree as it moves in the breeze is its leaves. All the shades of green and yellow, the reds and browns. You see the sway and shimmer. What you don't see are the trunk and branches. Without the trunk and branches, though, the leaves would be a pile you'd have to sweep up.

Structure is the trunk and branches of your script. There'll be no shimmer without them.

Or structure is like a glass bowl.

If you could hold the idea of your script, like a glass bowl, and tap it you'd hear it chime. It's that satisfying reverberation that tells you how good it is, how well it's made.

Structure is the reverberating chimes you get from a well-made bowl.

Structure is shape, pattern, plan, design, form. Your script will have a structure whether you think about it or not, so you might as well take some time to make sure it's got a good one.

Three approaches …

There are three ways you can approach structure:

1. *Plan first, write afterwards*: You can work out the bones of the story before you start; you can craft the plot in precise detail before you write a word of dialogue.
2. *Writing into the void*: You can ignore it altogether; you can dive straight in – dialogue, images, texture – without giving a thought to structure; and you can do this in a spirit of adventure and exploration.
3. *Stopping, starting*: You can combine both these approaches.

Plan first, write afterwards …

The advantage of meticulously plotting everything first is that you'll get every structural element in its most effective place. All your inciting incidents, crises, turning points, midpoints, obstacles and so on will be lined up and ready. You'll have a shape that works.

The disadvantage is that you may shut down options and take your story down a corridor of closed doors.

Every story will take your characters (and you as the writer) down a corridor to places where you have to make choices: two, three or more doors. You pick the door you want to open, you make your choice, and on you go, down the next bit of corridor. Each decision you make will change the journey. If you've mapped out the entire journey before you start, you know which doors you'll be opening, so you'll ignore the others whether or not there's something interesting or enticing behind them.

You can usually tell a script which has been 'pre-structured'. Attention has been paid to all the structural elements. They're all there and you end up with the inevitable race to the airport/station/hospital/spooky house to prevent some terrible life-threatening event. And you can picture the script meeting where someone has said, 'Let's put a clock on this' or 'Let's raise the stakes here' or 'Let's make it really hard for our guys'.

MIKE WALKER'S TOP TIP

Think about the third act... the one where, after putting your protagonist in the tree – and then throwing stones at her – you have to get her down out of that tree.

In the drive to generate excitement, all other considerations (truth and logic, for example) may be forgotten.

Of course, you *can* do all those things – raise the stakes, put a clock on the action, make things hard for your characters, and so on. In fact you *should* do them because they can give your script cohesion and pace. But they have to be applied to a story with a heartbeat. They don't work by and of themselves. If you apply those things to characters for whom an audience cares nothing, you'll still have a story that doesn't work.

Another disadvantage to working everything out before you start is that you can end up making everything too clear, too explicit and unambiguous. An over-structural approach can be inimical to ambiguity. And ambiguity, properly handled, can enhance a story.

'Explanation kills drama,' says John Yorke,[2] 'as does the impulse to make everything clear.'

[2] In his book *Into The Woods.*

THE FOOL'S TOP TIP

As the Fool advises King Lear: 'Have more than thou showest, speak less than thou knowest.'

Writing into the void

The second approach is to write without any kind of plan at all.

'I have this vague idea and I just want to write, to throw everything in and see where it leads me!'

And, indeed, that might lead to discoveries. All sorts of doors might be flung open and explored. And there's the possibility of an abundance of ambiguity. But the story will almost certainly meander, the script will be baggy and ill-conceived and it'll collapse.

In other words, simply writing into the void won't work. You can try it. You can dip your net into a swirling pool of imagination and possibility, but once you've seen what you've got in your net you'll have to sort it out. You'll have to attend to structure.

Stopping, starting ...

The way I work is to combine both these approaches by planning, then writing, then replanning.

I'll spend a lot of time thinking about the story – not writing anything, just thinking: walking about and thinking, waking up in the night and thinking, staring into space and thinking. Then I'll make notes, sometimes in different-coloured inks (I think that helps: I don't know why) and I'll draw diagrams complete with arrows. I'll also ask myself questions about what I'm doing. This one's from the current notebook:

> Q: Eleanor stands up for the underdog/outsider – is she perhaps a bit perverse in this?

The notebook is my conversation with myself so I write notes and questions in complete sentences like that.

No, this isn't working! Go back and look at your original list.

You can develop your own ways of doing notes and questions: handwritten in a notebook, recorded on some electronic device, tattooed on your thigh – whatever works best for you.

When I feel I've done enough thinking and note making (or when I can't put it off any longer) I start writing.

And once I've started writing I make new discoveries, about the characters mostly, but also about the shape of the narrative and the effectiveness of the original plan.

Don't put this bit at the end – it'll have more resonance if it's nearer the beginning.

Then I stop writing and replan: more notes and diagrams, more walking and thinking, and new questions to myself in the notebook. Then I write again, sometimes going back to the beginning and changing everything.

So the process is one of writing and restructuring, writing and restructuring. There's no single controlling plan but rather a series of draft plans and revisions. And, of course, the writing and the thinking about the writing sometimes happen simultaneously.

Because writing *is* thinking. And writing *creates* writing.

TOP TIP

I believe that the act of writing – hand to pen or fingers to keyboard – generates ideas.

This isn't the *fastest* approach to writing – in fact, it's probably the slowest of the three – but it does allow you to make what might be called mid-journey discoveries.

The scriptwriter Joe Ainsworth always said, 'Every good story has its own structure' and I think he's right. There's a difference between discovering the natural structure of the story you want to tell, and imposing a structure on it before you start.

Instinct ...

Peter Bowker said, in a documentary on BBC Four, 'I don't know what I'm doing when I'm doing it.'

What he means, I think, is that you can't plan everything you do, everywhere you go, when you write; you have to leave something to chance and discovery. There *is* a point, there is a plan, but you don't always know what it is until you look back.

You come to trust your feelings for what you're doing.

And John Yorke says something similar: 'The more I explore structure, the more I believe it to be instinctive.'

With thought and practice, though, you can develop and refine any instinct you might have, and you can do this in a number of ways.

EXERCISES

- Think about your story – get used to holding conversations and debates with yourself; go for a walk and think; think about the story's shape, the sequence of events, the things you include and the things you leave out, the way it starts and the way it ends; write notes and questions to yourself in your notebook, on a tablet, on a phone, your thigh, someone else's thigh, a tree trunk ...
- Read published scripts – to see how other writers use structure; read (or watch or listen to) plays that work and those that don't; you can learn from success and failure, your own and others.
- Practise structure – take an existing story (the story of Cinderella, say, or Little Red Riding Hood) and play around with some of the ways you might turn it into a TV drama or a radio play.

Find a way to get the structure right. Then you can apply the shimmering leaves.

A most delicate monster – voice

Nick Warburton

> *Four legs and two voices: a most delicate monster*
> Shakespeare – *The Tempest*

When you write a play you have to have a profound understanding of story and character, but you also have to know about those things that serve story and character, the things that make the story work and the characters live. Voice is one of those things. This chapter is about voice, how it relates to storytelling and how you can make use of it. It's partly about *direct address* – talking to the audience – and what the presence of a narrator or storyteller (sometimes several storytellers) can add to a script. But it's also about *varieties* of direct address, and how fluid and powerful they can be.[1] Most of it applies to writing for radio, but some of it has a bearing on TV scripts.

Peter Bowker, in an interview in the *Guardian*,[2] recalled learning something important about voice from the novelist and critic Malcolm Bradbury. Bradbury believed that, if you have a year to write a novel, the first ten months should be given to working out the voice you intend to use for telling the story, and the next two months for the writing of it. It's the voice that people will remember.

[1] Not all agree. See Jonathan Myerson's piece on p 108 for a robust alternative view.

[2] 18 May 2014.

> **MARCY KAHAN'S TOP TIP**
>
> **Voice**: How do you find your writing voice? Try writing. A lot.

More than one voice ...

We each have more than one voice. We use a different voice for work, for talking to friends, for the family, for meeting strangers, for answering the phone. We vary tone and even accent, sentence structure and vocabulary, often without realizing we're doing it.

We also have a voice inside our head. An inner voice. A head voice 'Now I am alone' Hamlet says to us, and then, when it's just him and the audience, he unburdens his soul. 'Oh, what a rogue and peasant slave am I!' He talks to us quite differently from the way he talks to anyone else. He's more reflective, and he tells us more.

The inner voice is the one that nobody else hears, the voice that runs through the waking day and much of the dreaming night, reflecting on what we see or hear. It is, perhaps, the strangest and most compelling of our voices.

Why use direct address?

If you think about it, you'll see that there are perhaps two main reasons for using direct address:

- Because direct address can tell an audience what they otherwise wouldn't know.
- Because the inner voice can take the audience into someone's head; by getting characters to 'think out loud' a writer has direct access to their feelings and motives.

And, if you think about it a little longer, you'll realize that both these reasons are suspect.

It's true that writing dramatic action on radio is sometimes difficult because no one can see your characters or what they're doing. So it might seem that the easy solution to that problem is to bring in a narrator to tell everyone what's going on.

> *NARRATOR: Legs and Harry walked into the bank and looked around. Legs joined the shortest queue while Harry went to stand with his back to the wall, where he could see everything ...*

But this is the weakest of reasons for using a narrator. It almost announces itself: *you can't see what I can see but this is what's going on here*. It's both lazy and distancing. It places the listener outside the scene and in need of an intrusive guide.

> *NARRATOR: Harry narrowed his eyes. His heart pounded and he was nervous ...*

So Harry's nervous because you tell us he is? Where's the drama in that? Where are the questions that keep us wondering? (Unless the questions are, 'Who are you that you know what's going on in Harry's head and heart? And *where* are you that you can see all this?') Again, this is narration that keeps us as listeners at a distance, that comes between us and the event.

This is one of those rules about writing stories: it's about showing, not telling. Don't tell us how your characters are feeling. Convert all that into action and events. Get everything moving, right in front of our eyes. Let us *witness* these things directly, come to those conclusions ourselves, and not have to be *told*.

Does this mean you should avoid *any* use of direct address?

No, because direct address *can* enrich a script. What it does mean is, consider the options first and know what you're doing.

Thinking out loud ...

Direct address is not 'thinking out loud'. If you get your characters to 'think out loud' the result will almost certainly be unnatural and clunky. People don't 'think out loud'. They talk to themselves sometimes, yes, or they talk to someone who isn't there, but they very rarely 'think out loud'. Talking to yourself, or to someone who isn't there, is not the same as 'thinking out loud'.

You can go inside someone's head and dramatize what they're thinking, but that isn't 'thinking out loud' either. It's just 'thinking' and it's often not particularly tidy or ordered. In Dennis Potter's great TV series *The Singing Detective* (1986) his hero Marlow is having his groin greased by one of the nurses. The only way he can get through this process without embarrassment is by thinking of the dullest, least stimulating things he can imagine. Dennis Potter takes us into his head where Marlow's thoughts speed up until they're almost impossible to follow.

Special pleading ...

By the way, don't think that allowing your characters to tell us what they're feeling will win any sympathy. An audience is more likely to withhold its sympathy from someone who asks for it. So don't use direct address for special pleading – unless, of course, you *want* your audience to withhold its sympathy.

Direct address and storytelling ...

This is how a story begins. You're sitting round the fire with the darkness at your back, or you've finished dinner with friends and the coffee comes round, and someone says, 'That reminds me of something I heard once.' Or, 'Did I ever tell you about the time I was in Italy ...?' Or:

In a hole in the ground there lived a Hobbit.

Then, if you're lucky, you're drawn into the story.

The line about the Hobbit is a good one because it's clear and simple and it plants questions. A Hobbit? What's a Hobbit? And why does it live in a hole? As soon as there are questions the listener is caught. She wants to know: Who? Why? They did *what?* And, most of all, what then? What happened next?

So what you're looking for is a simple, clear opening that generates some questions.

Last night I dreamt I went to Manderley again.

Manderley, where's that? And why would you dream of going there? Tell me more ...

The experience of listening to a radio play comes close to the experience of listening to a tale round the fire late at night, when you stare into the flames and follow your imagination. The thrill and intrigue of the story are brought out both by the story itself, the sequence of events *and* by the voice of the storyteller, its meaning and sound.

Forty years ago I heard J. Meade Falkner's novel *Moonfleet* read by Paul Rogers on BBC Radio. To this day I can recall the warmth and colour and the 'setting' of that voice, its rich Dorset tones. I remember the voice drawing me in. Of course, *Moonfleet* wasn't a drama – it was a reading of a novel – but there was something in the sound, about *direct address*, that made me realize how powerful and persuasive voice can be. Using direct address, I realized, does more than fill in the bits that are otherwise difficult to write.

Who's talking to you ...?

Look at those two openings again, the Tolkien and the du Maurier.

> *In a hole in the ground there lived a Hobbit.*

And

> *Last night I dreamt I went to Manderley again.*

They're both effective but they're different. The Tolkien is in the third person; it's the pronouncement of an external, all-seeing, probably all-knowing storyteller. The du Maurier is spoken by 'I', someone who's already been to Manderley so probably has a part to play in the story she's about to tell, and feelings about it. (But who, as it turns out, remains nameless, as storytellers often do.)

The difference is important. Our experience of stories is considerably influenced by who's talking to us.

VOICE CHOICES

So there are choices to make:

- Will you, for example, choose to make your narrator a man, a woman or a child? (Or none of the above? A dog, a cat, a chair, a room ...?)

- What's the relationship between your storyteller and the audience?
- What's the relationship between your storyteller and the other characters?

Ways of using direct address ...

There are several types of storyteller, and several different ways in which they can address us. Here's a quick look at some of them. You may discover more.

1. *The single third-person, all-seeing, all-knowing narrator*

This is the type of storyteller closest to those found in novels like *The Hobbit* or *War and Peace* or *Pride and Prejudice* – a Tolstoyan narrator, omniscient and ubiquitous. He or she may be objective:

> *This is what happened and what the characters felt about it. Make of it what you will.*

Or he or she may have a point to make, and a message to pass on:

> *The good are rewarded after adversity, whereas the bad perish unhappily.*

It's fairly straightforward and easy to write this type of storyteller because he or she can pop up as required and say as much, or as little, as you want. But in a drama it can look unadventurous, and it could be dull (though not, of course, in the hands of a Tolstoy or a Jane Austen). If you use it you'll need discretion: it's a form of narration that can tempt you into saying too much and not leaving the audience enough to do.

2. *The single third-person narrator with limited vision and knowledge*

This storyteller may not know what happens to all the characters or how the story ends. He or she tells it as it happens and the story unfolds before us both, storyteller and listener. The storyteller and the listener are thus brought a little closer to each other. This can be a simple matter of the tense you use:

> *NARRATOR: Legs and Harry walked into the bank and looked around. Legs joined the shortest queue while Harry went to stand with his back to the wall, where he could see everything …*

Which becomes more immediate – and therefore more dramatic – when it's done in the present tense:

> *NARRATOR: Legs and Harry walk into the bank and look around. Legs joins the shortest queue while Harry goes to stand with his back to the wall, where he can see everything …*

But it's still sounding a bit remote and rather more like a novel than a play.

3. *Multiple third-person narrators*

I can't think of many reasons why you might want to do this. If you have a narrator who stands outside the story and helps to tell it – and who sometimes comments on it perhaps – why would you need another narrator who does exactly the same thing? What would you gain?

The answer would seem to be 'not much' though Dylan Thomas does just this in *Under Milk Wood*. He has a First Voice who can see into every house and cottage in the village of Llareggub, and into the secret desires and dreams of all the inhabitants. Sometimes the First Voice hands over to a Second Voice and the Second Voice, we find, has exactly the same powers. I suspect Thomas did this for the sake of variety, to avoid long passages being carried by a single voice. But that's not a *compelling* reason for having multiple narrators, and it's not a cheap one either when you have to hire an extra 'voice'. Still, Dylan Thomas did things in his own eccentric and not always logical fashion and made them work for him.

4. *The single first-person narrator*

This is, in other words, the *involved* narrator. It is the 'I' of the opening of *Rebecca*:

> *Last night I dreamt I went to Manderley again.*

The two most obvious benefits of using a first-person narrator are the *authority* and the *intimacy* it can bring to a script. When one of your characters speaks directly to us and says, 'This happened to me', or 'I was there and I saw these things', the story gains some sort of authority; it seems more authentic. There was a witness to these events and this witness is talking to us. (We may, in fact, discover later that our storyteller *can't* be trusted, but up to that point we're content to take their hand and go with them.)

A first-person narrator also strengthens the bond between the story and the listener. It makes it more intimate. 'This is my story and I'm sharing it with you.'

A first-person narrator can also address us in the past or in the present; they can know the whole story at the outset, or they can find things out as we do, as the story unfolds.

> *LAURA: (Narrating) I have come to wait outside The Maypole. To speak to Roach.*

In this case, from my radio play *Foundling*, Laura is waiting for someone. We don't know if he'll turn up and nor does she, until he does. She's telling us the story as it happens; we're there outside the pub, waiting with her.

The stories in Alan Bennett's *Talking Heads* are told in the same way. None of his narrating characters knows how things are going to work out for them. Time passes in the intervals between their speeches to us; they have to tell their stories in stages.

First-person narrators can't, of course, go everywhere – they're bound by rules of time and space – and there's a limit to what they can know. They can't know what the other characters are thinking or feeling, though they may be inclined to guess.

5. *Multiple first-person narrators*

Dylan Thomas, as well as using two third-person narrators, also employs multiple first-person ones. Organ Morgan, like most of the inhabitants of Llareggub, speaks to us directly from his dreams where he finds there is 'perturbation and music in Coronation Street'. He then tells us exactly what he can see in his dreams.

When you make your characters address the audience directly like this, you change their relationship both to the story and to the audience. And all sorts of contradictions and ironies can come into play.

Here's an example of several storytellers speaking in a variety of different ways from a BBC Radio series I wrote called *Witness*, an adaptation of Luke's gospel.[3] Jesus is in a room with a group of people and he begins to tell them the story of the Prodigal Son. Two of the disciples, Peter and Judas, join in because they know the story; they've heard it before. Having three voices rather than one helps to break up the story. It also sets up different rhythms and resonances.

EXAMPLE

PETER: (Narrating) So the money went …
JUDAS: (Narrating) Of course it did.
JESUS: Everything. And then it went from bad to worse. The money was gone and there was nothing to eat, so he got a job looking after pigs. He watched them feed and he wished he could join them at the trough, share in their swill …
PETER: (Narrating) But he couldn't. He had nothing …
PETER: And there was no help.
JESUS: Then he said to himself …
PETER: My Father's got servants and they all eat. They eat and I starve.
SLOWLY CHEAT OUT THE SOUND OF THE ROOM. WE'RE MOVING IMPERCEPTIBLY INTO THE WORLD OF THE STORY.
JESUS: (Narrating) So he thought he'd go home and see his Father and plead with him.
PETER: I'll ask him to forgive me. Tell him I've wronged him and offended God. And it's true. I have and I'm fit to be no son of his.
JESUS: Maybe he'd take him on, not as a son but as one of his workers. So he set off, back to his Father.

[3] This is a passage also quoted in *So You Want To Write Radio Drama?* by Claire Grove and Stephen Wyatt.

BRIEF MUSIC TAKES US TO A BLEAK ROAD WITH A WIND BLOWING.
JESUS: Now every day this lad was away, his Father would leave the farmhouse and go out the front and up to the top of the rise. He'd stand there a while and look down the long track where he'd seen him once disappear. Nothing there.
JUDAS: So every day he'd take the lonely walk back to the house.
JESUS: Then, at last …
JUDAS: Far, far down the track …
JESUS: Someone was making his way …
JUDAS: And he knew …
JESUS: (Quietly) Oh, my son …
JUDAS: He was making his way home.
JESUS: My son!
HE BEGINS TO RUN …
JUDAS: He ran all the way down the hill, and flung his arms round him …
JESUS AND PETER CLASP EACH OTHER. THEY'RE BOTH OVERCOME.
JESUS: My son, my son!
PETER: Father!
JUDAS: And he kissed him. (Cold) He kissed him.
BEAT.
JESUS: You've come back. My son …
PETER: (Upset) Don't call me that. I don't deserve it …
(*Witness*, episode three, 2007)

You can see that the three storytellers talk both to the people and to us – some of the lines are delivered 'in the room', where the story's being told, and some are delivered directly to us as listeners. (The lines to us were recorded on a different 'narrating' microphone.) So we have a kind of trio of different voice sounds and rhythms.

But there's something else going on as well. Both Peter and Judas are also telling part of their own story. We've seen Peter, throughout the series, express self-doubt and a sense of worthlessness. And Judas has become increasingly impatient with a campaign that isn't heading where he thinks it should go. We've seen him becoming resentful. So Peter begins to say the lines of the Prodigal Son, and Judas those of the brother who stays at home.

When Judas says, 'He kissed him' he stops things for a moment to repeat the line. It's a moment charged with irony. We, as listeners, know the significance of the kiss in Judas's story, but at this stage he doesn't.

Incidentally this example also shows something of the ability of radio to move from place to place. We shift location – from the room where the story's being told to a bleak hillside – without announcing that that's what we're doing. We cheat in the world of the story. So we are, for a while, in two different places at once – something you can only achieve, I think, on radio.

Other types of direct address ...

All the narrators in these examples have been human, but they don't have to be. You can get the dog to speak to us; or the baby; or inanimate objects. You can even give an entire building a voice. The only limit is your own imagination – and your ability to convince.

Another type of narrative voice is the *written voice*, the kind of thing you might find in letters or diaries. A written voice is not the same as a spoken voice. It's more formal and measured and usually conducts itself in longer sentences. Most of the time you'll want to use the spoken voice but there may be occasions when a written voice is perfectly appropriate – as, for example, in the 'written' passages that are intercut with the lively dialogue in Hattie Naylor's *The Diaries of Samuel Pepys*. We get the juxtaposition of life lived at pace, and then life recollected and considered.

More variables ...

You can also play with the way we hear these voices. Samuel Beckett's *That Time* is a monologue in which we hear the same voice from three different locations with three different acoustics. Beckett's stage directions explain that the three voices come from both sides and above and that there's a sudden switch from one voice to the next. It just happens; the person we were listening to continues to address us, but from somewhere else or from some other time, perhaps.

That Time was written as a stage play – we see the face of the speaker, apparently suspended ten feet above stage level – but that doesn't matter: it works wonderfully well on radio, greatly helped by John Moffat's brilliantly disaffected, regretful and poetic performance.

In *The Disagreeable Oyster* (1957) Giles Cooper gives his central character Bundy two 'head' voices. Cooper's directions tell us that his central character, Mervyn Bundy, has been split between Bundy Major and Bundy Minor. The reason for this is that one of these Bundys is released to say some of the deep and secret things the other Bundy would never dream of saying out loud.

So to whom is Bundy talking? Often it's to himself. The difference here is that another voice – and a *different* voice, played by a different actor – answers him. The idea is clever and original but Giles Cooper's use of two-for-one narrators isn't just show: it serves the play. And, almost certainly, it could only be done on radio.

Conversation and chorus ...

Are your narrations, your 'head voices', ever heard by the characters whose story they're telling? The question might seem a strange one – obviously they're not – but it's possible to imagine a situation in which this can happen.

Think of an elderly woman telling us about something that happened to her when she was a girl. Her storytelling brings the girl to life; it presents her to her listeners. So the girl moves, and speaks, and experiences those events again. There are times when the woman wants to intervene, to talk to her younger self, to warn her or to comfort her. Logic dictates that she can't do this, but the desire to say something is very strong.

So she does.

She speaks to her young self.

What develops is a kind of conversation across time. It's largely a one-sided conversation but just occasionally we might wonder if some of what the woman says *is* heard, or perhaps half heard.

Here's an example of the kind of thing I mean. This is from a dramatization of Edmund Gosse's *Father and Son*. It's really a three-way exchange between the adult Edmund, his younger self and his father (Henry). Sometimes Edmund speaks as himself looking back; he 'narrates'. At other times he speaks as, and on behalf of, the boy he once was. And sometimes it seems that the young Edmund is responding as if he has indeed heard what his adult self has just said. But we're never entirely sure.

Young Edmund is present when Henry comes to complain to his wife about the baker's boy.

EXAMPLE

THE BREAKFAST ROOM. THE DOOR OPENS AND HENRY COMES IN.
HENRY: Emily, the baker's boy. He's again left the gate swinging. I shall have to have another word with Harding.
EDMUND IS SHOCKED AND CATCHES HIS BREATH.
YOUNG EDMUND: (Hushed) The baker's boy?
EDMUND: (Hushed) He means the butcher's boy.
YOUNG EDMUND: (Hushed) The baker comes himself ...
EDMUND: And always, always shuts the gate!
YOUNG EDMUND: Papa is wrong!
EDMUND: Wrong! (Narrating) I was standing on the rug, gazing at him, and I turned quickly, in embarrassment, and looked into the fire.
A CRACK OF THUNDER.
Here was the appalling discovery, never suspected before, that my Father was not as God.
YOUNG EDMUND: (Hushed) He does not know everything.
(*Father and Son*, 2005)

Adaptation ...

If you're dramatizing a novel – turning it into a TV script or a radio play – you'll probably have to make a decision about the novelist's voice. The essence of a novel is often as much in the voice of its author as it is in the narrative. This is particularly true for writers like Trollope or Dickens or P. G. Wodehouse. The writer's voice is so distinctive, and so rewarding, that we feel the story would be undone without it.

So can you find some way of keeping it? Or must you sacrifice the writer's voice to the greater demands of the story?

There's a passage in *Bleak House*, after the death of Jo, the crossing sweeper, in which Dickens sets aside any pretence to objectivity and delivers a damning speech about injustice:

> Dead, your Majesty. Dead, my lords and gentlemen. Dead, Right Reverends and Wrong Reverends of every order. Dead, men and women, born with Heavenly compassion in your hearts. And dying thus around us, every day.

I find this passage moving, not so much because of what it's saying, but because it shows Dickens' passionate concern for the underdog. He throws off the mantle of objective narrator and speaks to us directly. When Andrew Davies adapted the novel for BBC Television in 2005 he gave the speech to John Jarndyce, one of the centres of good in the story. Jarndyce steps away from the deathbed and delivers the lines, not as a voice-over, but out loud, into the room. He's not merely 'thinking'. He's doing what Dickens did – addressing his protests to an unseen audience. This seemed to me a brilliant solution. Andrew Davies is aware that first-person voice-overs do sometimes work, but that third-person voice-overs risk making everything seem remote and distant to an audience. They prevent viewers becoming involved. He, too, was attracted by Dickens' voice in this passage. When he checked an earlier dramatization – Arthur Hopcraft's 1985 version – he found that Hopcraft had given the speech to Jarndyce. So, thinking that this was a good solution, and also wishing to pay a kind of compliment to Hopcraft, he did the same.[4]

And that's another piece of good advice. If a writer has an interesting and successful way of doing something, feel free to borrow.

---

[4] See *Soft Soaping Dickens: Andrew Davies, BBC 1 and Bleak House* by Robert Giddings, Professor Emeritus, School of Media Arts and Communication, Bournemouth University.

'Whose story is it anyway?'

Sue Teddern

The many variations of voice, as described by Nick, show the versatility of radio. I've noticed, however, that some new writers, fearful of dialogue, write their first radio play as a straight monologue, which can, if they're not careful, resemble a short story read out loud.

It doesn't have to be like that.

One of my favourite radio plays, *12 Shares* by Dennis Kelly, recounts a year in the life of Kate, and her attendance at Alcoholics Anonymous, where she 'shares' her thoughts and experiences. *12 Shares* is funny, truthful and raw; and the device of Kate making her journey to wellness – if not one day at a time, then one share at a time – is ideally constructed for a one-voice play.

Context is all. As a listener, I like to know *why* my characters are narrating their stories as internal thoughts or retrospective accounts. Just as I can't handle musicals where someone suddenly breaks into song because they're happy or heartbroken, as a writer I need narrations and monologues to have a logical reason for being. *12 Shares* does just that.

The silent listener

In real life, people don't talk to themselves in full, coherent sentences. But if you give them a listening audience, as Kelly did in *12 Shares*, a character may open up and express thoughts or feelings for the very first time.

My radio play *In Mates* tells the story of an agoraphobic woman called Michelle, who sends a series of cassette letters to her pen-pal Randall on death row in the USA.[5] Because he's another 'in-mate', she can be honest with him. Up to a point.

Here she is, 'writing' to him at 2 am, when darkness and insomnia bring out some home truths.

MICHELLE *You know when you throw a pebble into a river and the ripples spread out. My life was like that, only the other*

[5] See Part 3, page 128.

way round. The ripples were coming closer and closer.
My boundaries were closing in until I'd avoid going to the shops, the library, even my own street.
I'm fine with it though. I really am. Because I know it can't last forever. I'll wake up one morning and it will be over. So I don't mind. I only mind when other people do. It's my life, not theirs.

Michelle is also an unreliable narrator, the only person in the play who can't see that her need to stay indoors is a problem. I've always enjoyed novels with unreliable narrators at their heart (*Notes on a Scandal* by Zoe Heller, *Gone Girl* by Gillian Flynn) and it works incredibly well on radio.

In my sixty-minute radio play, *Sad Girl*, about a young Jewish woman called Rachel who is trying to find a family painting stolen by the Nazis, was a little nervous about using flashbacks to the Holocaust. Would it be too 'big' a back story to introduce to a drama set in the present?

After a few failed attempts, I found my way in. I used the voice of Rachel's late grandmother as a link to the past. Lisel[6] relates her childhood, in several chunks of painful reminiscence, to silent ten-year-old Rachel.

Here she recalls her father and twin brother:

LISEL *Mama and Emmy and I left for England. Papa and Rudy stayed in Berlin. Papa said they would join us when the time was right. We got letters from them – so many letters, Rachel – saying they were fine and we shouldn't worry.*
And then it must have been nearly a year later, just as they were about to come to England, they were deported to Theresienstadt, then Auschwitz. Rudy swore on his life that he would take care of Papa and I know he tried. But he was such a sensitive little boy, Rachel, however much he pretended he wasn't.
I hope there weren't spiders in Auschwitz. Rudy hated spiders.

6 Lisel was played so movingly by the late Miriam Karlin that, even at the first read-through, she had us all in tears.

I'm certainly not advocating that every writer needs to justify the logic of how they use narration and monologue. This is how it works for me.

You will find your own way of working and your own 'voice'.

EXERCISE

Many radio dramas and comedies are epistolary, in the form of a correspondence of some sort. (*Ladies of Letters, Warhorses of Letters, Love Virtually, soloparentpals.com* ...)

- Choose a means of communication: work emails, voicemail, postcards, online forum, Facebook posts, the Christmas round robin.
- Think how you might develop a 45-min radio drama about two people who love-hate each other, who correspond using one or more of these methods.

Voice, meet POV!

Voice on the radio: the most natural place for it. Your clever audience will provide every element of the visuals. But can 'voice' have the same resonance on TV, where the visuals are created by a huge crew of technicians, from camera operators and lighting designers to props and make-up?

Is the TV equivalent of voice 'point of view' or POV?

It's essential not to confuse voice with voice-over. A voice-over narration is a useful tool, but it's only as good as the craftsman using it. If a narration is tacked onto the visuals to paper over any cracks in the plot, then your audience may subconsciously seek out other gaping holes. Sometimes a writer is 'encouraged' into adding a voice-over, after the edit, to clarify the narrative. Only 'A-list' writers have the clout to say no.

TOP TIP

Don't write a script that's so woolly and unclear that a voice-over is your only way of explaining what's going on.

EXAMPLE

A good example of retrospective voice-over is Jack Rosenthal's 1979 TV drama *The Knowledge*. This is an ensemble piece told through the eyes of Chris, a young would-be taxi driver learning his way around the streets of London.

We see Chris approaching the Carriage Office where he's regularly tested on his knowledge. His voice-over tells us how this process has taken over his life.

CHRIS *Normal people know time's gone by from what's happening in the world. Like President Carter shouts the odds on something or Elvis Presley dies or Liverpool win the European Cup . . . something like that. (Beat) Or a bloke and a bird slip up one night and then the next thing she has a little nipper.*

Well, then she sort of knows it was nine months ago when it happened, right? (Beat) With Knowledge boys, it's different. Time goes by from when they start road works in Camden High Street to when they finish or when they try a new one-way system in Seven Sisters Road and then jack it in again . . . something like that. All you know about Elvis dying is they put a show on about him at the Astoria Theatre, Charing Cross Road – and what's the quickest way to get there from the Hilton Hotel.

This use of voice-over is also extremely effective when the visuals don't match the voice-over. For example, parents have gone away for the weekend and ring their son to say they're returning early.

We *hear* the son's voicemail or phone conversation with Mum, telling them he's had a quiet weekend. But we *see* him running round the house, tidying up after a mega party. Who's this drunken stranger asleep behind the sofa and, oh hell, where's Fluffy the cat?

Many successful US TV series have used voice-over as an integral part of the format and premise: *How I Met Your Mother, My So-Called Life, Ally McBeal, Desperate Housewives, Grey's Anatomy, My Name is Earl.*

But voice-over can be seen as a gimmick if you don't have a good reason for using it or if you have yet to acquire the kind of writerly clout that makes people do what you say.

EXERCISE

Write a short voice-over that contradicts your visuals. Here are some prompts:

- A job application from a highly unsuitable applicant.
- A job description from a highly unreliable/unethical employer.
- A blind date – plenty of room for fun here!
- A two-way phone conversation between a couple, one of whom is lying.
- A postcard home. What's the lie and why?

Whose POV is it anyway?

Varying points of view can be revealed when one incident is recalled by several different characters and related accordingly, a little like that song from *Gigi, I Remember It Well.* John Hopkins' *Talking to a Stranger*[7] is a classic example.

I recall an episode of *thirtysomething,* which used this device to great effect: a disastrous evening is shown from three or four different points of view. Who's coming on to whom depends on each character's self-edited version of the evening.

The most literal example of playing around with point of view is Sam Bain[8] and Jesse Armstrong's hugely successful sitcom *Peep Show.* Mark and

[7] See 'Ten landmark TV dramas and comedies', p. 13.

[8] Read Sam Bain 'The art of Notiquette' Part 2, p. 85.

Jeremy (*The Odd Couple* meets *Steptoe and Son*) are reluctant flatmates and even more reluctant friends, whose lives self-sabotage on a regular basis.

We hear their inner thoughts. We see the world through their eyes. Cameras are mounted on the heads of actors David Mitchell and Robert Webb to catch their POVs. This device has become so integral to the look of *Peep Show* that it barely registers any more. Which is as it should be.

The talky bits: Writing dialogue

Nick Warburton

> *Sloppy is a beautiful reader of a newspaper. He do the police in different voices.*
>
> Charles Dickens, *Our Mutual Friend*

So this one's about dialogue and ... well, it's in two parts. It's in two parts because I thought, I was thinking ...

Well, let's just say it's in two parts ...

The first part looks at dialogue in general, what it is and what it does. It considers the difference between dialogue for radio and dialogue for TV. The second part suggests ways of playing around with dialogue that might improve what we've written. Possibly.

By dialogue I mean two things: the *sound* of speech and the *exchanges* between people when they talk to each other. I've broadened the definition to include not only speech between characters but also speech to an audience – monologues, head voices and so on.

Dialogue is more important than people sometimes allow. On radio it carries your play. On TV you can set up moments made of powerful images and resonant action which will be blown out of the water as soon as the characters open their mouths.

Unless you get the dialogue right.

What dialogue is

Spoken, not written

I should begin by saying that writing dialogue is an enjoyable activity. For many writers it's the most enjoyable stage in the process. Perhaps that's why they sometimes hurry, or skip entirely, the plotting stage.[1] I find it enjoyable because it involves direct engagement with our language.

I'm not talking about the language that people write but the language they speak. The two things are quite different and dialogue in scripts sometimes fails to come to life because its writer has put together sentences to be read rather than words to be spoken, and you can almost always hear the difference.

Here's a small example of spoken language, overheard years ago in a college canteen when I was queuing for lunch. The student in front of me couldn't speak English very well and didn't know how to convey that it was the potatoes he wanted on his plate. So he muttered, 'Ahm . . . ahm . . .' and tapped the glass nearest to the potatoes. The woman who was serving took offence at this. She stared at the floor and said under her breath, 'Don't you tap your fork at me, mate.' The line – I think of it as a line – has lodged in my memory ever since. I like its crispness and its aptness to the moment. It resonates like poetry and is made up of trochees, pairs of syllables in which the first has the strong beat, a stressed syllable followed by unstressed one.

Don't *you* ***tap*** *your* ***fork*** *at* ***me****, mate.*

This may sound fanciful but, as we'll see, rhythm is an important part of dialogue. You should hear dialogue, as the writer Nell Leyshon says, as if it's music.

NELL LEYSHON'S TOP TIP

Like music, dialogue is something we can hear or not and, for people who love dialogue, it has a mathematical quality and a beauty which I never tire of.[2]

By musical dialogue Leyshon *doesn't* mean pretty and lilting dialogue. There are many kinds of music, some of it deliberately dissonant and jarring.

---

[1] See Part 1, 'I've Written a Play'.

[2] 'Dialogue' by Nell Leyshon, *The Author*, Winter 2013.

You can experiment with rhythm not just within speeches ('Don't you tap your fork at me, mate!') but also across them. You can set short speeches against long ones. (See Andrew Davies' TV adaptation of *Wives and Daughters* mentioned below.) You can set short against short, in a run. The Greeks did this 2,500 years ago and called it stichomythia. It brings pace and energy to a scene.

In this example two people meet while walking on the fens of East Anglia. It's an exchange taken from an episode of my radio series *On Mardle Fen*. In it the restaurateur, Warwick Hedges, is talking directly to us when a woman with binoculars comes strolling along. At first Warwick is resentful – his splendid loneliness on the fen interrupted by an outsider – then he notices how attractive she is and suddenly he's happy to talk.

MEGAN: No, I'm a city girl, unfortunately. But I do like to get into the country when I can. Mostly day trips, you know.
WARWICK: (Narrating, suspicious) Day trips to the country. Neat little binoculars slung round her neck …
MEGAN: I'd like to stay longer, of course, but you know how it is …
WARWICK: (Narrating) Oh, no, please, not a birdwatcher …
MEGAN: One must work.
WARWICK: (Narrating) I can't stand birdwatchers …
MEGAN: But I am drawn to places like this …
WARWICK: (Narrating) Dangerously focussed people, humourless and bossy …
MEGAN: Specifically to the birds.
WARWICK: The birds?
MEGAN: Yes, I'm a birdwatcher.
WARWICK: Really?
MEGAN: Yes. Devoted, actually.
WARWICK: Lovely.
MEGAN: Are you?
WARWICK: Me?
MEGAN: Yes. Do you …?

WARWICK: Birds? Oh, yes!
MEGAN: Really?
WARWICK: Yes! Can't get enough of the little chaps. It's why I'm out here today, actually.

Warwick, as he often does, performs an abrupt volte-face – from anti-birdwatcher prejudice to ornithological enthusiasm – and this is marked by a sequence of two- or three-word exchanges, the brevity of which matches the nimble turnaround going on in Warwick's mind.

Dialogue is also linked to the way it's delivered and to the action that accompanies it. In the case of the tapped fork, the glare at the floor and the subdued delivery added to the conflict found in the words.[3]

HAMLET'S TOP TIP

Suit the action to the word, the word to the action.

Listening to speech

You can experience the sound of speech by going out and listening to conversations on buses and trains. Or you can read Robert Frost. And read him out loud.

Frost was a poet. He didn't write many plays but he was interested in the poetry of the spoken word and the way it carries meaning. In *The Death of the Hired Man* a farmer and his wife talk about what the word 'home' means:

'Home is the place where, when you go there,
They have to take you in.'

[3] The writer, you notice, doesn't step forward to ease the conflict; he merely makes a note of it. That's what writers do. They're like wildlife photographers, observing but not interfering.

'I should have called it
Something you somehow haven't to deserve.'

Here are two definitions of the word, quite complex and profound definitions, expressed in a handful of words and in the easy, unforced voices of ordinary people. The speech is not lilting and self-consciously lyrical, it's not 'poetry', but it is poetic, and musical.

When I say you should read Frost I'm being deliberately provocative, of course. He isn't the only writer who's aware of the musicality of speech. You can find others. Look at Harold Pinter, Jez Butterworth, Martin Crimp, David Mamet, Mike Bartlett ... and, of course, Shakespeare. Here's Viola summing up Olivia in *Twelfth Night*:

I see you what you are, you are too proud.

The line has the bounce and certainly of her sudden insight about another character. There's nothing flowery about the language; all the words are single syllable.

And here's part of a familiar exchange from *King Lear*. Lear asks his favourite daughter Cordelia to make a public declaration of her love.

EXAMPLE

LEAR: ... What can you say to draw
A third more opulent than your sisters? Speak.
CORDELIA: Nothing, my lord.
LEAR: Nothing?
CORDELIA: Nothing.
LEAR: Nothing can come of nothing. Speak again.
CORDELIA: Unhappy that I am, I cannot heave
My heart into my mouth. I love your Majesty
According to my bond; no more nor less.

It's written in verse but the rhythms are those of common, fairly fragmented exchange – at least, it is after the flowery formality of Lear's question. The undercutting economy of Cordelia's reply, the repetition of certain words, the question and counter-question, all these things take us out of the world of the court and into a much more private face-to-face world. It's done with an ear for the way ordinary speech sounds.

You can, of course, write dialogue without paying any attention to its music – it will still convey meaning – but it always works better if you have an ear for the sound.

EXERCISE

Those examples – the Frost and the Shakespeare – are favourites of mine. Look at some television and radio scripts, or some poems, and pick out three lines that appeal to your ear.

TV dialogue, radio dialogue

You can see reasonably effective TV drama in which the dialogue is poor. It works reasonably well because the sense of story and the structure are good. But I always feel that a good story with unconvincing, uninspiring dialogue is a missed opportunity. It's harder to get away with poor dialogue on radio (though it does happen) because on radio the words are the main focus. If they don't convince, the story won't work, so very often more attention is paid on radio to the colour and texture of the spoken word.

It's plain to see *why* dialogue sometimes seems less important on TV. It's the story that carries the drama, so the dialogue must serve the story. It must be functional. You can't afford to be indulgent with it. You can't let your characters hang around talking. There are certain things the audience needs to know. Get your characters to say those things and then move on.

All of which is, at least some of the time, true. But there is a fear of what some producers and script editors think of as 'talking heads'.

Alan Bennett's 1988 series of TV monologues was called *Talking Heads*, perhaps in defiance of this sort of producers' anxiety. One character on screen, talking directly to camera? And nothing else? That's not what TV drama is supposed to do. It can't work.

But it did work. *Talking Heads* was very successful – both critically acclaimed and very popular. They were funny and touching and truthful, though it's fair to point out that the best of them also had good stories, cleverly told.

The dialogue triangle

Dialogue is more than just a means to a dramatic end, a carrier of dramatic beats. At times it can be, and arguably should be, dramatic in itself. At its best it will *demonstrate* the nature of what it's saying.

> **TOP TIP**
>
> There is a kind of dialogue triangle, a perfect match of character, situation and speech.

Here's an example of what I mean from a 2001 episode of *EastEnders*, written by Tony Jordan. The Slater sisters are on a girls' night out when a row flares up between Kat and Zoe. The younger sister, Zoe, announces that she's going to Spain and the protective Kat objects. ('You ain't going anywhere!') Zoe storms out into the street with Kat at her heels.

'You can't tell me what to do!' Zoe yells, 'You ain't my mother!'

She turns and stalks off.

'Yes, I am!' Kat shouts after her. End of episode.

There are four reasons why this short exchange represents good dialogue:

- It's *spare and simple*. It uses not a word more than is necessary.
- It *conveys the story* – a huge amount of story in those last three words, in fact.

- It's *appropriate to character*; the sparring between Kat and Zoe was part of the *EastEnders* fabric. Good dialogue not only reflects character, it also defines it.
- And it's *clever*. Kat's great secret comes not in a planned and considered speech but in a day-to-day row; people throw things like that at each other – you ain't my mother. It's a casual insult that suddenly takes on a greater significance.
- That pair of speeches – fourteen words in all – perfectly illustrates the dialogue triangle – words, character and situation.

Banter

Banter is wordplay, the batting backwards and forwards of amusing one-liners, what used to be called wit. It's speech with one eyebrow raised.

Do not mistake it for genuine dialogue.

Dialogue is dependent on character and sometimes banter is inclined to sacrifice character for the sake of a laugh. Tempting as that might be, I think it's better not to do it. Saying funny or clever things should always come second to character because an audience will not believe in characters who are mere vehicles for one-liners. And if the audience don't believe in the characters, they won't care what happens to them. And then the story won't work.[4]

I was put off a very successful TV series because of a single speech in an early episode. A young man stood in a corridor delivering words of wit and sharp observation. After a few moments I stopped seeing the young man in the corridor and saw instead the writer at his desk, typing the speech and looking pleased with himself. I often see popular TV drama series in which all the characters talk in one-liners. I find that induces indifference.

However, it might be argued that the key words in these examples are 'successful' and 'popular'. If it works, why not do it? Maybe so. Maybe my argument – that truth should outweigh a joke – is merely a curmudgeonly one based on personal taste.

I'll leave it for you to decide. You're the writer.

[4] Banter *can* work in sitcoms but the best sitcoms have believable characters and believable characters will have individual voices. Or so it seems to me.

Playing with dialogue

Enough said

There's always a temptation to write too much dialogue and that should be resisted. Don't allow your characters to ramble on. As Nell Leyshon says in *The Author*, 'Every line of dialogue needs to be interrogated. Why is it being said? What objective does a character have at any one moment?'[5]

You can almost always make your dialogue more lean. Remember that exchange in *EastEnders* – fourteen words across two speeches. Nothing else needed to be said. Even the seemingly talky *Talking Heads* said what was necessary and no more. They weren't indulgent.

Another example of dialogue cut to the bone and to great effect comes in Andrew Davies' TV adaptation of Elizabeth Gaskell's *Wives and Daughters*, when the heroine (Molly) has about three speeches at the end of the series. The hero (Roger) is at long last proposing to her. They stand together in the pouring rain. Molly's speeches are all the same and consist of one word ('Yes'). It's just right. Not only is it appropriate to her forthright, no-nonsense character, but also the contrast with Roger's slightly insecure verbosity sets up a delightful speech-against-speech rhythm.

There are times (even on radio) when it's good to stop people talking. Or at least to restrict them.

EXERCISE

Think of a character and put him or her in one of these situations ...

- Having to explain why I'm leaving you
- Having to explain where I got that money
- Having to explain what I'll do if you tell anyone my secret
- ... and write a speech for them.

[5] 'Dialogue' by Nell Leyshon, *The Author*, Winter 2013.

Then write it again with the same sense but using under a dozen words.

Exposition

Sometimes your dialogue has to convey information. It's important to know where the money was hidden, or what Colin did last Friday, or what happened to Elizabeth when she left university. A string of facts, important to the story. This is a test of your dialogue-creating skills. How can you pass on this essential information without making it seem clunky?

Is there a way of injecting some tension into these exchanges? Can you make life difficult for your characters at the point when they have to deliver the information?

Is there, for example, a possibility that they might be overheard?

Must the information be given within a time limit? ('I have to know before she gets to the bank. And she's driving there now!')

Is the information carrier about to fall asleep, to lose the power of speech, to realize suddenly what's going on and refuse to speak?

Or can you find some way of disguising the information? Can you hide it in an anecdote or some exchange that seems to be about something else?

Can you cut it up and deliver it in separate chunks across several scenes?

And so on. How you do this will depend on what the information is, the nature of the story you're telling, and the personality of the characters who have to pass it on.

EXERCISE

Imagine it's vital to your plot that you have to explain, in exact detail, how to make a pot of tea. Or wire a plug.

Create two characters and write dialogue to convey this information in the most exciting or engaging way you can.

Naturalistic ... or not?

I once heard Barry Simner (writer/creator of the TV dramas *The Vice* and *Single-Handed*) tell a group of students that the trouble with most dialogue is that it's too measured, too careful and too tidy.

'What you need to do,' he said, 'is to mess up its hair'.

When people speak they rarely do so in complete and neatly constructed sentences. Speech is messier than that. You can make your dialogue less unnaturally tidy by noticing that people:

- repeat themselves,
- hesitate,
- are interrupted,
- sometimes fall silent.

Listen to the way people ask and answer questions. Sometimes the answers don't fit the questions. ('Where were you last night?' 'Last night? There was a full moon.') Sometimes the questions are ignored completely.

You can also introduce an element of natural untidiness – and play around with the rhythm – by changing the word order. ('Last night. Where were you?' 'A moon. There was a full moon.')

EXERCISE

Here's a fairly neat and tidy piece of dialogue ...

RUTH: It was such a pleasant evening I decided to walk by the lake.

PAUL: Which way did you go?

RUTH: I took the path that runs past The Cobbler's Vest. Old Simon was sitting outside with his pint.

PAUL: Old Simon's awfully fond of a pint.

RUTH: I'd gone about half a mile when the strangest thing happened.

Now, using the words of Ruth and Paul, mess up its hair. You can change its word order and emphasize its rhythms. You can throw in some hesitations, repetitions, questions and interruptions. You may use a smattering of 'yes', 'no' and 'well'.

Of course, dialogue with its hair messed up can, and sometimes should, still be rhythmic and musical. There are actors who, for sound-enough reasons, also believe that dialogue should have messed-up hair and they go about this by adding their own 'yes, wells', 'OKs', 'rights', 'listens' and an assortment of personalized hesitations. The result then is more mess than dialogue. Rhythm and musicality are spoiled.

By the way, I don't take it for granted that all dialogue should be naturalistic. Look at almost any piece of dialogue by Pinter: it has the rhythms of common speech but it's not naturalistic. The following exchange, from my play *Irongate*, is between Laura and a man called Teal. She meets him while walking the Thames Path and, after two or three encounters, she begins to suspect that he's following her. Here she sees him again in an underpass at Westminster where he talks to her about the way the tunnel walls change how we hear voices.

EXAMPLE

TEAL: Remember? You must've noticed.
HE STEPS CLOSER.
How it can make people seem further away than they are.
It's a natural phenomenon. Like the light. The way broken sunlight through the trees sometimes makes things look different.
You could see that on the Path.
People who aren't there.

> *Or you think you're on your own and then you find you're not.*
> *LAURA: Look, I don't know how you managed to follow me here but –*
> *TEAL: Did I? Follow you?*
> *LAURA: You waited for me at Chiswick –*
> *TEAL: Ah, yes.*

Teal in particular speaks with a kind of rhythm but in a manner that's not quite of this world.[6] We can see this partly in the use of punctuation. What might be written as 'It's a natural phenomenon like the light' becomes 'It's a natural phenomenon. Like the light.' Not a huge difference, you might think, but it's a significant one, I'd claim, and part of Teal's remoteness and his cryptic use of language. And 'The way broken sunlight through the trees sometimes makes things look different' is perhaps more elegiac than we might expect in conversation between strangers.

How articulate?

It's a good idea in general *not* to let your characters say exactly what they mean or what they want. Sometimes it works best if they don't even know what they want. There was an enjoyable character in the TV series *Budgie*[7] called Wossname who was so inarticulate he could barely remember the names of everyday objects. He used to say things like, 'I've left the car in town, parked outside the wossname.' But it's sometimes permissible, and equally enjoyable, to write the occasional uncommonly articulate character: Ed Reardon, say, from *Ed Reardon's Week* (BBC Radio 4) or Francis Urquart from *House of Cards* (Frank Underwood in the US version).

> **HATTIE NAYLOR'S TOP TIP**
>
> The choice of accent is political and can enhance your work further. It should be at the forefront of the choices a writer makes.

[6] And, as we eventually discover, he isn't of this world.

[7] Created by Keith Waterhouse and Willis Hall, played by James Bolam.

Period dialogue

Writing dialogue for characters who lived more than about thirty years ago presents its own difficulties. People spoke differently then and the further back in time you go the more differently they spoke. BBC producer Marion Nancarrow points out that in radio, dialogue also works as costume. We can't see the people speaking but what they say will help to place them for us. It will give us clues about their position in society and the period of history from which they come.

How can we achieve this?

A fey pastiche won't do. ('Unhand the wench, you blackguard!') It's tiresome and restricting, and it sounds false, as if you're writing a pantomime. But ignoring the problem by using a completely modern voice won't do either. ('I'm just saying, Sir Jasper, watch yourself, all right?') Such cloth-eared anachronisms will wrench an audience out of the world you've otherwise set up so carefully. (Hair messing has to be done with particular care when you're writing period dialogue. 'Rights' and 'OKs' must be shown the door.)

What you need to develop, I suspect, is a *period voice*. You must become so steeped in the language of the time that you begin to think in it. If you can put yourself in the world you're writing about, you can then perhaps begin to use language that won't threaten the sense of period. And you can use it with a sense of freedom and invention.

In Mike Walker's radio adaptation of *Barnaby Rudge* by Charles Dickens, Hugh, the wild stable hand, asks someone if he has anything more to say. 'Otherwise,' he adds, 'I've got horse-shite to shovel for more profit than I'm getting here.' I haven't reread the novel to check but I'm pretty sure 'horse-shite' doesn't appear in it. Nevertheless the line rings true to me. It's anachronistic only in the sense that it's not Dickensian. But horse-shite shovelling existed then, more than it does now, so, I think, it passes the test. It's understandable to us but doesn't wrench us out of the nineteenth century. It also goes with a bounce and is true to Hugh's character.

Punctuation

You can't write effective dialogue without a working knowledge of punctuation. This isn't a matter of making sure the English is correct, it's a matter of making sure that what you write sounds the way you want it to sound. It's especially useful at the end of lines.

LINE ENDINGS

Sometimes a line will come to a neat and natural conclusion. (The full stop or sparingly, for emphasis, exclamation mark!)

Sometimes it'll trail off because, well, the speaker is hesitant, or distracted or too embarrassed to ... (... to carry on; three dots.)

Sometimes it'll be cut off because –

Because someone else barges in with something to say. (The dash.)

I know of no rule that says three dots mean hesitation, trailed or abandoned speech, and that a dash means interrupted speech. Except my own. That's the way I use them. I also use commas, semicolons, colons, brackets (sometimes) and question marks. A question mark may seem obvious – you put it at the end of a question – but if it's used with what looks like a statement it changes the way the line reads.

Big Ben is not a clock. Big Ben is not a clock?

TOP TIP

Punctuation is a means to accuracy in what you write and the way lines are delivered.

If an actor is in doubt about a line you should be able to help him or her by saying, 'Play the punctuation.'

Set-ups

As well as what people say to each other, think about how and where they say it. They don't always have to be on chairs facing each other, or sitting round a table, or standing face-to-face in a corridor. There are other options.

You can consider the history, the location and the activity of your speakers.

The history is what they were doing immediately before they started speaking (or, to be precise, before we started to hear them). For example, a conversation will be affected by the fact that one (or more) of the characters has just come in from a run, or a swim, or has just woken up, or had too much to drink. And so on.

The location also makes a difference. Are your characters in a big, public space like a railway station? Or a small private room? Or in bed? Or under the bed? And how does where they are, and who they're with, change the way they speak to each other?

Consider, too, what your characters might be doing while they talk. They can be walking, sitting, running, rowing, skating, clipping a hedge, counting money, cooking and so on.

EXERCISE

Imagine a conversation in which Dangerous Tanya issues a strict warning to her employee, Edward. Whatever he's been doing in recent weeks she wants him to stop. She wants him to change his behaviour. She's arranged a meeting in the local park. They sit on a bench together There are children playing nearby.

Now imagine the same scene with Tanya feeding the ducks as she speaks.

Now imagine it in Tanya's kitchen. As she's gutting a fish.

Or she's arranging her stamp collection as she speaks. Sitting in an armchair, looking through a magnifying glass. Using tweezers.

The most obviously threatening of these scenes might seem to be the fish-gutting one, but I'm not so sure. I think the tweezers and the magnifying glass could be terrifying.

There's a series of compelling duologues in BBC Television's *Line of Duty* (the second series) by Jed Mercurio. They're often tense, close interrogations in which the power shifts backwards and forwards between the speakers. One of the best is when two women – Kate Fleming (Vicky McClure) and Lindsay Denton (Keeley Hawes) have a conversation in prison. There's already considerable animosity between the two and this is exacerbated by the fact that there's a glass barrier between them. The barrier distorts what they (and we) hear; it makes the exchange more strange, more difficult and alienating.

EXERCISE

Imagine an exchange between two people. Someone is breaking bad news to a friend. Or someone is trying to sell a sofa to a stranger.

Now think of three different ways of setting up that conversation. Try different histories, locations and activities.

Speech, speech!

Sue Teddern

We all champ at the bit to reach the stage when the planning's done, the plots and subplots are in place and we can finally 'hang out' with our characters. Time to show the world how funny, flawed, foolhardy or flippant they are by what they say and how they say it.

It's easy to get carried away with dialogue. If your characters are well drawn and three-dimensional, they can natter away for page after page. It's your job to rein them in when they get too garrulous or to give them a nudge if they're tongue-tied. They are relying on you to make their words work.

Here are my Twenty Commandments for writing dialogue:

See if they 'talk' to you.

1. Are your characters saying exactly how they feel? We don't do this in real life. We say everything's fine when it isn't. We laugh when we want to cry. Would subtext, irony, monosyllables or silence give a truer sense of how someone's feeling?
2. Is your dialogue overwritten? Try removing every alternate line.[8] Will you still get a sense of the scene? In nearly every case, less really is more.
3. What are your characters doing while they talk? Don't just put them on a sofa or in a pub. If you have them baking, jogging or cleaning while they talk, they'll reveal so much more about themselves.
4. Do your characters sound too much like each other? Swap around some lines. If your characters' speeches are interchangeable, they're not sufficiently distinctive.
5. Do your characters sound too much like you? Sometimes your way of speaking or brand of irony can slip onto the page. Again, the end result is a lack of distinctiveness which will cause your audience to disengage.
6. Avoid lazy clichés and platitudes – unless that's how your characters speak.
7. Are there too many long speeches? Is there a good reason for keeping them? If not, trim!
8. Can you join a scene in mid-dialogue and cut to the next one before all the goodbyes? There's no need to include every 'how are you' and 'see you later' but sometimes the logical bit of our brain thinks they're necessary.[9] Include them in your first draft, by all means. They'll probably be deleted at a later stage, if your script's too long.
9. Don't write your dialogue phonetically. 'Ain't' is fine but don't go all Eliza Doolittle. Actors hate being instructed on how to pronounce every word. That's their job, not yours. Awright?

[8] This tip comes from a crime writer friend. She removes superfluous clues to who-done-it and says it's like taking away every alternate rung of a ladder; a visual image I find very helpful.

[9] My early *Archers* scripts were full of waffle like this.

10. Don't overdo the directions. It's an insecure writer who precedes every line of dialogue with 'tersely', 'wearily', 'ironically'. If your dialogue is clear, your cast will know how you want it spoken. Only give a suggestion if it's absolutely necessary. For example, 'I will survive' can be delivered any number of ways. If you want it whispered or screamed, say so. But if you want the actor to find their own way of saying it, trust them and enjoy the surprise.
11. Is your dialogue speakable? Read it aloud if you're not sure. Novelists and poets can turn on the alliteration tap and see their sensual sentences swish subtly to a suitable stop. But this will be the line that causes an actor to corpse or fluff[10] because it's impossible to say. I'm not suggesting you avoid alliteration but be aware of the pitfalls.
12. Not every question needs to be answered. We don't do it in life so why put it in a script? For example:

    BARRY Can I have that £50 back?

    HARRY No. You'll get it next week.

    The 'no' is unnecessary. See how many yeses and nos you can remove from your dialogue. Yes, you can do it! No, you won't regret it.
13. You'll see a lot of scripts with 'beat' in brackets. It signifies a change of subject or tone. As in:

    CARRIE So I told him I wanted a divorce. (BEAT) Do you mind if I smoke?
14. Don't overdo beats, pauses and silences. Again this is something to leave to your talented actors.
15. I tend to avoid dot-dot-dots. What do they signify? What am I asking an actor to do here? This is my own little bugbear ... but ... maybe ... you like them.
16. Another bugbear: characters who keep using the other person's name. On radio, it can be confusing when two women of a similar age and accent are talking. 'How will listeners know who's who, unless I stick their names in?'

---

[10] Corpse = get the giggles. Fluff = mess up the line.

CARRIE Are you okay, Terri?

TERRI Yes, Carrie, I'm fine thanks.

CARRIE That's a relief, Terri.

On radio it can be justified – up to a point – for the purpose of identifying who's who. On TV, it simply isn't how we speak, unless we've been on one of those slick 'how to relate to your customer'-type courses.

17. It's tempting to underline all the words you want an actor to emphasize. Again, the rule of thumb is: only do it if the meaning might otherwise be misunderstood. Could that *be* any clearer?

18. Every writer has their own way of signifying interruptions or characters speaking over each other. This is mine:

BARRY Hang on, I haven't finished what– [I was saying]

CARRIE –too bad. It's my turn.

The words in brackets give Barry a sense of the whole sentence and they tell Carrie when to jump in.

19. Every line of dialogue should either move the story along or reveal something about the character. If it does neither, delete it.

20. Ignore all the above and make your 'talky bits' your own.

Hearing their dreams – the nuts and bolts of radio

Nick Warburton

> *From where you are, you can hear their dreams ...*
> Dylan Thomas, *Under Milk Wood*

The essential elements

The death of radio, like the death of the novel, is regularly predicted, but both continue to survive and, from time to time, flourish.

One of the reasons that radio keeps going is that you can hear it while you're doing other things. You can experience a play while you're having a bath or cooking an omelette. And now you can listen on the move – in cars, on trains, while you're running or walking. It surprises me that more radio drama isn't available on long flights. Better to hear a play, I would have thought, than to watch a moving postcard of a recent film.

The radio audience has tended to be more thoughtful, more middle class and older than audiences for TV. Occasional attempts are made to attract younger listeners, but I suspect that people discover the pleasures of radio as they mature. It is not, however, a docile audience. Try taking *The Archers* off the air and see what happens.

THE ELEMENTS OF RADIO

We're aware of five elements when we listen to a radio play:

- Words
- Sounds
- Music
- Silence
- Movement

These elements can be handled clumsily or with subtlety and imagination. (For the clumsy version you'll be well rewarded by seeking out, probably online, Timothy West's brilliant parody of a bad radio play: 'This gun that I have in my right hand is loaded.') I say quite a lot about using words elsewhere in the book[1] so here we'll concentrate on ways you can use the other four elements when you write a script. For our purposes, movement includes the notion of space.

Sounds

Because sound can both help to paint the picture and to tell the story, it pays to give it some consideration. I want to do this by talking first about what I call *sound setting* and then about *sound effects*.

Sound setting ...

The sound setting is the immediate sound environment of a radio play. It's the equivalent of scenery or set on screen or stage. It not only tells the listener where we are but also helps to create atmosphere and add texture.

Sometimes you can think about an overall sound setting for a play as well as the sound setting of each scene.

You can also ask yourself if the scene you're writing is an *internal* or an *external* one. Does it take place in a building or in the open air? (Is it INT or EXT?)

And, if you were to stand in this place, what would you hear?

The sound environment of a place is made up of lots of small surrounding and *continuing sounds* – birds, perhaps, heard outside the windows of a room, or nearby traffic, or wind – and the way the place affects the sounds made in it, its *acoustic*. Are you, for example, in a room that makes a voice sound louder, harder, softer, more 'alive' or slightly deadened?

[1] See 'A most delicate monster – voice' and 'The talky bit: writing dialogue' above.

EXERCISE

Think of a line of dialogue. It doesn't matter what it is or what it means. Imagine it – hear it with your mind's ear – spoken on a windswept mountain top.

Now hear it spoken in a swimming pool.

And again under a duvet.

Does hearing the line spoken in those different places make you want to change it? Or merely change the way it's spoken?

The combination of these two things – the continuing sounds and the acoustic – can also affect the way we feel about what we hear. So a small, close room with stone walls will not only sound different from a large, empty space like a museum or a barn, but we'll also feel slightly different about being there.

RACHEL JOYCE'S TOP TIP

Create a world the listener believes in, and you can take that listener anywhere. *Yes, this is not real but come with me. I am going to tell you a story and you won't want to leave me until you know the end.*

Think about what you might hear if you were standing on a seashore, or in a wood by a stream. And how you might *feel*. Or think about a crowded street, busy with traffic. Or a deserted street at night.

EXERCISE

Now create a distinctive sound environment of your own.

Consider the acoustic. And the atmosphere, the feeling it might convey.

Put two people there. Don't spend any time working out a plot or who precisely they are. Just make them different from each other and put the barest bones of character – a middle-aged man and his quiet friend...a smart woman and a nervous stranger ...

What do they say to each other? Give them a single line each, no more. Something that suits the sound setting.

Changing the sound setting from scene to scene can help with the overall rhythm of your play; it can add variety or contrast. This can have a similar sort of effect to the way you might use lighting in a television script: you set one scene, for example, in a small, dark room and the next in bright open air.

Here's an example of complex layers of sound designed to present an extraordinary world. It's from the opening of my adaptation of *Peter Pan in Scarlet* (from Geraldine McCaughrean's wonderful book):

EXAMPLE

SLOWLY BRING UP A LAGOON IN NEVERLAND. IT BEGINS QUIETLY, PERHAPS WITH THE SWOOPING CALL OF SOME UNIDENTIFIABLE EXOTIC, NOT QUITE NATURAL BIRD. THIS IS JOINED BY THE PECULIAR BURBLING OF INSECTS. MUSIC JOINS IN AND CONTINUES THROUGH AND UNDER THE DISTANT SPLASHING AND DIVING OF CHILDREN AT PLAY IN THE LAGOON. WE CLOSE ON THEM AS THEY SHOUT AND LAUGH.

JOHN: Mermaid! Here comes one!

WENDY: And rainbows! Look, John – reflections of rainbows!

JOHN: Tag, tag, tag!

NARRATOR: John was dreaming of Neverland again. And Peter Pan.

PETER: Cock-a-doodle-doo!

NARRATOR: All over London old boys were dreaming the same kind of dreams.

PETER DIVES. WE PLUNGE UNDERWATER WITH HIM. THE BIRD AND INSECTS ARE REPLACED BY A SWIRL OF BUBBLES.
PETER: (Underwater) Cock-a-doodle-doo!
HIS CRY SLOWS DOWN AND EVERYTHING ELSE SLOWS WITH IT.
NARRATOR: And what did they have in common, these dreamers?
WENDY: (Slow and underwater) Be careful, John …
THE SLOW, HEAVY SWIRLING OF WATER. THE MOOD HAS CHANGED. WHERE THERE WAS PLAY THERE IS NOW THREAT.

You won't always want, or need, to create such a multi-layered pattern of sounds. Creating a sound setting is often a matter of selection. *Othello* begins in Venice, a teeming, colourful world of contrasts that makes us think of carnivals and conflict. But the play is more concerned with the things people say to each other – with jealousy and suspicion – than it is with its surroundings. John Tydeman's 1988 production, with Paul Scofield as Othello and Nicol Williamson as Iago, begins with the sound of water lapping round wooden stakes in a canal. Then we hear Roderigo speak. That simple sound – a swirl of water – is all that's needed to set us down in Venice.

TOP TIP

Weather can also be used as part of the sound setting.

If you think about the scene you've just imagined, for example, you can now ask yourself what difference the addition of rain, or snow, or oppressive heat might make. If your play is set on a single day, how might the change of weather affect events – or how we feel about those events? If it starts in rain and the rain diminishes during the day until the evening is still and quiet, what difference will that make? Or what difference will it make if the reverse is the case? And if you set your play over a number of months, might you use the change in seasons to help tell the story?

But you should only use these things – continuing sounds, and acoustic and weather – if they help. Remember that some scenes can and should be played quietly. No weather. An uncomplicated, fairly clean acoustic. Not much in the way of environmental sounds. Just the words.

Studio managers, the immensely talented people who provide the sounds for radio drama, say it helps them if writers have, in the first place, thought carefully about the sound they want, and, in the second place, written precise descriptions of that sound.

Studio managers also like to be challenged. So when I wrote ...

Peter dives. We plunge underwater with him. The bird and insects are replaced by a swirl of bubbles

... I had no idea how that might be achieved, but I did know that it was what I wanted, and that there were people who could create the effect of us diving underwater with Peter Pan.

You'll have a lot of background sounds at your disposal so it's worth taking time to think about them, to consider the picture you're building and the story you're telling.

But don't do it for the sake of it, and don't overdo it. Remember Venice.

Sound effects ...

As well as the sound *setting* in that example from *Peter Pan in Scarlet*, there are also particular sound *effects*. The *setting* gives us the continuing, background sounds – the lagoon in Neverland, above and below water – the *sound effects* give us *events*. In this case we hear the call of an exotic bird, the children diving in the water and so on. Some of these are pre-recorded sounds that can be dropped in during studio recording or during the editing process. Others are spot effects – made 'on the spot' in the studio by actors and/or studio managers.

Sound effects can work in several ways:

- They can help to realize a scene by adding texture and making it seem real.
- They can help to tell the story – a gunshot, a breaking vase, a ship crashing on rocks, a creaky floorboard and so on. They let us know what's happening.
- They can comment on a scene or a character.

Texture and realism …

Using *some* sound effects can make a scene seem real. Using *a lot* of sound effects won't necessarily make it seem more real. It will, rather, make it seem as if your play is taking place in a studio with a trolley full of cups and saucers, pots and pans, jangling keys and coconut shells at the ready. Avoid the temptation to overdo sound effects. Be selective. Most of the time you only need to suggest what's going on.

Some plays are recorded on location and this can give a sense of muddy realism to what we hear. It adds a lively randomness to the sound, making it seem almost filmic. This suits some plays very well, but not all. So think about what you're writing: do you want intense, random realism, or sounds orchestrated, almost like music, to help tell the story? Or something of both?

You can have what you want. All you have to do is think about it first.

Telling the story …

Sound effects are events. A simple sound effect, well-placed and prepared for, can have a powerful impact. It can, in some cases, have an effect more immediate than words. Two examples are below: an ending and a beginning.

The first is really a series of sound effects. In *Albert's Bridge* (1967) by Tom Stoppard an army of 1,800 painters marches towards the bridge Albert's painting. We hear them coming; we hear them whistling as they advance. We know that they should break step when they reach the bridge. If they don't break step the rhythm of the marching, the bounce of feet will destroy the bridge. So we hear the tramp of feet … the whistling … the rivets starting to pop … and …

Well, you can listen to the play and find out.

The second example is from Angela Carter. In the introduction to *Come Unto These Yellow Sands*, her collection of radio plays, she describes how a sound effect made by accident, running a pencil along the top of a radiator, made her think of a long, pointed fingernail running across the wires of a birdcage … and the thought of that sound led to her writing *Vampirella* (1976). That play, about a lady vampire, begins with the sound.

EXERCISE

Instead of starting with the story, start with the sound. Think of a sound effect that will have a main impact on a story, that will be crucial to the climax. Avoid the obvious (gunshots, explosions and so on). Make it something unusual and distinctive.

Then think about how you might set up this sound effect.

An aside on doors ...

It's easy to forget that you don't always need doors in radio plays. People don't have to come in and out of doors, announcing themselves or being named and greeted as they do so. You can start a scene when the protagonists are already in place and launched on their conversation; you can end it before they leave and say their goodbyes.

However ... doors can be useful for the sounds they make.

A door opened tentatively can announce the arrival of an habitually nervous character, or a character made nervous by what's in the room.

A door flung open can make a very different kind of announcement.

A slammed door can both tell us about the mood of the slammer and make a sharp scene ending. Or beginning.

A door opened and then closed and then opened again can suggest something else.

And so on.[2]

Sound as comment ...

Sometimes a sound effect can be used to comment on the action. It can support or undermine what people say. An example is the best way to explain what I mean.

---

[2] You can use telephones – answered and unanswered – in a similar way. Their ringtones can add to the rhythm of the script.

In *Under the Loofah Tree* by Giles Cooper (1958), Edward Thwaite is looking back on his life as he takes a bath. He has with him toy boats and a plastic duck. He recalls proposing to his wife Muriel. We hear romantic music as he brings the moment to mind. He asks her to marry him and the music cuts out. But there were others, he remembers. He could have had his pick. He still could, he thinks. And the plastic duck quacks.

The quack of Edward's plastic duck is heard after each of his most self-regarding statements. It punctures his pomposity. It's a sound that does two things: it helps us picture the scene – an unprepossessing middle-aged man taking a leisurely bath – and at the same time it makes a critical assessment of what Edward's just said. Not many sound effects are this clever.

Music

In the script for my first radio play I made no reference to music. I naïvely assumed that someone at the BBC would add some at the beginning and end to see us in and out. But, since I didn't put that in the script, it was broadcast without music. It wasn't too great a loss in that case but it might've been, so ever since then I've thought about the music I want and the ways of using it.

Sometimes I know precisely which piece of music I want to use, but even if I don't I'll know the mood I want it to convey and the effect it should create at any given moment. I'll type

MUSIC. IT FADES UNDER

or

MUSIC TAKES US TO

or, for example,

CHILDREN SINGING FOR ASSEMBLY. A BIT ROUGH ROUND THE EDGES, NOT SWEET AND PERFECT.

And then I'll talk to the producer about the music that might work best. These are usually enjoyable conversations. Most radio producers have a good ear for music and a vast store of pieces they can call on. Sometimes a producer will persuade me away from my original idea, and when they do that they're almost always right.

Some pieces of music suggest themselves immediately; they seem to be the obvious choice for what you're doing. When this happens it's usually a good idea to think again. Don't be obvious. Unless you're being ironic and want to play against the mood of the music. As with all other aspects of writing, your first thought is sometimes exactly right, and sometimes it's the thing you have to ditch. The trick, of course, is knowing which is which.

Some ways of using music …

- Don't use it at all. Moving straight to action and dialogue can be effective because it has the potential to catch the listener off guard a little. That might be exactly what you want and entirely appropriate to the subject.
- Use it to bookend a play. Music takes us into the world of the play, prepares us for its tone, and brings us out of that world at the end. If the tone of the play has changed during its course, the music that brings us out can reflect that. (I'm thinking about music for a stage play I'm working on at the moment and I've found two slightly different versions of the same thing, one slightly more sombre than the other. One will start and the other end the play.)
- An aside on what I call plinky-plonky music. This is emotional signposting, music that tells us all too firmly what we should be feeling. Sometimes it even announces what we should be feeling before we get to the emotional moment. (*JO JOINS CHRIS ON THE PORCH. PLINKY-PLONKY MUSIC. JO PUTS AN ARM ROUND CHRIS. THEY HUG. SWELL PLINKY-PLONKY MUSIC.*)
- Thread music through a play. Use it to link scenes or episodes and move us from place to place. (*MUSIC TAKES US TO …*) You might have subtle changes of mood in moving from one scene to another. Music can help mark that. (You can also use silence between scenes. See below under *Movement*.) We used music to move the narrative forward in my series of plays *Witness*, adapted from St Luke's gospel. A lot of the story centred on journeys – travelling down to Jerusalem, the road to the cross and so on – and an imaginative score by the composer David Pickvance brilliantly

suggested this forward impetus. You can also use music within scenes, within speeches even, as a kind of punctuation. Remember Edward in his bath from Giles Cooper's play *Under the Loofah Tree*? There's romantic music, he proposes and the music cuts out. It cuts abruptly. Cooper uses the music here in bursts, almost as a sound effect – a quick burst of romantic music to set up the proposal, a quick cut of the music to deflate the mood.[3] Underscoring, by the way, can heighten emotion and emphasize drama. But be careful: it can also obscure the words. And the music should serve the words.

- Integrate it. Music can be the subject of the play, or at least an important element in it. Two examples of this follow. In Anthony Minghella's *Cigarettes and Chocolate* (1988) the talking and, in the case of the central character Gemma, the silence are powerfully set against passages from Bach's *St Matthew Passion*. And in Lee Hall's *Spoonface Steinberg* (1997) Spoonface, the little girl who speaks to us, begins by telling us about 'the olden days when they wrote the songs and the operas and all that' and her small, innocent voice is set against the mature, powerful voice of Maria Callas. It makes an important dramatic point and is an essential part of the play.

So it's a good idea to listen to music – all kinds of music – and make note of the pieces that might one day be useful.

EXERCISE

What music might you use – and how – in a scene from a familiar myth, legend or folktale? (For example, Orpheus leading Eurydice up from the underworld, or a scene in the Ark before the deluge.)

[3] You can also use sounds to link or punctuate scenes – wind, rain, birdsong, traffic and so on.

Silence

Silence can be a powerful element in a radio play. A long silence can create discomfort and unease. It can also provide a space through which emotions can reverberate. On the other hand, *too* long a silence will suggest there's something wrong with the radio, that you've lost the signal. So it behoves you to think about how you intend to use silence.

Not all silences are alike. They vary in length and quality.

Length

I tend to use about three types of silence.

THREE TYPES OF SILENCE

- *Beat* – the shortest possible silence; it might signify no more than a change of direction in a speech or the briefest of pauses for consideration.
- *Pause* – the length of a couple of beats; on the whole, it has more weight and significance that a beat.
- *Silence* – the genuine, golden article; deliberate dead air, or the sound of the place, the sound environment continuing for several moments without speech – the river running or the trees in the breeze, with your characters present but saying nothing.

Sometimes I'll add 'short pause' to that list. A short pause is, rather obviously, somewhere between a beat and a pause. Sometimes the script seems to need it. I can't always say why.

You can work out categories of silence that suit you best. It's important to be consistent – don't put 'silence' when you mean 'pause' – and to remember that the shorter silences are probably negotiable. Beats and short pauses are also part of the actor's armoury. Derek Jacobi once asked me, very politely, if he could ignore a beat in a certain line. 'It'll be funnier if I run it on,' he said. And, of course, he was right. I still include those smaller silences in a script, though, because they're part of the rhythm of the thing and you have to write what you hear in your head.

Incidentally, make sure you and your actors agree the meanings of the terms you use. I've noticed that some actors think of what I'd call a pause as a beat. They're not wrong: we just haven't agreed terms.

Silence is the most powerful member of the clan so it must be used sparingly. If you keep throwing in silences – proper, golden silences – they'll get weaker and less valuable as you go.

Quality ...

The quality of a silence will depend on what you place either side of it – the sound that leads up to it and the sound that follows it.

The silence that comes after a big, powerful, clashing scene will be different from the silence that comes after a quiet, intimate scene. And the silence that comes after a question will have a different texture from the silence that comes after a statement.

Movement

People often assume that when actors record a radio play they stand round a microphone and read. In fact a fair amount of movement and physicality is involved in even the quietest production. Sometimes they do stand round a mic and read. Sometimes they'll sit round it; and sitting to read is different from standing to read. At other times they'll run, march, crawl, fight, crouch under tables, cook, dig, hug, cuddle and jump up and down steps. So the writer for radio should always be aware of movement, position and space, and the opportunities they provide for adding energy, animation, contrast and variety to a script.

Take note of the way a character might approach or leave a scene. Or when characters might start or stop moving. Think about how far away they are from the listener (i.e. from the microphone) and what we might or might not hear from other characters in the background.

Background is an interesting concept on radio. Can you have two scenes running at the same time, one in the foreground and one in the background? You can quite easily on television but will it work on radio? Of course it will if you can pull it off without confusing your audience.

Here's an example of movement from an adaptation of Anthony Trollope's *Framley Parsonage*. The two characters aren't moving from place to place; they're side by side at a kitchen table. Lucy has come to look after Mr Crawley's sick wife. Lucy is bright and purposeful; Mr Crawley is helpless, cerebral and introspective. She is making pastry; he sits at the table with an open book in front of him talking about St Paul.

EXAMPLE

LUCY: Mr Crawley.
MR CRAWLEY: Hmm?
LUCY: Your book, in the flour ...
MR CRAWLEY: Oh, yes. Sorry.
HE MOVES HIS BOOK.
Yes, I'm bound to say that no one has lapsed so frequently as myself. Surely a man must throw himself prostrate in the dust and ...
LUCY CONTINUES TO THUMP THE PASTRY.
What are you doing?
LUCY: Making a goose pie.
MR CRAWLEY: Oh?
LUCY: I think your wife might try a little.
MR CRAWLEY: Ah.

The movement in this scene – Lucy's busy activity with the pastry – emphasizes the contrast between the two characters and highlights what the scene is, at least partly, about: on the one hand anxious self-contemplation and on the other practical love for a family in need.

Stereo recording can suggest movement from side to side – a car swishes by from left to right, an army marches past from right to left – and distance from the microphone can give backwards and forwards movement. Microphones – or rather the speakers or earpieces through which you hear radio drama – can't replicate movement up and down, but the writer can create that impression by the deft use of a word or two. Technology can help create movement, and depth, but I'm never particularly worried about how technologically advanced the device you listen on might be. If the play's good it should work just as well on the ancient radio you've kept in the bathroom for thirty years. If the script is clear enough the listener will always know who's moving where.

Jonathan Raban has argued that most radio drama is best served by mono- rather than stereo-recording because stereo imposes a kind of naturalism on everything that isn't always appropriate. Stereo doesn't necessarily help to create the intimacy that is one of radio's greatest strengths.[4]

The following thoughts on acting for radio drama, taken from a document prepared for those new to radio acting after an actors' workshop with BBC Radio Drama for World Service, shows how important it is to be aware of movement in radio drama.[5]

> Be aware of your physicality when recording and move around the space – away from the mic if possible – a director will always tell you if it's too much! Allow your body freedom of movement.... Connect as much as possible with other actors within a scene, through eye-contact, physical touch or gesture.

---

[4] In *Radio Drama* edited by Peter Lewis.

[5] Copyright of the BBC, by kind permission.

The visuals: Writing for camera

Sue Teddern

> *Don't tell me the moon is shining, show me the glint of light on broken glass.*
>
> Anton Chekhov

'Show, don't tell.' Isn't that the most familiar note to writers, along with 'write what you know'? It's good advice. Whether you're a novelist, poet, dramatist or scriptwriter, your work comes alive when you present those important moments as they happen, rather than reported retrospectively.

As a radio dramatist, all you need to do is give your listeners a few clues to where you are and what can be 'seen'. They're happy to provide the lighting, costume, props and sense of place.

When you write for TV, you become Executive Producer of all these elements. That's not to say you must take total command when your script is filmed. That would do you no favours and elevate you to diva/control freak status. At the writing stage, however, every element of the visuals is down to you: what to include, what to omit, how much to describe/dictate and how much to leave in the capable hands of your production team.

Scary and thrilling all at once!

The silent treatment

Earlier, we looked at 'the talky bits'. We understand the importance of strong dialogue but so much can be said without words. For all their hammy acting and OTT eyebrows, silent movies managed to tell compelling stories without any spoken dialogue. It's inspiring to realize much narrative can be covered without a single utterance. A picture really is worth a thousand words. It's up to the screenwriter to underpin the script with unspoken information, emotion and impetus.

One example that springs to mind is in Troy Kennedy Martin's seminal TV serial *Edge of Darkness*.[1] Craven (Bob Peck) is bereft at the murder of his eco-activist daughter, Emma. He wanders around her bedroom, searching for clues to who she was. It's visceral and shocking; we feel his pain.

EXERCISE

- Try to recall scenes for TV that were devoid of dialogue but packed with plot, information and impact.
- Find a scene in one of your own scripts and rewrite it without any dialogue.
- Is it better?
- Why? Why not?
- If it doesn't work, try another scene.

TOP TIP

As writers, our first instinct is to join up all the expositional dots with dialogue. As viewers, we like to be tantalized, to not be given all the best toys in the box in one greedy go. We relish making our own connections, coming to our own conclusions. We don't wish to be spoon-fed or patronized.

That's when non-dialogue scenes work their own magic.

Sound to vision

I write for TV *and* radio. Rarely does a TV script evolve into something for radio – or vice versa – because they were conceived with a specific medium

[1] The BBC series, made in 1985, is, in my opinion, the version to revisit, not the 2010 movie starring Mel Gibson and Ray Winstone.

in mind. I like the different sets of muscles that I exercise in each creative process, although many of the basics (structure, plotting, characterization, tone) overlap.

My serial, *soloparentpals.com,* was written specifically with radio in mind, because it suited an epistolary structure. Two lonely and bruised single parents, living 250 miles apart, meet in a single parents' online chatroom. Their sparky encounters evolve slowly into a will-they-won't-they relationship, via voicemail, email, phone calls, chatroom and forum. Ideal for radio and fun to write.

After five successful series culminating in the inevitable happy ending, I decided to rework the premise for TV. An early mistake was to retain the online, long-distance element. This is eminently doable on radio but hard to show visually. My solution was to have them living in the same town and meeting in the flesh at a support group for single parents.

The initial idea for this series came many years earlier from an image I'd had of inept Tom not knowing what to do when his six-year-old daughter Lily needed to go to the loo in a public place. This moment made its way into both the radio and TV versions because it illustrated his discomfort with his role of a Saturday dad, after being dumped by his ex-partner. Particularly because she went on to meet someone new and he didn't.

It may be useful to see how I dealt with this specific image in each medium. It becomes more 'tell' than 'show' for radio because of the chat room format. Apart from anything else, choreographing Tom's attempt to deal with Lily's comfort stop would have required a fair bit of exposition and clunky description.

EXAMPLE

This is series one, episode one, scene two, of my radio serial, *soloparentpals.com.* It features Tom's very first encounter with Rosie. (Reader, she married him!)

SCENE 2	**SOLOPARENTPALS.COM CHAT ROOM**
FX	FADE UP. EACH SPEECH BEGINS WITH A COMPUTERIZED BEEP
SPP.COM VOICE	Major Tom has entered the chat room.

GILL	Hi Tom.
TOM	(SHOUTING) HI EVERYONE.
ROSIE	Oi, don't type in capitals. Comes over like you're shouting.
TOM	SORRY. (beat) I mean, sorry!
<u>FX</u>	<u>CHAT ROOM ENTRY/EXIT BEEP</u>
SPP.COM VOICE	Tash the Lash has entered the chat room.
TASH	Hi All. Hi Tom. Found your way in then?
TOM	Hi Tash.
TASH	Everyone being friendly? Even Rosie?
ROSIE	(SNOTTY) I'm *always* friendly! So what's your story, Tom?
TOM	The usual one. Me and my partner split up. I have Lily at weekends.
ROSIE	Here we go. Another Saturday dad!
GILL	spp.com's brilliant for support from folk who understand, Tom.
TOM	And advice, I hope.
ROSIE	On what?
TOM	Public toilets. Seriously. What do I do?
GILL	Sorry, don't follow.
TOM	Last week we were at the park and Lily needed the loo. So I waited outside for her. And this woman thought I was a pervert.
GILL	No! Really?
TOM	So she phoned the police.
ROSIE	Can't blame her, I suppose.
TOM	I'm always getting funny looks. Like I'm up to something. But I can hardly go in the loo *with* Lily, can I!
ROSIE	Typical single dad. No initiative.
TASH	Oh-oh, Rosie's on her soapbox!
ROSIE	It ain't rocket science, Tom.
TOM	Okay, I'm getting the message.
ROSIE	If your girl wants the loo, find a friendly woman to take her in. End of.

FX	CHAT ROOM ENTRY/EXIT BEEP
SPP.COM VOICE	Major Tom has left the chat room.
TASH	Charming as ever, Rosie.
ROSIE	I tell it like it is, that's all.

So we hear Tom's cry for help and Rosie using it as a stick to beat all ex-husbands with because *she's* been dumped too. The same thing happens in the TV version when Tom asks for advice at his first single parents' support group meeting. Again, her harsh words send him scurrying away.

For the TV version, which I renamed *Fix You*, I wanted to show how Tom and Rosie get through a typical weekend, before I bring them together. Tom lives alone all week but has Lily from Friday to Sunday. Rosie and her son Calum are a single-parent unit all week but he stays at his dad's from Friday to Sunday. So Tom is suddenly thrown back into full-on parentdom while Rosie is reluctantly footloose and fancy-free.

EXAMPLE

This is how I 'showed' the toilet moment for TV, rather than 'told' it:

EXT. PARK — DAY

TOM and LILY 'work out' on some park exercise machines. LILY thinks her daddy is hilarious which, of course, is hugely gratifying.

Then they feed the ducks with a burger bun TOM kept back from lunch. It's all going really well.

Until ...

TOM

The film starts at 4. We better get going.

LILY

I need to wee.

TOM

Wait till the cinema, Pickle.

LILY

I need to wee now.

TOM

Please, Lills. The cinema loo's much nicer.

LILY glares at him. Why does he always make such a fuss? Then she stomps off to the public toilets in the park - someone has to take charge here.

TOM follows reluctantly. Here we go ... <u>again</u>.

CUT TO:

EXT. PARK PUBLIC TOILETS – DAY

TOM lurks outside, feeling uncomfortable. Every week they go through this!

A YOUNG MUM passes by with a buggy, gives him a worried look. Honestly, does he <u>really</u> look like a paedo!?

TOM

(shouts sotto)

Lills? You okay?

No reply.

TOM (CONT'D)

Get a wiggle on, lovely. We don't want to miss the film.

No reply. He sighs wearily. No option. He goes into the Ladies to see what's keeping her.

CUT TO:

INT. PARK PUBLIC TOILETS – CONTINUOUS

LILY has been to the loo. Now she stands on tiptoes at the sink, fastidiously washing her hands.

LILY

It's not very nice in here.

TOM

I said to hang on.

She dries her hands on a paper towel. TOM breathes a sigh of relief as they exit ...

CUT TO:

EXT. PARK PUBLIC TOILETS – CONTINUOUS

... and appear outside. The YOUNG MUM observes them suspiciously, alongside the PARK KEEPER she has now alerted. TOM can't help feeling irrationally guilty.

TOM

(for their benefit)

Lily, please will you tell those people who I am.

LILY

My daddy.

TOM stares them out. See! All perfectly normal.

LILY (CONT'D)

Actually, he's my <u>old</u> daddy. My new daddy is called Adrian.

And TOM's heart dies a little inside. A hollow victory.

He walks just a bit too fast for LILY's little legs as they head for the park gates.

Fade to or cut to?

If you haven't already done so, it's imperative that you understand the format of a TV script. The best way of doing this is by reading as many as possible. Scriptwriters use templates like Final Draft, not just because it's the industry vernacular but because, by using it, they're showing that they are professionals. Other versions are available which we'll cover on page 273.

When you read a good script, make a note of what's been included and why. Some writers include more information than others. It's vital not to overload the 'black stuff' or directions. This could make your script far longer than it actually is.

Once you get the hang of writing in the accepted industry format, you'll wonder how you ever managed without it. Final Draft learns the names of your characters and locations. It 'listens' to your instructions to start a new scene or add information in parenthesis. It adds 'continued' if dialogue is interrupted by directions and it ensures that speeches are not broken up at the end of each page. Be honest, could you be as punctilious or consistent while in the throes of filling your pages?

Don't include complicated camera shots unless it's absolutely vital. Just as you wouldn't appreciate script notes from the DOP (director of photography), why should you tell him/her how to do his/her job by overloading your descriptions?

Here's a list of abbreviations and shots to use in your scripts.

You shouldn't need any others.

V/O	Voice-over or dialogue that runs over the top of the scene.
N/S	Non-speaking character. For example, a policeman, passenger, party guest or whatever. Also known as background artiste or extra.
O/S or OOS	Off screen or out-of-shot. Perhaps someone is shouting from the next room but we can't see them.
POV	A shot which must be seen from a character's point of view.

F/G or B/G	Foreground or background.[2]
C/U	Close-up.
CUT TO:	Final Draft will include this at the end of each scene under 'transition'. The convention is to use CUT TO but it takes up space and can be accused of stating the obvious.
FADE IN or OUT	Convention also suggests that you use these at the beginning and end of your script. I rarely do, unless I specifically need a scene to fade. Don't forget to fade in for a new scene, if you faded out of the previous one.
INT and EXT	Interior and exterior. And if your scene is in a car, INT/EXT will do just fine.
DAY and NIGHT	No need to be more specific. Only use DUSK, DAWN, LATE AFTERNOON, TWILIGHT, etc. if absolutely essential.
CONTINUOUS	You'll see an example of this in my script, above, where Tom and Lily leave the public toilet and are confronted by the mum and park keeper. It's as if the scene is flowing in real time from one location to the next.
SOTTO	An audible whisper.
TIC	This is a very useful one I learned from Jan McVerry[3] when we were working on *Homefront*. It's an abbreviation of tongue in cheek. (Instructions like 'sotto' and 'tic' should appear in brackets after the character's name.)
ROSIE'S HOUSE	Some writers give a general location: house. I prefer to say ROSIE'S KITCHEN or BEDROOM if that's where I specifically want this scene played.

[2] Midground also exists but I've never used it!

[3] See Jan McVerry in Part 2, page 105.

TOP TIP

Here's another lesson about scene direction learnt from Jan McVerry.

I came to *Homefront* thinking: only write scene directions that you can see. In other words, you can't get inside a character's head so don't include thoughts or feelings.

Reading Jan's concise, pacey scripts, I realized that little hints at mood or tone can be extremely useful.

Some examples from my TV scenes, above, with Tom and Rosie:

- LILY thinks her daddy is hilarious which, of course, is hugely gratifying.
- If ROSIE wasn't feeling so misanthropic, she'd be amused by their banter.
- And TOM's heart dies a little inside. A hollow victory.

It's a matter of taste. A script editor may take you to one side and politely suggest you delete stuff like this. But I feel it gives an additional emotional layer to the script and it makes the script a more satisfying read. It may assist the actor too.

Purely from my POV, it can only be helpful.

INT. desk – day

How to start writing

Sue Teddern

> *Abandon the idea that you are ever going to finish. Lose track of the 400 pages and just write one page for each day. It helps. Then when it gets finished, you are always surprised.*
>
> John Steinbeck

> *I wish I had a secret I could let you in on, some formula my father passed on to me in a whisper just before he died, some code word that has enabled me to sit at my desk and land flights of creative inspiration like an air-traffic controller. But I don't. All I know is pretty much the same for almost everyone I know. The good news is that some days it feels like you just have to keep getting out of your own way so that whatever is that wants to be written can use you to write it.'*
>
> Anne Lamott, *Bird by Bird*

Right. You are here. Everything that came before – the musing and scribbling, the agonizing and 'ecstasizing', the plotting and planning – was all designed to bring you to this very point. Now it's time to start writing your script.

You are a writer. So go on then. Write!

Of course, you may have jumped straight into your script without going through all the previous stages. Your enthusiasm to fill those pages is all the momentum you need. Like Jack Kerouac's famous stream of consciousness, *On the Road*, maybe the words are pouring out of you faster than you can type them. Lucky you.

I, however, maintain that all the postponing and worrying is normal. It's how *I* work anyway. I liken it to stage fright. It may be debilitating and unpleasant but isn't it better to be nervous than to breeze in front of a camera or audience, assuming your performance will be a walk in the park. As soon as you think that, you'll fall and you'll fail.

We all worry in so many aspects of our lives that we're just pretending to be adults. '*This* is the all-important job interview/assignment/date that's going to have me exposed as an impostor.' (Or is that just me?)

These feelings of anxiety may seek you out when you start to write. '*This* is the script that will dash my hopes of ever getting a play on the radio or securing me a meeting with an unfeasibly enthusiastic TV producer.'

As that famous self-help book proclaimed: Feel the fear and do it anyway! This is normal. Get over it. Get on with it.

Why did I want to write this?

The other problem with doing all that vital preparation is that you may forget what drew you to the idea in the first place. You've been so busy making it into something substantial, relatable and (with any luck) sellable, that you've forgotten why it grabbed you in the first place.

TOP TIP

Scroll back to the very beginning. Remember that 'light bulb' moment when your passing thought turned into something special. For there will have been such a moment and there's nothing more thrilling.

Revisit your early notes, when 'the thing' wasn't even 'a thing' yet.

An analogy: instead of thinking of a fairground as a succession of dangerous, over-priced rides and bacteria-ridden snacks, go back to the time when it was a place of thrills, excitement and scrummy hot dogs.

In other words, don't dwell on the sensible logical bits; remember the first heady elation. That's why you're sitting at your keyboard. Because you thought of something brilliant and you need to do it justice.

Writing on spec

Motivation is hard to find when nobody's waiting for delivery of your script. If you have no deadline, it's all too easy to postpone the daily trudge to your desk. Why bother?

Nothing motivates more than a deadline and/or accompanying cheque. We all procrastinate. Or we put off the non-urgent job when kids have to be collected from school, the bathroom must be painted or the day job beckons.

If your script doesn't inspire you to just get on with it, maybe it isn't the script you want to write. Yet or ever. If you need a deadline, invert one. Maybe you have a party or wedding to attend and won't it be cool to tell those people you haven't seen for a while that you've just written a radio play or the first episode of a sitcom.

I have mixed feelings about writing competitions. Your script will be one of hundreds, maybe thousands, that will need to be sifted through before a shortlist can be compiled. You may be reducing the odds of your work finding a mentor when it's in a huge stack with all the others.

However, script competitions have deadlines. Your aim is to win but if you don't, you have used the momentum to get your script written. Dust yourself off and send it elsewhere.

If the aim of entering that script competition was for you to take yourself seriously and actually write something, you've just won first prize.

Where, when, how ...

Where you write is an important consideration. If you only have the corner of a messy kitchen table, it will have to do. Maybe you can appropriate it for two hours a day when no one else is around. There's always the call of the upscale coffee shop, where every table is taken up with people pretending to be writers. You will never be short of café lattes, muffins, wifi and a loo.

That said, you will take yourself more seriously if you can create a writing place that is yours alone, where your post-it notes and mind maps can cover every surface and creep up the wall.

TOP TIP

A proper typing chair is essential if you don't want to screw up your back – a common writers' ailment. The more your work space looks like a writers' work space, the more you look like a writer, the more you are a writer.

That day job may beckon and family commitments can't be ignored. But it helps if you clear your schedule of other duties for a specific time each day or week. That's when you're a writer. The rest of time, you can be plotting, ruminating, what-if-ing, until you're back at your desk, itching to get started.

This may sound daft, but I find it helps if I'm showered and dressed before I start work. I'm taking myself more seriously when my hair is brushed and I'm out of my dressing gown. A tracksuit is also good. No need for a business suit and full make-up.

Unless it gets you writing, of course.

Don't get it right ...

Yes, here's another one of those writerly maxims: 'Don't get it right, get it written'.

Easier said than done.

You can agonize over every dot and comma or you can crack on and get something – anything – out of your head and onto the screen. Likewise, if you're writing a comedy, it's all too easy to stay with a dodgy gag until you finesse it. Been there, done that. All this will do is make you think you're not funny and you better give up now.

I reckon it's better to write something like... *[insert hilarious joke about inedible dinner here]*... and come back to it when you're feeling more hilarious.

I tend to write in fits and starts because I'm easily distracted. The consequence is that everything feels disjointed and random. Where are the connections? Why is there no flow? If it feels woolly and waffly, it probably is. Just keep going. You can de-waffle and unpick the woolly bits later.

Don't get it right, etc., etc.

TOP TIP

I learned a hugely useful lesson from a seasoned writer in my early days on *Birds of a Feather*. I felt blocked. Why was it so hard to get this episode written? In my non-professional days, I'd been able to bash out a script in a couple of days.

I ran my self-pitying whinge past veteran writer, Anne Valery. She told me that all this meant was I was becoming a proper writer. Speed did not equate with 'good script'; the reason it was taking longer to finish was because I was now more discriminate about the words I chose.

Obvious, when you think about it.

That said, if you can write quickly *and* choose the right words, even better!

Beat a block

Writers' block is a reality. It need not last years, months, weeks or even hours in order to knock you for six. That doesn't make it any less scary. It's like sitting in a plane. Suddenly you see yourself there above the clouds and you think, this can't possibly work. How can I be up in the sky like this?

You stop believing. You stop writing.

In the early days, when self-doubt overwhelmed me, I occasionally resorted to watching the opening credits of something I'd written and pressing pause when my name appeared. 'See, Sue! You've done it before. You can do it again.'

While you await your first screen or radio credit, you can't do this. But you *can* revisit something you wrote that shows the essence of you and what you do best. You can also watch a favourite TV show or listen to today's radio drama to see how someone else did it. Why did it work? What can you learn from it?

TOP TIP

If the words aren't coming, go for a walk, go the gym, have a nap, make soup, complete a crossword. Whatever you do that takes you away from your desk will clear your head.

> You may even find a solution to that insurmountable problem in scene twelve while you chop carrots or find your Zumba groove.
>
> You can also scroll through what you've written so far. Pat yourself on the back for the bits that worked. See if there's anything you can use from them that will shift the block.
>
> You CAN do this. Maybe not today, but with every page you are closer to 'Fade Out' or 'Ends'.

You are not alone

It may feel like you've the only one at a laptop or tablet, putting yourself through all kinds of misery and self-doubt in the cause of art, drama and pratfalls. You are not alone.

You must know other writers, from workshops you've attended or via Facebook groups and forums. Share your agonies and successes with them and they will do likewise. Writing is a solitary business – unless you write with someone else – but it needn't be.

> Here are some writers' tips from friends:
>
> - How do I get started? Deadlines. Abject poverty. Freedom, a program me that shuts off the internet to let me work without constantly checking Facebook and Twitter. Any of these usually work. Sometimes all three.
> - I create a false deadline. I say I'll do something by a certain time, thereby forcing myself into the right timeframe. This may be as simple as arranging a lunch.
> - I set a timer so that I write in twenty-minute blocks. Keith Hjortshoj[1] says that unless you're physically writing, you're not 'writing'. So I write notes or diary entries in the morning to warm up.
> - False deadlines don't work for me. I need someone waiting for the script and/or money in the bank.

[1] *Rules for Writers 5e & Transition to College Writing* by Diana Hacker, Keith Hjortshoj.

- I structure my writing day like a day of Test cricket. Seriously. It works. I faff about in the morning and allow myself the right number of breaks in the afternoon.
- I leave a sentence unfinished at the end of every day. It plays hell with my slight tendency to OCD-ishness but there's nothing worse than trying to start the day with a brand new scene. Whereas any idiot could finish that sentence, then write the next one and before you know it ...

What do you want? A medal?

When I have doggedly cracked on and finished my first draft, I really do expect a medal. I started this whole project with a wisp of an idea and now here it is, written.

Job done. I won.

But it's only a first draft and there's much more to do before it's ready to go out and face the world. Enjoy the moment. For rewrites will follow just as surely night follows day.

Read on if you don't believe me.

Putting it off

Nick Warburton

I mention elsewhere the sequence of events, from the getting of an idea to the completion of the First Draft.[2] This is about how you begin what I'll loosely call Work. It's also about the things you might do to get started and the conditions that might help you to start. And one of the first things you tend to do is ... avoid Work.

I often begin by employing delaying tactics. I put off the moment of starting. Or, rather, I put off the moment I *think* is the moment of starting – at the keyboard, poised to strike the first key. By then the real starting point has

[2] See the next section, 'Writing is Rewriting'.

usually already happened, with the idea, and the thinking about the idea. But that moment with the keyboard and the blank screen – that's what I sometimes put off.

I'm not alone in this. Most writers are familiar with the urge *not* to write, with the fear of blankness. The English playwright and novelist J. B. Priestley wrote an essay on delaying tactics – pencil sharpening, desk tidying, list making, pipe cleaning (in Priestley's case) and so on. We tell ourselves this is essential preparation for the work ahead. And sometimes it is.

But not always.

Sometimes it *is* a kind of fear.

Jess, a character in Alan Ayckbourn's stage play *Improbable Fiction*, does masses of research and reading for the historical novel she wants to write, but makes no progress. She says this is because the *idea* of the book before she writes it is very nearly perfect. It is what she calls 'unsullied'. If she makes a start she'll spoil that ideal. I remember sitting in the theatre when I first saw *Improbable Fiction* and knowing exactly what she meant. The Idea of the thing you want to write is so *flawless* and, at the same time, so fragile that you fear it will be destroyed by the very attempt to put it into words. This is not merely an argument for delaying the start, it's an argument for never starting at all.[3]

In fact, it's not the moment in front of the blank page, the blank screen, that's so frightening. The moment when you first show what you've written to someone else, that's the frightening bit. And that's a long way down the line. You can cross that bridge when you get to it.

So by all means employ a few delaying tactics, as part of the ritual of writing, but then get on with it, because you're on your own and whatever you put first – a noun, a verb, the word SCENE in caps – can be changed, or deleted, or saved in case it turns out not be as bad as you first thought it was.

PWD

I try to put in a Proper Working Day. What I don't, and can't, do is wait for the Muse to stir. (Or wait till I feel like writing, which amounts to the same thing.)

---

[3] See also Camus's novel *The Plague*, in which one of the characters is writing a novel and spends so long rewriting the first sentence he never gets beyond it. It's the same thing.

There are two reasons for this. One is that the Muse might not stir for ages. She might be sleeping off a particularly heavy night on the nectar and have no inclination to come round and tickle your imagination. The other is that I believe that writing – the act of putting words on paper, or on a screen – generates writing.

EXERCISE

Face the blank page. Write down a word. Make it an active verb – run, for example, or place, or control.

Add to it. Write down someone who is performing this act – 'the queen is running' or 'John Wayne is placing'.

Now add to it again. 'The queen is running to (or from)...what?' or 'John Wayne is placing the saddle/letter/kipper...or what?'

Now – slightly more demanding – think about what you've written and become dissatisfied with it. It's good, yes, but it could be better. So make some changes.

What you were doing, if you did that, was writing. Of course it was. And it was writing without the aid or prompting of a muse. Perhaps it was done without even the inclination to write. But that's how it works.

Writing generates writing.

Another advantage of a Proper Working Day is that it can give you an unbroken, uninterrupted rhythm to your thinking. As far as I'm concerned, the ideal conditions for working are a flow of time in a remote place that offers no rival stimulation (not a beautiful place: that can be distracting[4]) and where unseen servants leave food at your door at regular intervals. And reasonably, though not completely, quiet. I can cope with birdsong, weather, even traffic, but not talk – not snippets of overheard conversation. But you

[4] Jim Hitchmough, writer of the sweet and funny sitcom *Watching*, told me he once worked in a caravan which he turned round so the window *didn't* face the view.

can't have everything. Just as you shouldn't wait to be stirred by the Muse, so you shouldn't expect those ideal conditions. Jane Austen wrote at a small table, by a window for light, in snatched moments when domestic duty didn't call her away. Anthony Trollope started writing at 5.30 every morning, put in a regulation 250 words a page, at an average of forty pages a week, and after three hours of writing went off to work for the Post Office. 'I found it to be expedient,' he wrote in his autobiography, 'to bind myself by certain self-imposed laws.' In other words he put in a Proper Working Day as a writer before going out to do a Proper Job.

You will have to find your own Proper Working Day.

Not writing

You're also writing when you're not writing – when you've stopped putting words down to make lunch or a coffee; when you're sitting and thinking, or daydreaming, or sometimes just sitting; when you go for a walk; when you're sleeping. When you're writing you must, in a sense, remove yourself from one world and take up residence in another – the world of the story. Joseph Conrad wrote about the finishing of his novel *Nostromo*: 'On my return I found . . . my family all well, my wife heartily glad to learn that the fuss was all over, and our small boy considerably grown during my absence.'[5] The story is set in an imaginary South American country and that's where Conrad had been during the telling of the story – in his imaginary country.

You can also spend time not writing by planning, reading and doing research. This is not, in the strict sense of the term, 'putting it off'; it's necessary preparation.

Selection and discretion

Something else to consider in the early stages of writing is how much to leave out. Storytelling isn't just about what you say; it's also about the things you leave unsaid, the information you deliberately *don't* pass on.

[5] From Conrad's introduction to the novel.

> **SHERLOCK HOLMES' TOP TIP**
>
> A certain selection and discretion must be used in producing a realistic effect.
> (*A Case of Identity*)

The decisions you make about what you put in or leave out, where you choose to start and end your story, which of your characters you choose to put at the heart of the script, will make a considerable difference to the story you tell. And how well it works. Have a look, for example, at the first series of the political thriller *Homeland* (based on the Israeli series *Hatufim*, created by Gideon Raff). Its clever scripts are almost entirely driven by what we, as audience, are *not* told.

I've included this idea – about selection and discretion – in a chapter on how to start writing, but it could just easily be included in a section on what to do when you've finished. You look at what you've written (a tense psycho drama about a girl going to take her grandmother essential supplies) and you see that there's an entire section you don't really need (those scenes in which the wolf dresses up as grandmother). Not only do you not need them, but the story works better without them (we find out about the deception at the same time as the girl does).

Irongate – a case study

Here's an example of how a radio play was written, from start to finish. The play is called *Irongate*[6] and it's a kind of ghost story about a woman who takes a walk along the Thames Path in London. She walks from Kew to Tower Bridge and she seems to be stalked by a strange man who knows what she's doing and why she's doing it. The sequence of events in the writing of this play went as follows.

6 *Irongate*, 2013, directed by Peter Kavanagh, starring James Fleet and Emma Fielding.

1. The idea – which in this case came from talking (and listening) to someone; so it was their idea, and generously given, until ...
2. The thinking – which is the interrogating of the idea and which made it mine, rather than a dramatization of someone else's. The first question I had to ask at this stage was, 'What is it about this story that attracts you to it?' And at this stage it could have become any one of several sorts of story. This is where I realized it should be a ghost story.
3. The plotting/planning – which is the playing around with the shape of the story, looking at the sequence of telling, how many characters and so on.[7]
4. The walk – at some point, early on, I had to do the walk, on my own, with a notebook; I had to look and listen and keep an open mind.
5. The putting off – which is a mixture of cowardice (Jess's fear of spoiling a good idea by writing it) and wisdom (not starting because I hadn't thought enough about it).
6. The start – the moment alone with the blank page/screen; this is when you need the Proper Working Day – or whatever method of getting on with it that suits you best, or that circumstances allow.
7. The restart – which is when you realize that there were aspects of this idea that just won't work; you need to start again.
8. The First Draft – arrived at via the first draft.
9. The missing link – in the case of *Irongate* this was the realization that there was still something that didn't quite work. It came from several conversations with the director, Peter Kavanagh. He could see there was something missing and agitated until, during a long phone call, I said what was only a half-formed idea at the time about the identity of the man who appeared to be doing the stalking. This part of the process needed the perception of someone else; it needed Peter's persistent agitation and my trust in his judgement.
10. The Final Draft – including the missing link.
11. The recording – when the actors and the studio managers also have considerable contributions to make and should be listened to.

---

7 See 'The building blocks' above.

Numbers one to five on this list produced very little in the way of written material – a few notes and observations, perhaps, that found their way into the final version – but they were an essential part of the process. The play itself was a journey, as are all plays, and to get from one to eleven I needed to put off, procrastinate and plan, and then to find my own disciplined approach to working at the desk.

Writing is rewriting – or what to do about drafts

Good, better, best

Sue Teddern

Interviewer:	How much rewriting do you do?
Ernest Hemingway:	It depends. I wrote the ending to *A Farewell to Arms*, the last part of it, thirty-nine times before I was satisfied.
Interviewer:	Was there some technical problem there? What was it that had stumped you?
EH:	Getting the words right.

Some years ago, I wrote a commissioned radio drama which only went to two drafts before it was recorded. There are two possible reasons for this:

1) It was utterly brilliant.
2) The producer was busy with another project and thought 'it would do'.

Every so often I think about this play. I liked it then and I still do. But brilliant? Hardly.

My idea was cute, though unoriginal; the characters were sufficiently different to make the dialogue fun to write; the casting was perfect and we had a hoot recording it on location, to give a sense of the 'great outdoorsy' story.

I don't, however, regard it as a great play and that's because it must have needed a few more drafts and it didn't get them. Everything can be improved. Nothing is perfect in its raw state, when the metaphorical ink is barely dry.

Rewriting is part of the process. If that doesn't suit you, scriptwriting's not for you. As I said earlier, we do feel like we've earned an Olympic medal for finishing that pesky first draft. But there's so much more to do after that.

You will instinctively rework and adjust as you write your first draft. You'll make changes as you go, adding a scene here, dropping a character there. You can call it your first draft, but it's been through numerous filters and rethinks while you were writing it.

When it's ready to show the world, you may ask for feedback from a friend or partner. Only do this if you think they're going to say something that will assist you, rather than set you back or put you off. If they love you and know how hard you've worked, they might pull their punches. You'll be grateful that they do, but it won't help your script.

You, the writer, may not see the wood for the trees with your finished script. You may miss a huge hole in the structure or not spot some clever contrast between plot and subplot. That's where someone else's observations can prove so invaluable.

Scriptwriter, edit thyself!

Before you show it to anyone else, study your script through the eyes of a script editor and ask yourself the kind of questions they might ask.

Questions like:

- Are my characters real?
- Do they all sound different to each other?
- Can I tell how they tick, what motivates them?
- Do my characters achieve their objectives?
- If they don't, do they learn something about themselves and their lives?
- What propels the story? What's my 'story engine'?
- What's the conflict?
- What's at stake?
- Is it overwritten?

- Can dialogue and directions be pared down to what's essential?
- Does the story get stuck while characters tell us stuff?
- Is there sufficient story?
- Is it just a string of situations or do I have a narrative through-line?
- Does the script have changes of pace, tone and intimacy?
- If it's a comedy, is it funny?
- No, *really*. It has to be funny!
- If it's a comedy, does the humour come from character and truth or are the jokes tacked on for easy laughs?
- Do my twists and turns work?
- Is it surprising? Is it predictable?
- Does my ending work?
- Will my audience be satisfied?
- Will they 'care'?
- Is the theme clear?
- If it isn't, is that what was intended?
- Are all the characters necessary?
- Does it surprise?
- Does it feel derivative?
- Even if it has a familiar setting/genre/premise, does it have a voice/tone which makes it 'fresh'?
- What can I do to make the next draft better?

Don't be too hard on yourself. It isn't always easy to spot the clunky bits or pick up on repetitious dialogue when you've been immersed in your script for weeks or months.

TOP TIP

A good writer is not someone who knows how to write but how to rewrite.

William Goldman

My preferred technique is to get away from the computer screen and give my eyes a rest for as long as I can. A day or two after completing and then ignoring my first draft, I like to print up a hard copy[1] and take it with me to a new location: the sofa downstairs, a local café or, if the sun's out, a park bench.

A few days' holiday from your current project does wonders. You see the things you missed or meant to get back to and didn't. That lame joke should be punched up. This complicated line of dialogue can be replaced by a simple shrug of the shoulders.

Making changes with a pencil – preferably with an eraser on the end – is a great way of polishing and perfecting. If you use a bulldog clip to hold it all together, you can also move scenes around or dump them completely.

Then, when you take these changes back to your computer screen, you're simply inputting data. The work is mechanical and it gives you time off from the stressful work of creating.

TOP TIP

In his book *Screenwriting*, Ray Frensham lists the six stages of a rewrite. You can't address every issue in one go, so it makes sense to trawl through your script in a methodical way, examining different elements each time.

> First stage: Understandability. Are some elements only clear to me? Whose story am I telling?
> Second stage: Structure. What are the purposes of each act? Do the plots and sub-plots work?
> Third stage: Characters. Are there too many? Are they memorable?
> Fourth stage: Dialogue. Is it over or under-written? Dull? Not distinctive enough?
> Fifth stage: Style. Is the pace good? Is the tone good? Is there enough dramatic action?
> Sixth stage: Polishing. What have I missed?

[1] Printed on the back of an old script to save paper, naturally!

Making changes

In Part 1, we covered the different kinds of feedback you'll get when you submit your script.[2] The drafts that follow, if you go into production, will be based on notes given by a script editor or producer.

This stage of feedback can be helpful or awful; often a combination of the two. It's up to you to take on board all the good suggestions, subtly sidestep the ones you don't agree with, and generally show that your only desire is to get the script into the best shape it can possibly be, before it's filmed or recorded.

I've been a script editor myself and know how it feels to be the bearer of bad news. It's made all the more awkward because, more often than not, s/he is merely the conduit for notes from the producer, the exec producer, the director, the Network, the commissioning editor, grumpy Dave who empties the recycled paper bin and nice Maria who refills the coffee thermos.

Notes can come in a number of forms:

The meeting

You go in for a chat with the script editor or producer, talk through the script and take copious notes. In the case of a radio script, this process is invariably helpful and supportive and you go away feeling reasonably optimistic about the next draft.

TV scripts require more discussion because the drama or comedy in question is a much bigger beast, with important considerations regarding sets, props, locations, extras, hair and make-up, catering, honey wagons,[3] the lot.

A TV script meeting around a conference table is more unwieldy because you'll be getting feedback from more than one person. The script editor will also be writing up all the comments so what you miss, s/he will have minuted. It can be daunting, frantically writing down other people's comments, whilst also processing what they've said and, where necessary, putting down your pen to fight your corner.

---

[2] See Part 1, page 57, on dealing with feedback.

[3] Portable toilets used on location when filming.

TOP TIP

If you disagree with what's being suggested by your script editor, of course you're free to say so.

If you don't want to appear stubborn or precious, the best technique is often to say 'Yes, sure', you'll try to trim that scene or adjust that sub-plot.

Then take a proper look at the implications of what's involved when you get home.

I attended an interesting discussion at a BBC Writers Festival a few years ago entitled *Are you a difficult writer?* A heated exchange followed, from both writers and script editors. The question: is it wrong to dig your heels in and refuse to change one single word? The answer: yes.

But is it equally unproductive to accept every note you're given? Of course it is. In the past, I've occasionally been too amenable and I've regretted it. Producers want you to put up some passionate resistance, but only up to a point. It's a tough call and one project may require more defensive behaviour than another.

The phone call

If geography or time constraints are against you, notes can arrive via a long phone call. It's pretty much the same juggling act of noting what's said, whilst agreeing or disagreeing. But you'll also be required to balance a phone under your chin (unless you use the 'speaker' option) and will have to request comfort/meal/sleep breaks, if it goes on too long.

TOP TIP

Face-to-face or over the phone, neat writing is essential if you want to make sense of your copious notes the next day. Don't let a vital plot alteration rely on the one sentence you were too tired or browbeaten to write down clearly.

Written notes

In many ways, written notes that are emailed to you are easier to deal with than the face-to-face encounter because no eyes are upon you when you read them. You can punch the air if the changes are minimal. You can kick the swing bin or eat half a packet of biscuits if they aren't.

Having said that, there are written notes and there are written notes.

The notes you *want* are clear, chronological and, above all, positive. The notes you *don't want* are twenty single-spaced pages of random, unedited thoughts; the script editor has regurgitated everyone's feedback into a document, leaving you to make sense of it. This can be because they are short of time or because they don't have the confidence to edit the vague comments and off-the-cuff ideas into a writer-friendly form.

Sometimes there's an opportunity to go through the notes with your script editor before you start rewriting so that you can clarify any confusion or highlight the bits that don't work for you. But if time's against you, you'll be expected to roll up your sleeves, brew some high-octane coffee, say adieu to your loved ones and get on with it.

Let the rewrite begin

If your notes are in a cogent form, you can work through them logically, changing as you go. Sometimes it helps to change all the easy stuff first – a word here, a stage direction there. The big changes will take more thought, time and caffeine.

Be thankful for technology. Scenes can be cut and pasted from act one to act three and back again in a matter of seconds. Characters' names can change with the click of a key.[4] I once deleted a subplot in ten minutes when my producer and I agreed that it wasn't needed.

It's a laborious process and, while you're doing it, it's easy to think you're merely rearranging the deckchairs on the *Titanic*. When you're in the middle

---

[4] I changed a character's name from Mad (short for Madeleine) to Sarah. Thus every 'madness' or 'made' became 'Sarahness' and 'Sarahe'. There's an apocryphal tale of an author who changed the name of his hero from David to Geoff and sent off his manuscript, only to realize later that a pivotal scene set in Florence now took place beside the statue of Michelangelo's Geoff.

of it, how can you tell what works and what doesn't? Are you even sure you know who you are and why you're here? Just crack on, get to the final page and have a good night's sleep.

What may seem like obfuscation and unnecessary tweaking will make sense in the cold light of day. And if it doesn't, just remember, it probably isn't your last draft anyway. But you're one lap closer to the finish line.

The final draft may read very differently to the naïve, shiny, optimistic, clunky 'duck' you created oh, so long ago. That's because it's been refined, finessed and reconfigured into a sleek, polished, professional 'swan'. That's the idea anyway!

EXERCISE

Take one of your finished scripts and reassess your scenes in script-editor mode:

- What is this scene about? What happens? What is it for?
- What does each character in this scene want to happen/ want NOT to happen?
- Where does this scene take place? Why here? Is a conversation at a zoo or in a lift more interesting than in a kitchen or on a sofa?
- Can you alternate plot and subplot scenes?
- Can you alternate small, intimate scenes with big, populated scenes?
- Can you alternate serious scenes with lighter scenes?
- Is this scene necessary? If in doubt, cut it out!
- Is it in the right place?
- What happens in it to move the story forward?

- Is it day, night, sunny, hot, raining, snowing? Can the weather, time of day or location enhance or contrast usefully with the scene's content?
- Is this scene too long?
- Is there conflict? Is it resolved?
- Can you use this scene to reveal back story?
- Are the stakes raised by the end of this scene? If so, how?
- Is your protagonist one (big or small) step closer to his/her goal?

The vanishing dream

Nick Warburton

> *The beauty of my dream vanished.*
> Mary Shelley, *Frankenstein*

First Draft or first draft

Remember Dr Frankenstein, creating the Monster? And then being disappointed with it?

'Now that I had finished,' he says, 'the beauty of my dream vanished, and breathless horror and disgust filled my heart'.[5]

A lot of writers will sympathize with that. And they'll know the solution to his problem. He should've done another draft. The Monster (Draft Two) might well have been quite personable, and a lot less trouble.

A First Draft hardly ever suffices. In fact, it's often the First Draft that reveals the flaws. I don't want to be dogmatic about this – as I've already said, there

5 According to Mary Shelley.

are different rules for different writers – but you need *at least* three drafts. The first to find out what's wrong with your plan; the second to put that right. The third to fine-tune those corrections.

And it's worth saying that there's a difference between the First Draft and the first draft.

The *First Draft* is the one you send out into the world. It will be the first time a producer or script editor sees it. The *first draft*, on the other hand, is the one you've been working on, pulling in and out of shape, changing, ditching, restarting as you go. All that is drafting – first drafting. When you've done enough of it, or run out of time, you will have produced a First Draft and that's what you send out. (People do, sometimes, send in uncorrected first drafts, and they do themselves no favours.)

What you don't do is (a) have an idea, (b) make a plan and (c) write the script, straight out, as it comes. Unless you're very, very lucky. Which you won't be.

There will come a point, though, when you have to stop drafting. The temptation will be to go on tampering with the script. (In my case it's beginning and endings I can barely leave alone; sometimes it's hard to stop myself rewriting them. And that can be dangerous.[6])

What should you do once you've wrestled the first draft to the floor and forced it to become the First Draft? To begin with you ought to put some distance between you and your script. Distance will help you become objective about it. You might already have the strength of mind and the will power to read your own script with a cold and objective eye. If not, you can pretend that it's by someone else, or you can pretend that you're someone else (a script editor or a producer). More efficaciously you can put the script in a drawer for two weeks and move on to something else.

But be objective. That's the aim.

If you are, you'll be in the right frame of mind to deal with notes. There'll be two sorts of notes to consider: external notes (those sent to you by producers and script editors) and internal ones (those sent to you by yourself).

[6] Remember that character in Camus's novel *The Plague*? The one who spends so long rewriting the first sentence of his novels he never gets beyond it?

External notes[7]

Notes sent by script editors or producers can also be divided into two categories. There will be General Notes about large areas of the script (like structure and characters), and there will be Specifics, about particular lines of dialogue and comparatively small details.

A General Note might be something like, 'I'm not sure the talking goat is really working for us. Can we get rid of him?' Or, 'What would happen if Amanda *fails* to steal the tractor?' Or, 'Most of the first act is too expositional – it's slowing everything down.'

You might bristle about some of these but a good General Note from a good and sensitive producer or editor can help you to improve your script in ways you hadn't thought about.

Specifics might be something like, 'Tony's third speech in scene 4 – can we cut this?' Or, 'How about giving her a handbag rather than a rucksack?' Most of them are easily addressed and some are rendered pointless by the General Notes. 'Scene 12: the dog shouldn't bark at this point – or, if he does, he should do so in an ironic manner.' If you've already had a General Note instructing you to lose the dog at the end of scene nine, its barking – ironic or otherwise – will be irrelevant. Even so, you'll probably still get notes like this.[8]

There's another way of categorizing the notes you get back on your script: those worth arguing about and those you can accept with obedient alacrity. You'll have to decide for yourself which are the ones to fight about,[9] but you should remember that putting on radio and TV dramas is a collaborative process. There will be some notes you don't like but which are not worth shedding blood over. ('Part 3, "The vanishing dream": shouldn't that be "over which it's not worth shedding blood"? What do you think?')

---

[7] Rewriting and notes are closely linked so see also 'Notes on notes: dealing with feedback' in Part 1.

[8] See *A Martian Wouldn't Say That* compiled by Leonard B. Stern and Diane L. Robinson. It will cheer you up. The title is taken from notes sent back on a TV series called *My Favourite Martian* – 'Please change the dialogue on page 14. A Martian wouldn't say that.'

[9] You'll hear stories of writers who threaten to have their names removed from the credits, or throw things around the room. A writer once told me he'd thrown a typewriter out of a window. I remember thinking I couldn't *afford* to do that. A pencil, maybe. But a typewriter?

I once had a sympathetic script editor who half-suggested that we left a couple of faults in a script so that they could be weeded out in the next draft: 'To give the producer something to find.' A rather cynical but entirely appealing approach. I can't remember if we did it.

Internal notes

I'm going to suggest seven headings for things to look out for when, after two weeks, you take your script out of the drawer and prepare to read it with that cold eye. You might think of other things to look out for, or you might find something in the script that doesn't come under any of these headings but just sounds wrong. It's the things that *sound wrong* or *feel wrong* that you'll need to do something about.

1. *Structural changes* – these will be the most worrying because they may require major rebuilding work. The way you've organized the story beats might be wrong – or not as good as it might be – and you might discover when you read through that you've mishandled time (by sticking to a chronological telling, or by *not* sticking to a chronological telling, or by starting too soon …) and so on.
2. *Beauty treatment* – or its opposite; this might involve roughing up the dialogue to make it more believable.[10] It might equally involve fine-tuning the language.
3. *Cutting* – removing characters, speeches, phrases, words that are superfluous; removing beats that do too much of the audience's work for them; getting rid of scenes that are 'on the nose' and explain themselves
4. *Adding* – it will be rare that you want to add something new, but it's not impossible; if you've carried on thinking about your script, you might well come up with something you can plant early in the narrative, say, to make the story work better.
5. *Looking at the joins* – how scenes and acts connect; how your script moves from one scene to the next, from one mood to the next.
6. *Punctuating* – is the punctuation doing what you want it to do?

[10] See pp 210 in 'The Talky Bits: Writing dialogue'.

7. *Scrutinizing the best bits* – 'In writing,' said William Faulkner, 'you must kill your darlings'. He meant beware of your favourite passages. They're likely to be less beautiful and resonant than you think they are, and far more overwritten. In years to come you'll be glad you got rid of them.

When you've done all this, and incorporated (or reasonably rejected) the External Notes, you should be in good shape to move on to the second draft (and subsequently the Second Draft) ... and so on until you achieve the Final Draft. Or you're overtaken by a deadline.

The finishing line

Now what?

Sue Teddern

You did it. Your script is finished and polished to perfection. Friends and family have read it and told you how clever you are. You have read it and you can't help agreeing with them.

There were one or two moments of self-doubt. But you hacked your way through the forest of fear and emerged triumphant. You are a scriptwriter. With a script.

Now what? Let's see if we can help with a few final tips and pointers.

TV script layout

You've seen an example of a TV script layout on page 241. Final Draft is the industry-preferred format for screenplays and TV drama. Some long-running TV shows create their own in-house variation, with helpful shortcuts for their team of writers, but they'll have based it on Final Draft.

It isn't cheap: £150–£160 or thereabouts. But if you're serious about presenting your script like a pro, bite the bullet and buy the software. It's tax deductible and you're worth it.

If, however, you feel it's too big an investment just yet, perhaps it's best to hold off until you're sure you can justify it. If that's the case, the BBC Writersroom website offers pdf templates in a number of formats: screenplay, screenplay for TV, taped drama, taped sitcom and some US variations. Copy or clone the template you require and this will suit you fine until you're ready to splash out on some professional software. Or check out Celtx, which is free if you opt for the most basic package.

UK TV sitcom scripts have a specific style of layout. See below a page from a sitcom script of mine. Every writer has their own way of doing things but the principle is the same, with the body of the words on the middle-to-right side of the page. Here's an excerpt from a script of mine, to show how I do it.

EXAMPLE: UK SITCOM LAYOUT

SCENE 10. INT. PAULA'S LIVING ROOM (NIGHT)

PAULA AND MIKE SIT AT EACH END OF THE SOFA, DRINKING COFFEES.

MIKE
You're alone. I'm alone. That can't be right now, can it?

PAULA
Who says I'm alone?

MIKE
Little bird.

PAULA
Mia can't just wave a magic wand and make us The Waltons again.

MIKE
I think it's sweet. I was very touched.

PAULA
Yeah well. You cry at loo roll commercials.

MIKE
Only that one where that little ginger kid thought he'd lost his teddy bear. (PLEASED) Hey, you remembered.

PAULA

I've been dining out on it for years. Whenever I need to explain just how sad you are.

HE PUTS HER FEET ON HIS LAP AND MASSAGES THEM. SHE'S TRYING HARD TO BE ON HER EMOTIONAL GUARD BUT HE'S FOUND HER ACHILLES' HEEL. QUITE LITERALLY.

TOP TIP

If a script is brilliant but it's in the wrong format, it won't matter. But you will always look more professional if you lay it out correctly.

Agents

The word 'agent' means someone who works for you. If you pick the right one, it will evolve into an equal relationship; you need each other. S/he sorts your contracts and waves a big stick when necessary and you earn her/him a percentage (10% to 20%) every time your work is commissioned.

Yes, it helps to have an agent when you're starting out, but it isn't essential. Besides, an agent probably won't take you on until you can show that you'll be earning them money. I wasn't signed up until I got my first TV commission.

Radio rates are standard, on a sliding scale depending on your credits. So an agent can't increase your fee or wangle a limousine to the studio. Maybe you won't need one if you intend to work only in radio and you establish good contacts with producers and indies.

But s/he can help with rights and negotiations if a radio idea has legs and could transfer to TV, become a novel or movie.

In TV, I'd say it's vital to have an agent. S/he doesn't just deal with the small print and wait for the cheque. S/he also has a good relationship with programme makers, knows what's being commissioned and whom you should meet. S/he can oil the wheels and make contacts on your behalf. Having an agent's name on your script proves you're a 'player'.

TOP TIP

When you start looking for an agent, ask around. Can any writer friends recommend theirs? Google a few agencies and see how you'd fit in with their current client list. You don't want to be competing with all the big names but, at the same time, if they have no successful writers on their books, they might not be sufficiently established to be taken seriously.

I asked my agent in what format she prefers to receive a script from a potential client: a hard copy or an electronic version? This is her reply:

> So many people read on screens now, so I'd say: send electronically. I can't remember the last time I read a hard copy script. The writer should ask the agent whether they want to read a sample of work (unless their website submissions guidelines say no) and then they'll be told how best to submit. That way, the writer knows their script has been asked for, rather than sitting in a slush pile with no idea whether it'll actually get read.

Don't go for the first agent who offers to take you on. Make sure you're right for them and they're right for you. It could be the difference between success and failure, so trust your instincts.

Submitting scripts

When I started out, I thought it would be okay to submit half a script. If someone liked it, they'd pay me to write the rest. Fortunately a writer friend set me straight. Producers (and agents!) want to know you can do middles and endings, as well as beginnings.

Just as you shouldn't submit half a script, it's advisable not to submit a few sketchy pages of your idea and wait for that big-bucks commission. What everyone wants to know is: can you write it?

A completed script, correctly formatted and well presented, is what's required. It's known as a 'calling card' script. It may never be produced but it shows what you can do. It's a sample of your wares so it has to be good.

Again, it's good to check in advance whether the producer prefers a hard copy or an electronic version. There may be guidelines on their website or you can phone, find the right person to ask and clarify before sending.

Some experts advise that your calling card script should be an episode of an existing series, written to slot right in with the style and tone of a successful show. Not a bad idea. It might even get you a commission to join the writing team.

My feeling is that if nothing comes of this script, there's nowhere else you can go with it. It was written solely with that series/serial in mind. But if your calling card script is an original piece, it's more suitable for sending off to a wide range of producers. It might even get commissioned.

In recent years, the BBC has streamlined its submissions process. Time was when you could submit scripts all the year round, but they've now opted for specific 'offers windows'. The theory is that it saves resources (and paper – it's by e-submission!) and concentrates the development process on those writers who show talent.

These submissions windows are by genre, for both TV and radio, so you might have to wait a year before the next opportunity occurs to submit your sitcom or radio drama.

If you haven't already, make yourself familiar with the BBC Writersroom website. Their opportunities page lists all the relevant deadlines, genres and requirements, plus essential information on how to submit your script electronically.

Be professional

Nick Warburton

You should always try to maintain a professional approach to writing for radio and TV – to any kind of writing, in fact. Being professional means meeting deadlines, making sure your manuscripts are properly set out and carefully corrected. So submit First Drafts, not first drafts.[1]

---

[1] See 'Writing is rewriting', page 268.

It also means learning to work with other people.

You can argue the case for your script, fight your corner, raise your voice, but you can't dismiss everyone else on the team as a complete fool and storm out. Not often, anyway. Remember, writing drama of any kind is a collaborative business.

Learn to talk

Writing for radio and TV is not just a matter of putting stories and ideas into documents; it's also a matter of talking about them. Poets and novelists, on the whole, only talk about their work when it's finished. It makes sense for novelists to keep their ideas to themselves until they know what shape those ideas are taking. P. D. James offered ten tips to help aspiring novelists and number nine was 'Never talk about a book before it's finished.' But for radio writers, and even more so for TV writers, talk is part of the process. You'll *need* to talk – to producers, editors and, sometimes, other writers. You'll have to present, to pitch your ideas.

If, like me, you're not a natural talker, if you can't pitch an idea to a producer with confidence, you may find yourself at a disadvantage. There's a story by Garrison Keillor[2] about Aunt Myrna, a brilliant cake maker who was so self-deprecating that she persuaded other people her wonderful cakes weren't really up to much. A chocolate cake entered in a competition, and an obvious winner, came tenth because when Aunt Myrna talked to the judge she convinced him it was disappointing, not nearly as good as cakes she'd made in the past, too *gummy*. You can't afford to be like Aunt Myrna if you're trying to sell your idea. ('It's not a bad idea, I think, though it has been done before, and far better, by Charles Dickens.')

Story conferences, at which writers and producers discuss the way series and serials might develop, are often dominated by quick thinkers and fast talkers. If you're neither it doesn't mean you're not a proper writer, nor does it mean you haven't got a contribution to make, but it does mean you'll have to prepare. Sometimes these talking sessions take place in what the industry calls The Room. (This is actually *a* room, but calling it The Room

[2] 'State Fair' in *Leaving Home*, Garrison Keillor (Faber and Faber, 1988).

somehow sounds more dynamic.) Being in The Room is, in theory, completely democratic. Everyone comes up with ideas in a brainstorming kind of way. Everyone's opinion is listened to and no idea is dismissed out of hand. For the time that you're in The Room, status is set aside. In practice, of course, everyone knows who the execs are.

I suspect I'm not alone in finding it difficult to talk about ideas with ease and confidence. To compensate for this I try to prepare for meetings by working out what the strengths of the ideas might be and then running through what I want to say about them a few times in my head. There's nothing spontaneous about this but at least it means the meeting won't stutter into silence when it's my turn to say something.[3]

Research

If you're writing about a world or a time you're not familiar with, you must do some research, and research is another of writing's great pleasures. Incidentally, people will tell you 'You must write about what you know', but that doesn't mean you can't write about, say, the Battle of Trafalgar on the grounds that you weren't there. You might not 'know' what it's like to fight against Napoleon's navy, but there's every chance that you will know what it feels like to be afraid and excited at the same time, and to think of loved ones far away as an event of huge significance approaches. What you know about is what people think and feel. The details of how they lived, what they did, wore and ate are to be discovered in research.

TOP TIP

There are three tricky corners to negotiate when you're doing research for a script:

- The first is to know when to stop reading and start writing. The reading can be so fascinating that you're tempted to delay the moment when you start writing.

[3] There are courses and workshops on how to improve your pitching technique, but I've never done one so I can't tell you how effective they are.

- The second is to avoid putting into your script anything that's not necessary to the story. Hemmingway talks about leaving out 'the underwater part of the iceberg', the things you know, or have discovered. You may have learned something of great interest about the men who fought at Trafalgar – about, say, the buttons on their coats – but the fact that it's of great interest is not in itself enough to earn it a place in the story.
- The third and trickiest of these corners is to make the research *belong*, to avoid it sounding like a piece of vital information that you're passing on to us because we really will need to know about it. You have to handle this sort of research the same way you handle exposition. All nougats of essential fact must be bedded in so naturally that we, the audience, don't realize we're being given them. And we must be fascinated by them.

Actors

Most actors are happy to talk about the characters you've given them and the script in general.

I wrote a dog in my very first radio play. We might've used pre-recorded material to provide various barks and yaps, but because we wanted this particular animal to react to what was going on in the play, an actor was cast to play the dog. The actor turned up with his own lead and chain, and when we talked about the play after the read-through, he was keen to know what sort of a dog it was – how big, what breed, what sort of personality.

Good actors have insights about the people they play and it will reward you to listen to them. Do not, however, 'direct' them. If you have something to say to an actor about what they're doing, say it through the director. You might, for example, want an actor to play *against* the emotion of a scene, rather than with it. Talk about that to the director. And don't be tempted to give line-readings. When I write I hear the lines in my head and when an actor speaks them the lines usually sound as I first heard them. There are times, though, when an actor will surprise me with a reading. Very often I end up admitting that I like what they're doing.

I remember watching the recording of a scene with two brilliant actors[4] playing father and son in the radio series *On Mardle Fen*. It was about the great but unspoken love they had for each other. Theirs was a difficult relationship, marked by resentment and neglect, so the scene was also a kind of reconciliation, and a farewell. In studio it felt to me as if the actors were throwing it away, that it was all done with such lightness that there was almost no feeling in it at all. When I listened back, though, what I heard was a pitch-perfect valediction full of love and forgiveness.

One of the greatest pleasures in writing for radio and TV is that you can find yourself working with actors capable of doing this.

Layout (radio)

If you look at the script samples quoted in this book, or at some of the scripts on view in the BBC's Writers' Room, you'll find a variety of different layouts for radio plays. Some, but not all, have numbered scene headings, some, but not all, use **bold** and *underlined* for sound effects. What they will have in common is the fact that they make a clear and observable distinction between what characters say and the writer's instructions for movement and sound.

TOP TIP FOR RADIO LAYOUT

Anyone reading a radio script will need to know ...

- who's speaking,
- where characters are; sometimes this might include an indication of where they are in relation to the audience (is the audience, for example, in a character's head?),
- a precise indication of the sound environment,
- a precise indication the sound events (or effects, or FX) that play into the scene.

Here's an example from my script for *Tommies*.[5]

[4] Trevor Peacock and Sam Dale.

[5] BBC Radio 4. This is from the first series, 14 October 1914. The series was devised by Jonathan Ruffle; this episode was directed by Jonquil Panting.

EXAMPLE

SCENE 1: BOULOGNE STATION.

FX: MUSIC. WE ARE IN THE MIDDLE OF CHAOS. AT THE MOMENT IT'S MOSTLY STEAM AND METAL. THERE ARE NO DISTINCT VOICES BUT SOME ENGINEERS ARE SHOUTING AS THEY HAMMER AWAY AT A FAILED ENGINE. A TRAIN COMES CLANKING AND STEAMING TOWARDS US, SLOWING LABORIOUSLY. FADE UNDER ...

1. ***COMMENTATOR:*** **The station at Boulogne. The 14th of October 1914, a little after seven in the morning.**

FX: THE TRAIN HALTS AND A FEW MEN JUMP FROM THE WAGONS. MARJORIE AND OTHERS ARE THERE TO RECEIVE THEM. INSTRUCTIONS AND COUNTER-INSTRUCTIONS BEGIN TO FLY AROUND. ONE OR TWO OF THE WOUNDED CALL OUT IN PAIN.

(MARJORIE BLAIKLEY IS 40. SHE'S A NURSE AND A VETERAN OF THE BOER WAR. SHE'S TOUGH AND SEEMS TO BE QUITE SINGLE-MINDED, BUT SHE'S JUST ABOUT HOLDING HERSELF TOGETHER.

CYRIL WALTON IS TWENTY-TWO, A CORPORAL IN THE RAMC, FROM SOUTH WALES. HE'S BEEN A STRETCHER-BEARER IN FRANCE AND WAS DETAILED TO ACCOMPANY THE WOUNDED TO BOULOGNE. HE'S A QUIET, OBEDIENT YOUNG MAN WITH A HIGHLY DEVELOPED SENSE OF DUTY AND AN UNQUESTIONING RESPECT FOR HIERARCHIES.)

2. MARJORIE: (SHOUTING ABOVE THE NOISE) Don't let those men off yet! ... Wait! Did you hear me? I said wait!

3. **COMMENTATOR:** **A train's just pulled in. A long, slow journey across France. Four hundred sick or wounded.**

4.	MARJORIE:	Stretcher-bearer! You!
5.	CYRIL:	(A LITTLE WAY OFF) Just a moment, miss.

You can see that instructions about sound, character descriptions and speech have all been indented. What the Commentator says is in **bold** so we know that she'll be on a narration mic. The scene is numbered – t's easier to work with numbered scenes in studio – as are the characters' speeches. Speeches are numbered so that it's easier to refer to them during recording. ('We'll re-take from speech 3 on page 2.') The numbering will start again, from speech one at the top of the next page. For your First Draft you won't have to number speeches.

Sometimes the scene heading will include the information INT or EXT. I notice that I haven't given that here: perhaps I thought the heading BOULOGNE STATION was enough of a clue.

Templates which give standard layouts can be restricting, though. If they use the abbreviation FX for sound instructions, they might lure you into thinking that your responsibility as the writer is to think about effects only. Sound is a more complex part of the process than that.[6]

[6] See 'Sound setting' in 'Hearing their dreams – the nuts and bolts of radio', pp 223.

Reading (+ viewing + listening) list

Here is a selection of books, scripts, CDs, DVDs, websites, etc. that we've found useful or which offer examples of good practice. It is a *selected* rather than a comprehensive list. You'll certainly be able to augment it. Some of the books here are out of print but they're still worth seeking out on the second-hand market.

Scripts

Samuel Beckett: *Collected Shorter Plays* (Faber and Faber, 2006)
Angela Carter: *Come Unto These Yellow Sands* (Bloodaxe, 1985)
David Chase (creator): *The Sopranos Scriptbook* (Channel 4 Books, 2001)
Giles Cooper: *Six Plays for Radio* (BBC, 1966)
Giles Cooper Award Winners: *Best Radio Plays* – 14 volumes (Methuen/BBC, 1978–1991)
Russell T Davies: *Queer as Folk – The Scripts* (Channel 4 Books, 1999)
Ray Galton and Alan Simpson: *The Best of Steptoe and Son* (Robson Books, 1988)
Lee Hall: *Spoonface Steinberg and Other Plays* (BBC, 1997)
Rebecca Lenkiewicz: *Plays 1* (Faber and Faber, 2013)
Christopher Lloyd (Introduction): *The Best of Frasier* (Channel 4 Books, 1999)
Hattie Naylor: *Ivan and the Dogs* (Methuen, 2010)
Dennis Potter: *The Singing Detective* (Faber and Faber, 2003)
David Pownall: *Radio Plays* (Oberon, 1998)
Jack Rosenthal: *The Chain; The Knowledge; Ready when You are, Mr McGill* (Faber and Faber, 1987)
Tom Stoppard: *Parade's End* – Adapted from the Novels of Ford Maddox Ford (Grove Press, 2012)

Tom Stoppard: *The Plays for Radio, 1964 – 1991* (Faber, 1994)
Dylan Thomas: *Under Milk Wood* (Penguin, 2000)
Richard Webber, Dick Clement, Ian La Frenais: *Porridge – The Complete Scripts and Series Guide* (Headline, 2005)
Stephen Wyatt: *Memorials to the Missing* (Stephen Wyatt, 2008)

DVDs, CDs, etc.

DVDs of most of the TV dramas mentioned in this book are readily available in boxed sets or can be viewed via channels like Netflix. You will also find CDs and downloads of some radio drama. These are mostly comedy adaptations of classic novels or crime, but a few original radio plays may be found.

Samuel Beckett: *Works for Radio – The Original Broadcasts* (British Library CD)
Christopher Douglas and Andrew Nickolds: *Ed Reardon's Week* (BBC CD and download)
Charles Dickens (adapted by Mike Walker): *A Tale of Two Cities* (BBC CD and download)
Lee Hall: *Spoonface Steinberg* (BBC CD and download)
Katie Hims: *Lost Property: The Complete Series* (BBC download)
Marcy Kahan: *Incredibly Guilty* (BBC download)
Jonathan Myerson: *Payback* (BBC download)
Hattie Naylor: *The Diary of Samuel Pepys* (BBC CD and download)
Jonathan Ruffle, Michael Chaplin and Nick Warburton: *Tommies* (BBC CD and download)
Tom Stoppard: *Tom Stoppard Radio Plays* (British Library CD)
Dylan Thomas: *Under Milk Wood* (BBC and others, original and subsequent productions CD and download)
Mike Walker: *Dickens Confidential* (BBC CD and download)
Nick Warburton: *On Mardle Fen* (BBC download)
Stephen Wyatt: *Double Jeopardy* (BBC download)

Books about radio, TV, writing

Rafael Alvarez: *The Wire – Truth Be Told* (Canongate, 2010)
Sam Boardman-Jacobs (ed.): *Radio Scriptwriting* (Seren, 2004)

Annie Caulfield: *Writing for Radio – A Practical Guide* (The Crowood Press, 2011)
Tim Crook: *Radio Drama – Theory and Practice* (Routledge, 1999)
Paul Donovan: *The Radio Companion* (Harper Collins, 1991)
John Drakakis: *British Radio Drama* (Cambridge University Press, 1981)
David Edgar: *How Plays Work* (Nick Hern Books, 2009)
Lajos Egri: *The Art of Dramatic Writing* (Simon and Schuster, 2007)
Ray Frensham: *Screenwriting* (Teach Yourself Books, 2003)
William Goldman: *Adventures in the Screen Trade* (Abacus, 1996)
Claire Grove and Stephen Wyatt: *So You Want to Write Radio Drama?* (Nick Hern Books, 2013)
Anne Karpf: *The Human Voice* (Bloomsbury, 2007)
Stephen King: *On Writing* (Hodder Paperbacks, 2012)
Anne Lamott: *Bird by Bird* (Anchor Books, 1995)
Peter Lewis (ed.): *Radio Drama* (Longman, 1981)
Rob Long: *Conversations with My Agent* (Faber and Faber, 1996)
Shaun MacLaughlin: *Writing for Radio* (How To Books, 1998)
Brett Martin: *Difficult Men – From The Sopranos and the Wire to Mad Men and Breaking Bad* (Faber and Faber, 2013)
Robert McKee: *Story* (Methuen, 1999)
Charlie Moritz: *Scriptwriting for the Screen* (Routledge, 2008)
Flannery O'Connor: *Mystery and Manners: Occasional Prose* (Faber and Faber, 2014)
Larry W. Phillips (ed.): *Ernest Hemingway on Writing* (Pocket Books, 1999)
David Pownall: *Sound Theatre* (Oberon, 2011)
Ian Rodger: *Radio Drama* (Macmillan, 1981)
Linda Seger: *Making a Good Script Great* (Samuel French, 2010)
Leonard B. Stern and Diane L. Robison (compilers): *A Martian Wouldn't Say That* (Tallfellow, 1994)
Christopher Vogler: *The Writer's Journey* (Michael Wiese Productions, 2007)
Meg Wolitzer: *Fitzgerald Did It* (Penguin, 1999)
John Yorke: *Into the Woods* (Particular Books, 2014)

Websites, etc.

The Diversity Website – www.suttonelms.org.uk (a very useful archive of material about radio plays)

The Literary Consultancy – www.literaryconsultancy.co.uk (offering script-reading and mentoring services)

New Writing Partnership – www.newwritingpartnership.org.uk (works to highlight, develop and support creative writing)

The Writers' Practice – www.thewriterspractice.com (offers assessments of screenplays for TV)

The BBC Writersroom – www.bbc.co.uk/writersroom (advice about writing and sending scripts; a library of scripts you can download)

The Radio Academy – www.radioacademy.org (concerned with all aspects of radio production)

Creative Skillset – www.creativeskillset.org (helps creative industries to develop skills and talent; covers both radio and TV)

Final Draft – www.finaldraft.com (the industry format for script layouts)

Celtx – www.celtx.com (an alternative to finaldraft.com, popular with many writers)

Facebook – don't underestimate the shared experiences of other writers who use social networks to pass on tips and contacts; offer advice, congratulations, commiserations and knowledgeable support. Facebook groups and pages come and go but if you 'search' writer-related names, you'll find the ones that are relevant to you. Or start your own!

Courses and workshops

Part- and full-time courses on writing for radio and TV are offered by many universities and colleges. You'll also find short courses at centres like those run by The Arvon Foundation (www.arvon.org). These courses tend to be residential and in remote but rather beautiful surroundings. Some of these places also offer writers the chance to take a retreat so they can work without distraction on their next novel, opera, poem sequence, play and so on. The courses are led by experienced writers who provide a programme of workshops, tutorials and, perhaps most importantly, a concentrated time to write.

The question is – do they work?

We went on several courses, both as tutors and participants, and found that they did work, and in several useful ways:

- They can help you discover things you want to write about and ideas you want to develop.
- As you're away for the best part of a week, and most of your time is spent writing (and thinking about writing) you may be able to find a rhythm of work that's unachievable during the rest of the year.
- They can teach you some of the technical aspects of writing – and writing for radio and TV is more technical than most forms of writing, simply because of the performance/broadcast elements it includes.
- They can inspire you to carry on writing.

What they can't do is provide would-be writers with the talent to write. Neither can they dole out shortcuts to success. To succeed as a writer you'll still need those three ingredients mentioned in the introduction – talent, luck and stamina.

Acknowledgements

Sue Teddern

I would like to thank:

Nick Warburton, my wise and witty collaborator.

Carole Angier and Sally Cline.

Our guest contributors.

Abigail Gonda and Scribes.

Lucy Fawcett at Sheil Land Associates for being such a supportive agent.

Rachel Calder.

BBC Radio Drama's inspiring producers, especially Marion Nancarrow and David Hunter.

The Arvon Foundation.

The Royal Literary Fund.

Nick Warburton

I would also like to thank my collaborator, Sue Teddern, who has both taught me a lot and made me laugh.

Carole Angier and Sally Cline.

Our guest contributors.

Rachel Calder.

Marion Nancarrow.

Nell Leyshon.

Barry Simner.

The BBC Radio Drama Department.

The University of Chichester.

Index